The Wonderful World of COOKIE JARS

*All our very best Regards
Ellen & Mark Supnick 6/23/95
D.O.A*

By Mark and Ellen Supnick

A PICTORIAL REFERENCE AND PRICE GUIDE

© 1995
Mark and Ellen Supnick

ISBN#: 0-89538-032-3

Additional autographed copies may be purchased
from Mark & Ellen Supnick • 2771 Oak Brook Manor •
Ft. Lauderdale, FL 33332 • Phone # 305-389-3911

Published by: L-W Book Sales
                P.O. Box 69
                Gas City, IN 46933

Please write for our free catalog.

Attention Collectors . . . if you would like to contribute photographs or
information of your collection (possibly for profit), please call L-W Books
(toll free) at 1-800-777-6450 Tuesday thru Friday 9am to 3pm EST.

Other books written by Mark E. Supnick include
Collecting Hull Pottery's "Little Red Riding Hood", and
Collecting Shawnee Pottery. Published by L-W Book Sales.

Table of Contents

Dedication

To our son, Todd Michael Supnick, who made us parents in 1972, and has grown into a wonderful young man of whom we are very proud, and to our son, Matthew Adam Supnick, who is a breath of fresh air, and from the very beginning, a gift from God.

Introduction

So many people have asked us over the years how did we ever get started in this? And this is how it goes . . . .

In approximately 1940, Mark's mother and father acquired Shawnee Pottery's Puss in Boots cookie jar. For many years, it sat in the Supnick kitchen, admired by all. In 1976, Mark and I were at an antique show and lo-and-behold we found the matching salt and pepper shakers to the cookie jar. We were so excited. Two hours later, we found the matching creamer. We were HOOKED!

What is this pottery that we are in love with all about?

We asked many questions and formed some wonderful friendships. In about two and a half years, we had the largest Shawnee collection in the country. At this point, Mark was inspired and all collectors across the country were begging for a complete Shawnee pottery book. We were glad to help. In 1983, Mark's first book, "Collecting Shawnee Pottery" hit the bookstores. We were very young and very inexperienced at writing books. There weren't many people at that time that were able to really help us, so we just decided that we would do the best job that we knew how, and hoped that the collectors would like it. It is now eleven years later, and over 50,000 copies have sold. Many refer to it as, "The Shawnee Bible".

In 1989, Mark's second book, "Collecting Hull's Little Red Riding Hood" hit the bookstores. This pictorial reference and value guide pictures and identifies all known items of "Hull's Little Red Riding Hood Collection." This book has remained the mainstay for identification of this beautiful line of pottery.

Over the past four years. Mark and I have become leading cookie jar dealers, specializing in top quality cookie jars. We also try to provide something for everyone. The enthusiasm and excitement of all of our customers has given us the strength to continue in this business and write this book.

Cookie jar collectors and dealers across the country are continually asking, "Is this the beginning or is this the end?", "Has the market bottomed out?", or "Is this the right time to buy?" No, the market has not bottomed out. YES, it really is just the beginning. Every day, new people are becoming cookie jar collectors, adding to its popularity. It is the most exciting collectible in the U.S.A. We wish that everyone could hear the happy, excited customers on the phone when they receive their special jar. Many ask, "What are the best selling cookie jars?" Everything is wonderful. A wonderful jar is the one that you want. Some of our favorite manufacturers are, of course, Shawnee, Metlox, Brush, American Bisque, Red Wing, McCoy, Regal China, California Originals, and all Walt Disney Productions. These companies have brought to the American people a beautiful part of our history.

Many collectors are now branching out and collecting the "new jars" and the very beautiful "artist" jars. "New Jars" are being made in the United States as well as different parts of the world – Japan, Taiwan, China, Portugal, England, and Italy. Most Japan, Taiwan, and China made cookie jars are light in weight and can be recognized readily from U.S.A. pottery. Over the past nine years, artists across the country have "popped-up" with their works of art. One the first to produce a beautiful original cookie jar of her own design, was Carol Gifford-McCalip of Wanette, Oklahoma. Carol started producing her set of five jars in 1986, and has not stopped since. Shirley Corl, of Caro, Michigan, started producing her magnificent works of art in 1990. Shirley manufactures more cookie jars than anyone else in the country. Sam and Denise Alfano, of Pearl River, Louisiana, have also made their mark in the cookie jar world. They produced top-quality, original designs, that are the very best. Most of their jars sell out immediately and sell on the secondary market extremely well. We must not forget to mention J.D. James in Buckeye Lake, Ohio, who started with some beautiful reproductions and is now designing and producing his own original cookie jars. Bob and Gale Gerds, of West Allis, Wisconsin, also produce beautiful reproductions and are now venturing into their own designs.

All of the above people need special recognition for a job well done! They will all be a part of history.

Acknowledgments

While writing this book, we learned very quickly that it is impossible for one single person to physically research and photograph all of the material. Therefore, we would like to take this moment to recognize all of the many people across the country who graciously used their own time and resources to assist us in completing this book, which we believe to be the most comprehensive collection of cookie jars today.

Steve Johnson and Wayne Bollin of Sioux City, Iowa, spent many hours photographing parts of their collection at their own expense to make our book complete. Steve and Wayne are two very special people who we have spent time visiting with in their home and who will always mean a lot to us. Thanks guys!

Karen Ceja, of Kent, Washington has been a customer and a friend for a very long time. Karen recently called me to see if she could be of any help. Thanks Karen for some beautiful photographs as well as being there for us all these years.

We'd like to thank Shirley and Clyde Cole of Idaho, who were the first to come forward and offer us anything they had in their collection for the book.

Shirley and Bill Corl, of Caro, Michigan, have been very important in our lives. Shirley is the talented artist and ceramicist who produces all of our Commemorative Shawnee Cookie Jars and other Special Editions for us.

William and Jean Correll of Bedford, Indiana are two very special people who has been very unselfish with their time, photography, as well as a shoulder to lean on. About two years ago, the Corrells visited us in our home and we spent a wonderful afternoon together. We cannot wait for Bill and Jean, along with their two children to come back and visit again.

Karen Constantine of Fort Lauderdale, Florida, who taught us how to use this computer and has spent many hours working on this book with us. We could not have done this without you, Karen. There aren't enough words of appreciation that Mark and I have for you. As long as this book is in print, you can always feel proud that you were a major factor in writing this book. Thanks Karen.

To Dennis Haase of Fort Lauderdale, Florida, how can Mark and I thank you for sharing your most treasured girlfriend, Karen? All of the days and all of the hours that Karen spent in our home, we have you to thank, Dennis, for being so unselfish.

My special friend Donna Gainey, of Oklahoma City, Oklahoma, no one has ever made me sick from laughing - but you! I hope we will always be friends.

Mary Jane Giacomini of Ferndale, California, I just want to say, "Thank you for being my friend." Mary Jane unselfishly provided us with the most beautiful American Bisque pictures and all she kept saying was, "Are you sure you don't need more?" M.J. is known across the country as being "Ms. Bubbly".

Thanks to John and Norma Grogan of Mesquite, Texas, your pictures were the best! I know I called you towards the end in a panic, and your kind words and reassurance meant so much. Thanks John!

Linda and Richard Guffey of El Cajon, California. Linda, you are one of my treasured friends. You have unselfishly given of yourself and your time just because you're a good person.

Steve Horelica of Texas generously supplied us with some photographs at the very last minute. Thanks for your help Steve!

Sam and Joani Klein of Boca Raton, Florida, our special friends, who have been a source of encouragement throughout the writing of this book.

Thanks to Reba Klimas of Federal Way, Washington, for being there when I needed you and for being a great friend. Your Friendship is very important to me.

Mike Kranz of Hudson, Wisconsin, was a big help with the Black Americana section. Your friendship over the years has meant a lot to us. Thanks Mike!

If it wasn't for Leonard Lindstrom, of Lubbock, Texas, we would not have the Red Wing section in our book. About 95% of the pictures are of his personal collection. Leonard spent many hours taking pictures for us, people that he didn't know. I hope that all collectors of Red Wing Pottery are happy with this section. Thank you Leonard, for all of your hard work.

Thanks to Chris Mahloch, of Onawa, Iowa, owner and operator of Treasure Shack Antiques. Her expertise and enthusiasm was greatly needed and appreciated. Chris and I have shared many wonderful laughs.

John Martin of California, a special friend and customer who also spent many hours photographing much of his collection.

Terry and Lisa McClellan of Rochester, Minnesota, were extremely helpful in pricing of the Red Wing Cookie Jars, the information given on Red Wing, and also some of the photography. Lisa and Terry have been very good friends over the years.

Richard O'Donnell of Latrobe, Pennsylvania came through for us at the very last minute with some beautiful pictures. Richard, your pictures were terrific. Thanks.

Dennis and Arlene Roth, our friends in New Jersey, shared their entire Black Americana and Walt Disney Production collections with us. Dennis is responsible for a majority of the entire Black Americana section, not only providing the photos, but seeking out other sources as well. Dennis spent many days on photography and Federal Expressing all photos for our approval. Many were to be reshot, and never did Dennis lose his enthusiasm. We thank you Dennis!

Neil and Terry Smith of Greensboro, North Carolina, spent many days photographing their entire collection and have been a tremendous source of encouragement from the very beginning, when we "just weren't sure if we could do this." Neil said, "Don't worry about anything. We will be there to help in any way, shape or form that you need." Neil and Terry were originally our customers, but now have become our treasured friends.

Charlie and Rose Snyder of Charlie's Collectibles, Independence, Kansas, also helped with photography. They are special friends and always share their knowledge with all cookie jar dealers and collectors across the country.

I'd also like to acknowledge Nyla and Phil Thurston of Cortland, New York, owners and operators of Classique Cookie Jars. Nyla and Phil, we will never forget September 30, 1993, that magical phone call when you ordered 66 cookie jars from us. The fun we shared that day will never be forgotten. A very special thanks to you both.

Kathy Turner of Jupiter, Florida, opened her home to Mark and Brett for an entire day of photographing many of her jars, an experience that neither Mark nor Brett will ever forget. Mark's words when he cam home from Kathy's house was, "Kathy has the most rare and unusual cookie jars that I have ever seen!" Thanks Kathy!

Janice Wise of El Segundo, California is someone who puts a smile on my face. Janice worked diligently on photography for many days and we have shared many wonderful hours on the phone.

Lauren Carroll of Bellmore, New York, your photography was incredible. Your pictures were the best! Thank you for all of the hours you put in photographing Pat and John Yohe's collection.

Pat and John Yohe of New York, two very special friends who started as customers. When I called on Pat for help, all she said was, "Anything you need Ellen, consider it done." Thanks Pat and John – you're very special.

At this time, Mark and I would like to say a very, very special thank you to Sharon and Michael Helmke, who came to us as customers and have become our very dearest friends. While Mark was suffering through Hurricane Andrew, I was in Iowa, visiting Sharon and Michael. Thank you both for the beautiful pictures of the most magnificent collection of Shawnee Pottery. I know you interrupted your field work to get it done for us. You guys are the best!

Mercedes DiRenzo of Jazze Junque, Chicago, Illinois has been a friend from the very beginning. She has sent us many pictures this year. Mark and I were lucky to go and visit Mercedes and her daughter Hillary in Chicago in 1993. We've shared some wonderful times on the phone together. Mark and I want to say how very important your friendship is to us. Thank you Mercedes!!

We must not forget to thank our parents, Sophie and Philip Gale, of Tamarac, Florida, and Mrs. Pearl Supnick, of Tamarac, Florida. Our parents have been a tremendous source of encouragement and inspiration throughout our lives. We wish everyone could be as lucky as we are to have such wonderful parents.

Last but not least, and most important, Neil Wood of L-W Book Sales, Gas City, Indiana, for making this dream come true. Thanks Neil, for being persistent.

Mark and I hope that these acknowledgments are just the beginning of many hours to come, enjoying our book. We would like to thank our friends, customers, and fellow dealers, who helped make this book possible.

Special Acknowledgment

We would like to take this time to recognize a very special young man, Brett Aaron Reynoldson, of Plantation, Florida. Not only is Brett our son Todd's best friend, he is our best friend. For the past three years, without Brett's help, our cookie jar business and this book could not be possible. In November 1992, Brett became my extra pair of hands and learned very quickly the art of packing a cookie jar. He has never stopped learning. He has also become quite experienced in all aspects of the pottery business. Brett has spent many days in 100 degree plus temperatures photographing cookie jars with Mark in our warehouse, visiting collector's homes, and just being Mark's extra pair of legs when necessary. Brett, Mark and I want to say, "Thank You! We are proud of you. You will always be the third Supnick son."

Pricing

This single subject is the one subject that evokes so much controversy. It does so because most people need to understand what the prices in the reference guide are representing. This guide represents a market value. The World Book Dictionary defines market value as,

"the probable price at which an article would be bought or sold at a given time on the open market."

In order to establish market prices for this book we have used the following to aid us in this endeavor: the prices stated in mailing lists, prices as advertised in the *Antique Trader*, prices from auctions, advertisements in newsletters, prices at shops and malls, items sold through our cookie jar business, "Sunshine Collectibles", as well as many collectors and dealers that stepped forward to help. Many of these same people are listed in our acknowledgments. Again, we thank them for their help.

Remember that condition is of utmost importance. Prices in this book are market prices for cookie jars that are free of damage. Cookie jars with hairlines, chips, etc. are to be priced accordingly.

This price guide, as with most price guides, was designed to assist both the collector and the dealer. The prices quoted are to be used as a guide only, and were not intended to set prices. The authors assume no responsibility for any losses that may occur as a result of consulting this book. As is always the case, prices will vary from one location to another as supply and demand set a market value.

In closing, I would like to quote from an article that I wrote in 1992.

"We have been collecting and dealing in collectibles for over fifteen years and have authored two books, Collecting Shawnee Pottery, and Collecting Hull Pottery's Little Red Riding Hood, as well as being a contributing author to Schroeder's Antique Price Guide and the Warman's Antique Guides.

Pricing is affected by many factors: rarity, supply and demand, inflation, condition, and the increased amounts of collectors in the market, are just a few of the reasons that cookie jars, as well as many collectibles, go up in price. Cookie jars are unique, since most of the jars that we seek were made in the years 1950 through 1970. With such a short history, you will be hard pressed to find collectors who are not bying for the now harder to find jars. These factors have caused prices to increase not just in cookie jars but in almost every collectible that we can think of.

In the March 16, 1988 issue of The Antique Trader, I find the following cookie jar for sale in the (China Glass For Sale) section: 'Milk Glass Westmoreland Cookie Jar $52.00'. It is the only cookie jar listed and this was just three years ago. Talk about demand. Open up the Trader today and count the jars. Supply and demand . . .

In the 1982 Price Guide of Brenda Roberts, The Collector's Encyclopedia of Hull Pottery, she lists three Little Red Riding Hood cookie jars at $25-30 each. Today, in Joan Hull's Hull, the Heavenly Pottery, the same cookie jars are listed at $300-$400 each – an increase of ten times the retail price. By the way, in the 1981 Robert's Guide, The Little Red Riding Hood Advertising Plaque was priced at $100-$150. Today it sells for, and has sold for, $15,000.00. Regarding other collectibles than cookie jars, let me say that the Hull Tropicana Basket was listed in 1981 at $40-$50. Today, is listed at $600. In 1966, a guide book of United States coins by R.S. Yeoman, the 1932 Denver Mint quarter was priced at $250. In mint condition, in 1976, the price was $425, and in 1991, it is priced at $5,500.00. This coin is called a key coin since it is the one that would be considered a key to complete the collection. Key coins come in every denomination. Do we not have many cookie jars that could be key jars? We sure do.

Ellen and I have purchased back many cookie jars and pottery that we have sold, and we have purchased them from the very collector that we sold them to. And yes, they did make a profit. You see, collecting and dealing go hand in hand. Buy what you like and buy what you can afford. History has proven that today's high prices are tomorrow's great deals."

I hope this point of view helps some of the collectors out there understand pricing. I would like to buy cookie jars at last year's prices also, but life goes on.

Recommended Newsletters

"The Cookie Jar Collector's Club News"
595 Cross River Road
Katonah, NY 10536
Phone: (914) 232-0383
Editor-in-Chief: Louise Messina Daking

"Exclusively Shawnee –
The Shawnee Pottery Lover's Newsletter"
P.O. Box 713
New Smyrna Beach, FL 32170
Phone: (904) 345-0150
Editor: Pamela Curran

"Learn Your ABC's – American Bisque
P.O. Box 404
Ferndale, CA 95536
Editior: Mary Jane Giacomini
Published Quarterly – Subscription Price is $12/year

Our McCoy Matters
Parksville, MO
Kathy Lynch, Editor

Cookie Jarrin
Rt. 2 Box 504
Walterboro, SC 29488
Joyce Roerig, Editor

The Cookie Jar Collectors Express
P.O. Box 221
Mayview, MO 64071
Sheryl Dabbs, Editor
816-584-6309

Pottery Restoration

Quoting a distinguished expert on restoration, Richard Beggs, "I think it is important to distinguish between a "repair" and a "restoration". A repair merely patches the piece to make it more visibly acceptable, whereas a restoration restores the piece to its original beauty."

There are many companies and individuals across the country involved in the restoration of pottery. Although many are reputable, some are not.

There are many quality restorers throughout the country. Before you trust your valuable piece with a restorer, be sure to check their references. Listed below are three quality restorers that we have had the occasion to use:

Richard Beggs, Kernersville, North Carolina

Mark Dorian, Fresno, California

George Honchar, Greenwood Lake, New York

Reproductions and Refired Cookie Jars

<u>Reproductions</u>: Reproducing or being reproduced, a copy.

<u>Refired</u>: Refired to a high enough heat to be able to add gold trim or non-original treatments, such as decals, to falsely increase the value of an item.

Knowledge and a good working relationship with reputable dealers are the key to your success. I hope the following hints help you identify both reproduced and refired cookie jars:

1. Cookie jars that are cast from originals tend to be about 10% smaller in girth and height. Most reproductions also lose some detail, weight, and will most likely be whiter than the originals.

2. Trim colors should match the colors on already established trimmed items, as the refired and reproductions have been found in newer and more modern colors.

3. Many refired items show a black "peppered type" of impurity that floats up to the top of the glaze. This impurity also shows up in a small degree in some of the real decorated items, but in larger amounts in those that have been refired.

4. Decals of the older type are harder to find. Study the details in our book as well as others. Count the petals, stems, leaves, lettering, and check the color. If what your looking at does not match either, beware.

5. Refired items, in many cases, have a sandy feel as the glaze thins when refired. Particularly check the bases, as this happens often.

6. We have been collecting and dealing in cookie jars for over 20 years and find it very hard to believe a booth could have <u>many</u> gold trimmed items with <u>matching</u> decals and trim. Beware . . . .

7. Items that have been refired at a later date and gold trim added can sometimes be identified with a magnifying glass. Check closely the gold trim that has gone over a craze. In a refired item, the gold will dip down into the craze as opposed to separating with the glaze craze. Refired gold trim on a jar that has crazing will also show some gold falling away from the applied line and flowing into the craze adjacent to the trim.

8. Most important is buy from a dealer who is knowledgeable and has a return policy. Do not buy questionable or decorated items from a dealer that you do not know or a dealer that states, "All Sales Final." Protect yourself . . . .

We have attempted throughout this book to identify many cookie jars that are being reproduced. Educate yourself. Remember, "if in doubt, don't", "if it looks too good to be true, it probably is."

About The Authors

Mark Elliott Supnick, was born March 19, 1945, in the Bronx, New York. Mark lived in the Bronx until he was 15, when, at that point his family moved to Teaneck, New Jersey, where Mark graduated from Teaneck High School in 1962. Then Uncle Sam called. Mark enlisted in the United States Navy where he served active duty for four years. Three years were spent in Africa and one year aboard the U.S.S. Independence Aircraft Carrier CVA 62. After the service, Mark became sales manager for the Smith Corona Marchant Corporation of Saddlebrook, New Jersey.

For the past 21 years, Mark has been in the furniture business in South Florida and is proud owner of 19 sleep centers. Mark has authored two other books, "Collecting Shawnee Pottery, A Pictorial Reference and Price Guide," published in 1983, and "Collecting Hull Pottery's Little Red Riding Hood, A Pictorial Reference and Price Guide," published in 1989.

Ellen Jane Supnick, was born in the Bronx, New York, June 16, 1947. Ellen lived in New York until the age of seven, when her family moved to Fair Lawn, New Jersey. Ellen graduated from Fair Lawn High School in 1965, and then began working in Midtown Manhattan for a major department store chain as a buyer in the small appliance division. Ellen then changed positions to a new company, Smith Corona Marchant of Saddlebrook, New Jersey, where she met Mark.

Two years later, Ellen and Mark were married on March 14, 1971. Fifteen months later, their first son, Todd Michael, was born, and they shortly thereafter moved to Florida. A few years later, Matthew Adam was born, when at that time Ellen was involved with Mark's company. About five years ago she decided that her love of collecting and dealing was what she wanted to do. Mark and Ellen live with their son, Matthew in Ft. Lauderdale, Florida, where Matthew attends the University School of Nova University, while their son Todd attends the University of Florida in Gainesville.

We both hope that everyone enjoys our cookie jar book. We have tried to do our best – that is all we can do.

Bibliography

Cookie Jarrin:
>   The Cookie Jar Newsletter, Joyce Roerig, Editor, January-February 1995, Vol. 5 #1,
>   Article written by Carl Gibbs Jr.

Curran, Pamela:
>   Exclusively Shawnee, Pottery Collector's Club, New Smyrna Beach, Florida.

Curran, Pamela:
>   Shawnee Pottery A True Encyclopedia, Schiffer Publishing, Atglen, Pennsylvania, 1995

DePasquale, Dan & Gail; Peterson, Larry:
>   Red Wing Stoneware and Identification value guide, Collector Books, Paducah, Kentucky, 1983.

Giacomini, Mary Jane:
>   American Bisque Collector's Guide with Prices, a Schiffer Book for Collectors,
>   Schiffer Publishing LTD, Atglen, Pennsylvania, 1994.

Gibbs, Carl, Jr.:
>   The Collectors Encyclopedia of Metlox Potteries. Collector Books, Paducah, Kentucky, 1995.

Lehner's, Encyclopedia of U.S. Marks on U.S. Pottery, Porcelain, and Clay. Collector Books, Paducah, Kentucky, 1988.

Nichols, Harold:
>   McCoy Cookie Jars, From the First to the Last, Nichols Publishing, 1991.

Pfaltzgraff, America's Potter, Historical Society of York County, York, Pennsylvania, 1989,
>   The Pfaltzgraff Company, Researched and Compiled by David A. Walsh and Polly Stetler.

Roberts, Brenda:
>   The Ultimate Encyclopedia of Hull Pottery, Walsworth Publishing Company, Marceline, Missouri 1992.

Roerig, Fred & Joyce Herndon:
>   The Collector's Encyclopedia of Cookie Jars, Collector Books, Paducah, Kentucky, 1991.

Roerig, Fred & Joyce Herndon:
>   The Collector's Encyclopedia of Cookie Jars, Book II, Collector Books, Paducah, Kentucky, 1994.

Schneider, Mike: The Complete Cookie Jar Book, Schiffer Publishing, LTD., Atglen, Pennsylvania, 1991.

Simon, Delores: Red Wing Pottery with Rum Rill Identification and Value Guide,
>   Collectors Books, Paducah, Kentucky, 1980.

Supnick, Mark E.: Collecting Hull Pottery's Little Red Riding Hood, A Pictorial Reference and Price Guide,
>   1992, L-W Book Sales, Gas City, Indiana 46933

Supnick, Mark E.: Collecting Shawnee Pottery, A Pictorial Reference and Price Guide,
>   1994, L-W Book Sales, Gas City, Indiana 46933

Westfall, Ermagene: An Illustrated Value Guide to Cookie Jars, Collector Books, a Division of
>   Schroeder Publishing Company, Inc., Paducah, Kentucky, Last Updated: 1993.

Westfall, Ermagene, An Illustrated Value Guide to Cookie Jars Book II, Collector Books,
>   A Division of Schroeder Publishing Company, Inc., Paducah, Kentucky, 1993.

A Company of Two

David Brdecko and Russ Morris are "A Company of Two." David designs and sculpts the cookie jars. Russ does public relations, promotions and advertising. Their cookie jars are sold all over the United States, plus a gift shop in Puerto Rico and the Museum of African Art, Los Angeles, California. New additions are constantly being produced. Originally from Albuquerque New Mexico, they now live and work in Shawnee, Oklahoma. All jars are Limited Editions.

Sister Chubby Cheeks
marked "A Company of 2" in a circular mark,
"David Brdecko Original Limited Editions".
Value: $150-195

Sister Chubby Cheeks
marked "A Company of 2" in a circular mark,
"David Brdecko Original Limited Editions".
Value: $150-195

Higby the Butler
marked "A Company of 2" in a circular mark,
"David Brdecko Original Limited Editions".
Value: $150-195

Higby the Butler
marked "A Company of 2" in a circular mark,
"David Brdecko Original Limited Editions".
Value: $150-195

Jelly Belly
marked "A Company of 2" in a circular mark,
"David Brdecko Original Limited Editions".
Value: $125

Izzy
marked "A Company of 2" in a circular mark,
"David Brdecko Original Limited Editions".
Value: $150-195

Hosefa Sal
marked "Sunshine Collectibles",
"A Company of 2" in a circular mark;
"David Brdecko Original Limited Editions".
Value: $150-175

Hosefa Sal
marked "A Company of 2" in a circular mark,
"David Brdecko Original Limited Editions".
Value: $150-195

A Little Company

A Little Company – Owned and operated by Michael Buonaiuto and Shelly Tincher Buonaiuto of Santa Fe, New Mexico. Both were educated at the University of Massachusetts Art School. Michael and Shelly, originally from New York, have traveled extensively around South America and other parts of the world, coming home to Santa Fe to design pottery, which is often humorous, whimsical, and stylish from their own experiences, the people they have met, and the places they have traveled.

Edmund
Edmund was a Friend of
Shelley & Michael Buonaiuto in New York.
Value: $175

Blanket Couple
12" high, (no longer being made),
marked "A Little Company Copyright 87".
Value: $200-250

Blanket Couple
12" high, African Americans,
(no longer being made)
marked "A Little Company Copyright 87".
Value: $200-250

Blanket Couple
12" high, (no longer being made)
marked "A Little Company Copyright 87".
Value: $200-250

Diva
marked "A Little Company 1991 Copyright ".
Value: $175

Italian Couple
12" high,
marked "A Little Company 1991 Copyright".
Value: $175

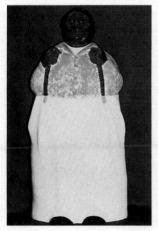

Edmund
As African American, 19 1/2" high.
Value: $175

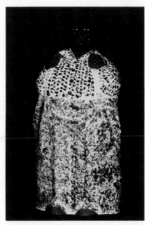

Edmund
Different Design.
Value: $175

Edmund
Different Design.
Value: $175

Edmund
Different Design.
Value: $175

David
19" high, A Friend of the Buonaiutos in New York
marked "A Little Company 1991"
Custom Tailored to Collector's Delights.
Value: $175

David
19" high, marked "A Little Company 1991"
Custom Tailored to Collector's Delights.
Value: $175

David
19" high, marked "A Little Company 1991"
Custom Tailored to Collector's Delights.
Value: $175

Fats the Piano Man
marked "A Little Company 1992 Copyright"
Limited Edition of 250.
Value: $225-275

Stella
She accompanies Fats at the Piano
15" high; Limited Edition of 250.
Value: $225-275

Stella and Fats
(shown together).
Value: $450-550/set

Stella
Limited Edition,
Slightly Different Design
Value: $225-275

Stella
Limited Edition,
Slightly Different Design.
Value: $225-275

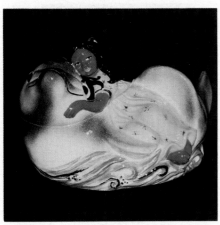

Dolphin with African American Girl
Limited Edition.
Value: $160-175

Dolphin with White Girl
Limited Edition.
Value: $160-175

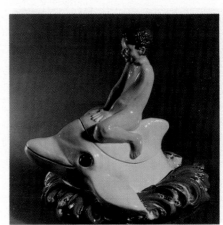

Dolphin with White Boy
11" high, introduced in 1994.
Limited Edition of 300.
Value: $160-175

Dolphin with African American Boy
11" high, introduced in 1994.
Limited Edition of 300.
Value: $160-175

Secrets
12" high, introduced in 1991.
Limited Edition of 150.
Value: $175

Secrets
12" high, introduced in 1991.
Limited Edition of 150.
Value: $175

Secrets
12" high, introduced in 1991.
Limited Edition of 150.
Value: $175

Grandma with Child
15" high, introduced in 1991.
Limited Edition of 150.
Value: $175

Grandma with Child
15" high, introduced in 1991.
Limited Edition of 150.
Value: $175

Woman with Scarf
11" tall. Limited Edition of 100.
Marked "A Little Company 1992 Copyright".
Value: $175

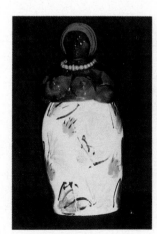

Earth Goddess
1991
Value: $175-225

Earth Goddess
16" high, introduced in 1985.
open edition, available as nude.
Value: $175-225

Gospel Singer
Limited Edition
Value: $160-175

Sugar Blues
Designed by Shelley Buonaiuto,
Limited Edition of 150, 1992
Value: $175-250

Diva
14" high, Introduced in 1987
Value: $175

Smile
Open Edition,
marked "A Little Company"
Value: $175

Santa Fe Railroad Station
8" high, Introduced in 1992, Open Edition
Value: $150

Pegapuss
7 1/2" high,
marked "A Little Company 1992 Copyright"
Value: $160-175

All are marked "A Little Company 1992 Copyright"

Small Pig
7 1/2" high
Value: $125

Medium Pig
9" high
Value: $150

Large Pig
10" high
Value: $175-190

Blanket Couple
Open Edition
Value: $200-250

The Abingdon Pottery Company

The Abingdon Pottery Company was located in Abingdon, Illinois; and started production in the early 1930's. 95% of Abingdon Cookie Jars have an ink stamp on the bottom, "Abingdon USA" and an impressed serial number. Abingdon jars are very collectible.

The Windmill
10 3/4" high,
marked "Abingdon U.S.A. #678"
Value: $350-450

Cookie Time Clock
9" high,
marked "Abingdon U.S.A. #653"
Value: $195-250

Money Bag
7 3/4" high,
marked "Abingdon U.S.A. #588"
Value: $150-175

Mother Goose
12 1/4" high,
marked "Abingdon U.S.A. #695"
Value: $900-1,100

Little Bo Peep
12" high,
marked "Abington U.S.A. #694"
Value: $450-500

Little Miss Muffett
11 1/4" high,
marked "Abington U.S.A. #622"
Value: $425-475

Little Old Lady
9 1/2" high,
marked "Abingdon U.S.A. #471".
Value: $550-595

Little Old Lady
Ranges from 9 1/2"-10" high,
marked "Abingdon U.S.A. #471" (different color).
Value: $550-595

Little Old Lady
10" high, marked "Abingdon U.S.A. #471".
Value: $550-595

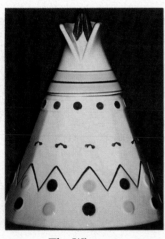

The Wigwam
marked "Abingdon U.S.A. #665".
Value: $700-900

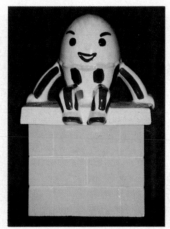

Humpty Dumpty
11 1/2" high, marked "Abingdon U.S.A. #663".
Value: $395-450

Train
7 1/2" high, marked "Abingdon U.S.A. #651"
Value: $350-450

Hobby Horse
10 1/2" high, marked "Abingdon U.S.A. #602".
Value: $350-450

Pineapple
10 1/2" high, marked "Abingdon U.S.A. #664".
Value: $175-195

The Daisy Jar
8" high, marked "Abingdon U.S.A. #677".
Value: $90-125

Hippo
8 1/4" high,
marked "Abingdon U.S.A. #549", solid color.
Value: $350-400

Hippo
8 1/4" high, marked "Abingdon U.S.A. #549",
hand decorated flowers.
Value: $650-750

Hippo
8 1/4" high, marked "Abingdon U.S.A. #549",
hand decorated flowers.
Value: $650-750

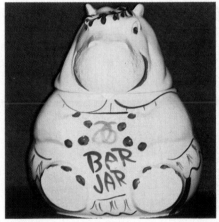

Hippo
8 1/4" high, bar jar,
marked "Abingdon U.S.A. #549".
Value: $850-900

Witch
11 1/2" high, marked "Abingdon U.S.A. #692".
Value: $1,800-2,200

Jack In The Box
marked "Abingdon U.S.A. #611".
Value: $850-950

Jack-O-Lantern
marked "Abingdon U.S.A. #674".
Value: $550-595

Advertising

Many different companies across the USA have produced cookie jars as advertising premiums.

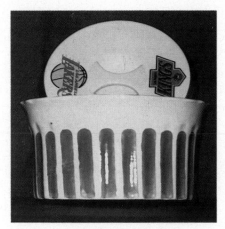

The Great Western Forum
marked "Another Darling Bear Production".
Value: $400-495

The Great Western Forum
(different view), marked
"Another Darling Bear Production".
Value: $400-495

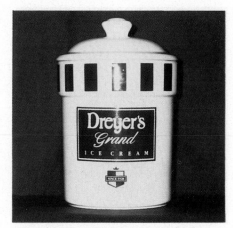

Dreyer's Grand Ice Cream
marked "Copyright Treasure Craft U.S.A.".
Value: $500-600

Dreyer's Grand Ice Cream
with different lid, the lid reads "Cookie's &
Cream All Natural Ice Cream", jar unmarked.
Value: $600-750

Coca-Cola Jug
sold thru catalogs,
made in Taiwan (nice quality).
Value: $50-60

Coca-Cola Jug
sold thru catalogs, shown with different lid,
made in Taiwan (nice quality).
Value: $50-60

Kentucky Fried Chicken
glass, marked "USA".
Value: $250-300

Entemann's Chef
promotional cookie jar in New York area
for purchases of $100.
Value: $300-400

Romper Room
"Laurel Sales, Cleveland, Ohio",
paper label "DO-BEE, E-2200" made in Japan.
Value: $550-600

Quaker Oats
marked "Regal China" below recipe.
Value: $150-175

Pepperidge Farm Bag of Cookies
offered thru catalogs.
Value: $90-95

Jazz'e Junque Cookie Shop
shop owned and operated by Mercedes DiRenzo,
3831 N. Lincoln Ave., Chicago, IL 60613.
Produced by Kathy Wolfe, limited edtion.
Value: $225-250

Century 21 House
1994
Value: $200-225

Century 21 House
older jar, first in series.
Value: $1,000-1,400

Case Tractor
celebrating 150 years of Case Tractors, 1993.
Value: $185-225

Green Giant Sprout
12" high, made in Taiwan. Benjsmin & Medwin,
marked "Copyright 1988 Pillsbury Co."
Value: $150-175

Liv-R-Snaps Dog
marked "USA Liv-R-Snaps Copyright"
Value: $125-150

Original Nestle's Toll House Cookies
9 ³/4" high, unmarked, recipe on back,
(possibly holiday designs).
Value: $200-225

Harley Davidson Hog
sold in Harley Davidson stores throughout the
country, marked "made by McCoy Pottery,
copyright 1984 HD"
Value: $600-750

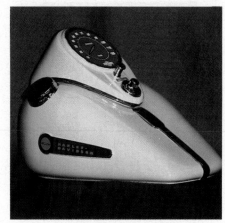

Harley Davidson Gas Tank Cookie Jar
made in Taiwan.
Value: $150-175

Human Bean
marked "Human Bean Copyright 1981
Morgan, Inc., LTD Enesco".
Value: $125-150

Pure Cane Sugar
unmarked.
Value: $125-150

Coca-Cola
marked "Doranne, made in the U.S.A.".
Value: $150-195

Coca-Cola Can
marked "Made by McCoy 1003 U.S.A.".
Value: $150-195

Famous Amos Sack of Cookies
marked "Treasure Craft Copyright
made in USA".
Value: $150-175

Famous Amos Sack of Cookies
made by Sigma, paper label marked "Sigma The
Tastesetter", handpainted, meets FDA guidelines.
Value: $175-200

Famous Amos Sack of Cookies Bank
marked, "Sigma".
Value: $60-65

Kraft-T Marshmallow Bear
marked "By Genuine Regal China,
T-Bear Pawprint".
Value: $300-395

Pillsbury All-Purpose Sack of Flour
Benjamin & Medwin, Taiwan.
Value: $95-110

Nestle's Toll House Cookies House
sold thru cookie jar offer in supermarkets.
Value: $65-75

Blue Bonnet Sue
11 3/4" high, Benjamin & Medwin, marked
"Made in Taiwan Copyright 1989 Nabisco".
Value: $75-95

Snowman
Dayton Hudson Department Stores, 1992.
Value: $125-150

U.S.S. Enterprise
Star Trek Cookie Jar,
made by Pfaltzgraff, York, PA.
Value: $125

Mr. Peanut
Benjamin & Medwin, marked "Copyright 1990
PLC", made in Taiwan.
Value: $125-160

Eddie Bauer Bear
marked in script "Made in Japan for Eddie
Bauer", stamped "Outdoor Outfitter".
Value: $65-75

Tony The Tiger
7 3/4" high, plastic container,
marked "Copyright Kellog Company 1968".
Value: $150-175

Avon Bear
made for Avon by California Originals
in 1979, unmarked.
Value: $150-185

Neiman Marcus Annual Christmas Bear
marked "1994 made in Taiwan".
Value: $150-175

Neiman Marcus Christmas Cowboy Bear
marked "1993 made in Taiwan".
Value: $175-195

Pillsbury Doughboy
Benjamin & Medwin, marked "Copyright
1988 The Pillsbury Company".
Value: $45-50

Red Wing Morning Glory Crock
extremely rare jar with advertising in lid, unmarked.
(two views – Lid showing advertising.)
Value: $1,100-1,500

Elsie The Cow
ink stamped "Pottery Guild".
Value: $400-450

Elsie The Cow
(slightly different color variations)
Value: $400-450

Quaker Oats
10" high, marked "McCoy No. 208 USA", 1970.
Value: $650-800

Avon Upside Down Panda
made by McCoy, marked "210 USA".
Value: $150-175

Spuds McKenzie
wearing blue sweater, marked "Taiwan".
Value: $300-350

Pillsbury Doughboy Funfetti
Benjamin & Medwin, marked "Copyright 1992
The Pillsbury Company, Made in Taiwan".
Value: $40-45

**Original Great American Chocolate
Chip Cookie Company**
marked "USA".
Value: $350-425

Parker Quink
Parker Pen, "Made under License of Parker Pen
Company" "1982, The Silver Crane Co., England".
Value: $400-495

Hamm's Bear
marked "#148 U.S.A. Made by McCoy".
Value: $350-400

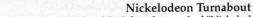

Nickelodeon Turnabout
one side marked "Nick at Nite" the other marked "Nickelodeon". Exclusively made for the
Nickelodeon channel, as a premium gift for employees only, approximately 2,500-3,000 total jars
were made. (These are both the same jars but two different views).
Value: $850-1,100

Horserace Track
unmarked.
Value: $350-395

Racoon Cookie Bandit
Shirttail character, limited edition, marked
"Made in Taiwan, Copyright 1981 Hallmark Cards",
(front and back views).
Value: $500-600

Jim Beam Commemorative
marked "Made for San Joaquin Valley
Collector's Club by Regal China".
Value: $175-200

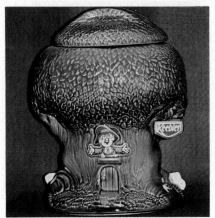 

Keebler Tree House
made by McCoy, unmarked.
Value: $125-150

Myer's Rum Crock
unmarked
Value: $50-65

Campbell Soup Kids
unmarked
Value: $550-650

Campbell Soup Kids Nodder
unmarked
Value: $600-650

The RSO Bull
RSO recording company, marked "Season's
Greetings 1988 from the RSO Family", company
recorded theme music from, "Saturday Night Fever".
Value: $500-600

Ken-L Ration Dog
marked "F & F Mold & Die Works,
Dayton, OH".
Value: $150

Carnation Malted Milk Cookie Jar
unmarked
Value: $350-400

Olmeca Tequila
unmarked
Value: $300-350

Campbell Soup Kids
marked "1990 Campbell Soup Company",
made in Taiwan.
Value: $75-95

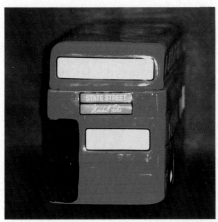

Picadilly Circus
made for Marshall Fields – (front and back views).
Value: $850-1,100

Campbell Soup Kids
(older jar)
Value: $95-125

Campbell Soup Canister Set
(older set)
Value: $195-225/set

Dunnell Co-Op Creamery Crock
Red Wing Pottery advertising cookie jar.
Value: $900-950

Hershey's Chocolate Bank
Value: $125-150

Ernie the Keebler Elf
9" high, marked "F & F Mold &
Die Works, Dayton, OH".
Value: $150-195

Milk Bone Dog Biscuit House
marked "Roman, made in Thailand".
Value: $150-195

Volkswagen
made exclusively for Lord and Taylor.
Value: $150-195

Century Brothers Circus Parade
made by Enesco, marked "Century Bros.
Circus Parade Copyright 1980".
Value: $250-350

Train
made for Marshall Fields, unmarked.
Value: $250-350

Clock
made for Marshall Fields, unmarked.
Value: $250-350

Avon House
(part of a set)
Value: $125-150

Mario Andretti Race Car
North American Ceramics, limited edition of
10,000, marked "ACCJ 10 NAC USA",
signed by Michael Andretti.
Value: $500-600

Frango Mint Truck
marked "Made in Italy Expressly for
Marshall Field & Co.".
Value: $600

President's Choice Cookies
made in Canada, unmarked.
Value: $175-195

Cookies Cylinder
marked "McMahan's Furniture
74th Birthday 1919-1993".
Jars were given away with purchases of $100.
Value: $300-350

Coca Cola Bear
sold thru catalogs, made in China.
Value: $45-55

Santa Bear
made for Dayton Hudson Dept. Stores, 1992.
Value: $95-100

Gulden's Mustard
(glass jar)
Value: $85-95

Fivers Jar
marked "Walter Kendall, Registered, Fivers".
Value: $300-350

Aramis Bear Jar
(older jar), marked "Aramis" in raised letters.
Value: $250-275

Oreo Cookie Server
2 1/4" x 10", marked "Copyright 1985,
Think Big, New York City". No longer being
made, but may be revived soon by company.
Value: $75-100

Oreo Cookie
made by Think Big, New York City,
(full view), marked "Made in the USA".
Value: $75-100

Entenmann's Chef
missing decal, marked "B & D Copyright".
Value: $225-250

Happy Face
made in ceramics class by Hillary DiRenzo,
age 9, marked "Made in USA".
Value: Priceless!

Mrs. Field's Cookie Sack
sold in Mrs. Field's Cookie Stores
throughout the country, paper label
marked "Made in Taiwan".
Value: $75-80

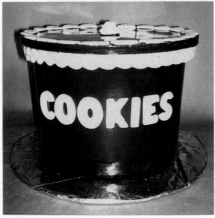

Happy 25th Anniversary Cookie Jar
made of solid chocolate for Mercedes DiRenzo as a gift from her husband, John.
(front and back views).
Value: No Value

Archway Cookie Bus
coupon to buy cookie jar with
oatmeal cookies, 1993.
Value: $60-75

Cookie Crock
for Jazz'e Junque, marked "Designed by K. Wolfe, Produced by the
The New Collection of Rose". (front and back views).
Value: $50-60

Grandma
Mary Englebriet for Hallmark Stores, 1993.
Value: $250-300

Happy Days Jukebox
Value: $200-225

Cookie Cylinder
(front and bottom views and a view showing the box)
Bottom view shows the advertising on this cookie cylinder.
Value: $175-195

Alfano Art Pottery

Alfano Art Pottery – Sam and Denise Alfano, Pearl River, Louisiana. Sam is a metal engraver and Denise has been a watercolor artist for many years. Sam and Denise started in cookie jars about 2 1/2 years ago. Their first jar was the Jazz player. Sam played professionally in a band in New Orleans which gave him the inspiration for this jar, as well as their second jar, B-Flat Williams. Sam and Denise produce only their own original designs, each in a Limited Edition.

Merlin the Magician
designed and created by Sam & Denise Alfano, limited edition of 50,
marked "Copyright Alfano Pottery USA". This jar sold out in 8 days.
(front and back views)
Value: $450-550

Ruby
African American, only 15 were made as
African American, sold out in 2 hours,
marked "Copyright Alfano Pottery USA".
Value: $400+

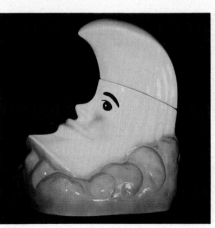 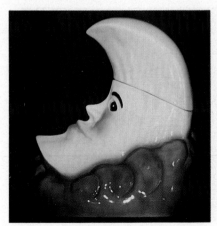

Man in the Moon
prototype, one-of-a-kind "Copyright Alfano Pottery USA".
Value: $150-175

Man in the Moon
marked "Copyright Alfano Pottery USA",
limited edition of 100.
Value: $150-175

Ruby
white faced, limited edition of 60,
marked "Copyright Alfano Pottery USA".
Value: $225+

Jazz Player
limited edition of 100, 1991
marked "Copyright Alfano Pottery USA".
Value: $195-250

B-Flat Williams
limited edition of 100,
marked "Copyright Alfano Pottery USA".
Value: $195+

The Paperboy
limited edition of 50,
marked "Copyright Alfano Pottery USA".
Value Issue Price: $200

Merlin the Magician
one of a kind experimental design,
never put into production.
No Value

American Bisque Company of Williamstown

American Bisque Company of Williamstown, West Virginia, was owned by the A.N. Allen family for sixty years. The company was in the business from 1919 until 1982.

Tugboat
8 ³/₄" high, bell in lid, marked "U.S.A."
Value: $275-325

Majorette
11 ¹/₄", marked "U.S.A."
Value: $475-550

Milk Wagon
9' high, marked "U.S.A. 740".
Value: $125-150

Yogi Bear
10" high, marked "Copyright Hanna Barbera Productions USA 1961".
Value: $475-575

Yogi Bear
light green hat and tie.
Value: $800-900

Standing Chef
12" high, marked "U.S.A.".
Value: $150-200

Grandma
12 3/4" high, gold trim, marked "U.S.A. 1958".
Value: $295-325

Grandma
12 3/4" high, yellow dress, brown hair,
marked "U.S.A."
Value: $175-195

Grandma
12 3/4" high, green dress, marked "U.S.A."
Value: $175-195

Pinecone Coffee Pot
9 1/2" high, marked "U.S.A."
Value: $40-50

Pup on Pot
11 1/2" high, most common style of this jar,
marked "U.S.A. 1958".
Value: $75-95

Pup on Pot
11 1/2" high.
Value: $125-150

Boy Pig
11 1/2" high, marked "U.S.A. 1958"
with patch on knee.
Value: $275-300

Boy Pig
11 1/2" high, variations in color and design,
no patch on knee.
Value: $175-250

Churn Boy
11 3/4" high, marked "U.S.A."
Value: $200-250

Ring for Cookies
10" high, bell in lid, common jar,
marked "USA".
Value: $65-75

Chick
12 ¼" high, marked "U.S.A. 1959".
(different color variations).
Value: $60-65 ea.

Yarn Doll
12" high, marked "U.S.A", (different color variations),
can also be found with gold trim.
Value: $250-275 ea.

Corner Acorn Jar
9 1/2" high, marked "U.S.A."
(different color variations).
Value: $325-350 ea.

Corner Chiffonier
marked "U.S.A."
Value: $325-350

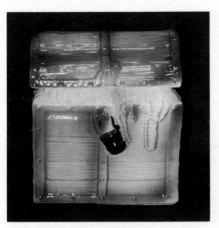

Treasure Chest
8 3/4" high, marked "U.S.A."
Value: $165-250

Treasure Chest
very rare and hard to find jar, 8" high,
marked "USA".
Value: $400-425

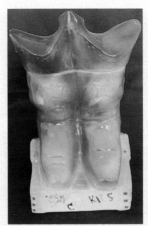

Cowboy Boots
12 1/2" high, marked "U.S.A. 742"
Value: $250-300

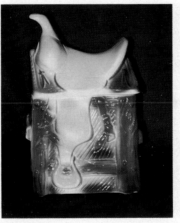

Saddle without Blackboard
12" high, marked "U.S.A."
(two different color variations shown here)
Value: $550-600 ea.

Strawberry
marked "Sears Exclusively,
USA Patent Pending".
Value: $125-150

Casper Candy Jar
11 3/4" high, very rare, marked "U.S.A."
Value: $1,800-2,200

Casper Cookie Jar
13 1/2" high, marked "U.S.A."
This jar is being reproduced.
Value: $900-1,100

Casper Bank
8 1/2" high, marked "U.S.A."
Value: $450-525

Popeye Bank
7" high, marked "U.S.A."
This bank is mising the corn cob pipe.
Value: $450-525

Popeye Cookie Jar
marked "U.S.A."
This jar is being reproduced.
Value: $1,100

Olive Oyl
10 1/2" high, marked "U.S.A."
This jar is being reproduced.
Value: $2,200-2,800

Swee Pea Bank
8 1/4" high x 6 1/2" long, marked "U.S.A.".
Value: $900-1,100

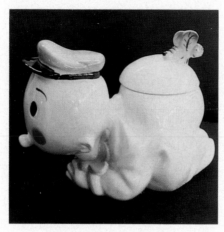

Swee Pea Cookie Jar
9" high x 12 1/2" long, marked "U.S.A."
This jar is being reproduced.
Value: $3,200-3,800

Icecream Freezer
9 3/4" high, marked "U.S.A."
Value: $475-500

Magic Bunny
12 1/4" high, marked "U.S.A. 1959".
Also available in green and blue.
Value: $140-175

Umbrella Kids
11 1/2" high, marked "U.S.A. #739".
Value: $395-495

Kitten on Beehive
11 3/4" high, marked "U.S.A."
Value: $130-145

Elephant with Baseball Cap
10" high, marked "U.S.A."
Value: $195-225

Pig in a Poke
12 1/2" high, marked "U.S.A.", made in 1958.
(two different color variations).
Value: $195-250 ea.

Baby Elephant
ranges from 11 1/2" to 13 1/4" high,
marked "U.S.A.", with gold trim.
Value: $300-325

Baby Elephant
ranges from 11 1/2" to 13 1/4" high,
marked "U.S.A."
Value: $225-250

Blackboard Hobo
14" high, raised lettering, marked "U.S.A."
Value: $400-495

Blackboard Boy
12 1/2" high, marked "U.S.A."
Value: $475-575

Blackboard Clown
13 1/4" high, marked "Patent Pending USA".
Value: $425-450

Blackboard Girl
13" high, marked "Patent Pending USA".
Value: $475-575

Blackboard Girl
13" high, marked "Patent Pending USA",
(different sign).
Value: $475-575

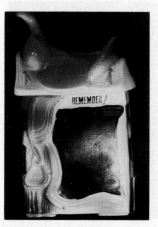

Blackboard Saddle
12 1/4" high, marked "Patent Pending USA".
Value: $295-350

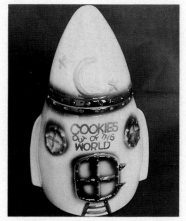

Cookies Out-of-this-World Spaceship
12 1/4" high, marked "U.S.A."
Value: $400-450

Jack-in-the-Box
12" high, marked "U.S.A.",
impressed in back
Value: $175-195

Hot Chocolate
9 1/4" high, marked "U.S.A.", a common jar.
Value: $195-250

Bear Flasher
10" high, corner cookie jar,
marked "#804 USA".
Value: $525-575

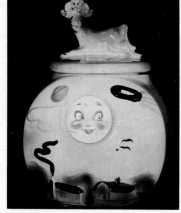

Cow Jumped over the Moon Flasher
11" high, marked "#806 USA", (most beautiful of all flashers
and hardest-to-find). (two different color variations).
Value: $1,500-1,800

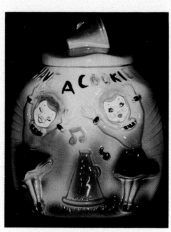

Cheerleader Flasher
11" high, (three sided jar),
marked "#802 USA".
Value: $475-525

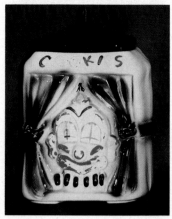  

Clown on Stage Flasher
9 3/4" high, marked "#805 USA". (Color difference in curtains).
Value: $375-425 ea.

Tortise and the Hare Flasher
9 3/4" high, marked "#803 USA",
(this is a harder to find flasher).
Value: $700-850

Sandman Cookies Flasher
9 3/4" high, marked "#801 USA",
(left: Dog on TV flasher – right: Clown on TV).
Value: $525-575 ea.

Cookie Railroad
7 1/2" x 11 3/4", marked "USA 200", gold trim.
Value: $150-160

Cookie Railroad
7 1/2" x 9 1/2", (smaller jar then previous picture),
different color variation, marked "USA 200".
Value: $150-160

Boy Turnabout

Girl Turnabout

9" high, made by APCO.
(The girl is the reverse view of the boy jar, safety pin trimmed in 22-24 K Gold".

Value: $175-225

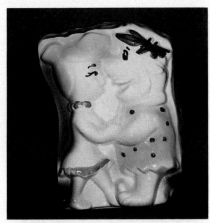

Fred & Wilma Bank
8 1/2" high, (on back, carved in stone,
"Fred Loves Wilma").
Value: $425-500

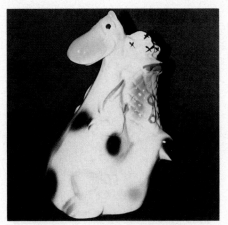

Dino with Golf Clubs Bank
8 1/4" high, incised, "Dino" on tail,
marked "USA".
Value: $500-550

Dino with Golf Clubs Jar
12 1/2" high, marked "Hanna Barbera Copyright".
This jar is being reproduced,
marked "USA, Made in 1960".
Value: $1,200-1,400

Wilma on the Telephone
"Flintstones" written on the arm of chair,
this jar has been reproduced, marked "USA".
Value: $1,500-1,800

Fred & Dino
first in Series, "Flintstones" is impressed
on bottom of base. Marked "U.S.A.".
14 1/2" high, this jar being reproduced.
Value: $1,100-1,300

The Rubbles House
10" high, marked "USA'.
This jar is being reproduced.
Value: $1,100-1,300

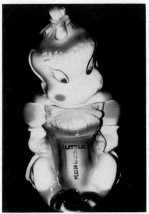

Little Audrey Cookie Jar
13 1/2" high x 8 1/2" wide, very rare,
and very hard-to-find.
Value: $4,500-5,200

Little Audrey Bank
8 1/4" high.
Value: $550-700

Davy Crockett
12 1/4" high, unmarked.
Value: $400-475

Davy in the Woods
11" high, marked "USA".
Value: $750-800

Santa
9 3/4" high, marked "USA",
(not an easy jar to find).
Value: $600-700

Oaken Bucket with Dipper Finial
10" high, marked "USA".
Value: $400-450

Pennsylvania Dutch Girl
11 1/4" high, marked "USA".
Value: $500-600

Pennsylvania Dutch Boy
11 1/2" high, marked "USA".
Value: $600-650

Peasant Girl
10 1/2" high, marked "USA".
Value: $750-900

Churn
10" high, marked "USA".
(common jar)
Value: $35-40

Cookie Time Clock
9" high, marked "USA 203", with gold trim.
Value: $125-175

Liberty Bell
9 3/4" high, marked "USA".
Value: $250-275

Collegiate Owl
11 1/4" high, (can also be found with gold trim).
Value: $85-95

After School Cookies
10 1/4" high, marked "U.S.A. 741",
with bell in lid.
Value: $50-60

Coffee Pot
9 1/2" high, marked "USA".
Value: $85-90

Bear with Hat
11 1/2" high, marked "USA".
(different color variations shown here).
Value: $160-195 ea.

Lamb with Hands in Pocket
10 1/2" high, marked "U.S.A."
Value: $225-250

Dancing Pig
(Ranges in size from 10" to 11 1/2" high),
marked "USA", with gold trim.
(front and back views)
Value: $225-250

Dancing Pig
marked "USA", no gold trim.
Value: $150-195

Cat with Hands in Pocket
11 1/2" high, marked "U.S.A.".
Value: $150-175

Dancing Baby Elephant
unmarked.
Value: $165-195

Dutch Girl
12 1/2" high, marked "U.S.A.".
Value: $95-110

Star Cylinder
8 1/2" high, marked "U.S.A.", red is cold paint applied after glazing.
(two views)
Value: $125

Dutch Boy
12 1/2" high, marked "U.S.A.".
Value: $65-70

Dutch Boy
13" high, paint under glaze,
marked "USA APCO".
Value: $95-110

Toy Soldier
11 1/4" high, also called Sentry, marked "U.S.A. 743".
(two different color variations shown here).
Value: $195-250

Fire Chief
12 3/4" high, made of clay, very collectible.
(two different color variations shown here).
Value: $225-300

Preacher
12 3/4" high.
Value: $300-325

World War I Soldier
8 3/4" high.
Value: $275-300

Jolly Pirate
13" high (all these jars come
in many color variations).
Value: $375-400

Cookie Truck
11 1/2" high, marked "U.S.A. 744".
(Also available as 13 1/4" high).
Value: $95-100

Chef with Cookie Tray Lid
7 1/2" high, marked "603 USA",
(a harder jar to find).
Value: $400-450

Snacks Jar
all trimmed in gold, marked
"American Bisque Company, U.S.A. 24kt. Gold".
Value: $150-160

Coach Lantern
13" high, not a common jar.
Value: $250-300

 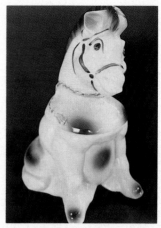

Herman & Katnip
11 1/2" high x 9" wide. The rarest of all American Bisque Jars.
On back marked "U.S.A.", stamped on bottom "Harvey Cartoons 1960".
(two different views shown) only about six jars are known to exist.
Value: $6,500-8,000

Sitting Horse
11 1/2" high, very hard to find,
marked "U.S.A.", this jar is being reproduced.
Value: $1,200

Cookie Bear
11 1/4" high, marked "U.S.A.", with lacy rompers.
Value: $150-175

Cookie Bear
11 1/4" high, marked "U.S.A.", wearing a bib.
Value: $150-175

Pig
11" high, marked "AB CO".
Value: $175-185

Lamb
11 1/2" high, produced by Apco and Abco.
Marked "Designed Pat. 132170 AB CO".
Value: $150-175

Lamb with Hands in Pocket
10 1/2" high, marked "U.S.A.".
(two different color variations).
Value: $225-250 ea.

Fluffy the Cat
12 1/4" high, marked "U.S.A. 131-A".
Notice the indented dots.
Value: $150

Fluffy the Cat
12 1/4" high, marked "U.S.A."
Value: $165-200

Dancing Pig
11 1/2" high, cold painted,
indented dots.
Value: $150

Pig
with a scarf, indented dots.
Value: $150

Sailor
cold painted, marked "U.S.A."
Value: $125-150

Air Force Officer
no paint.
Value: $125-150

Crowing Rooster
12 1/2" high, with green base, unmarked.
Value: $75-90

Rooster
11" high, marked "USA".
Value: $75-90

Multi Colored Rooster
10 3/4" high.
Value: $125-150

Multi-Colored Rooster
9 1/4" high, chick on back.
Value: $175-200

Multi-Colored Rooster
10 3/4" high.
Value: $125-150

Animal Cracker Cylinder
8 1/3" high, marked "U.S.A."
Value: $65-85

Daisy Cylinder
9 1/2" high, marked "USA".
Value: $50-65

Cat with Tail Finial
10 1/4" high, marked "CJ5 USA",
U-shaped footing, probably Ungemach.
Value: $200-225

Poodle with Bone Finial
10 1/4" high, marked "CJ5 USA",
U-shaped footing, probably Ungemach.
Value: $200-225

Candy Cane Babies
10 3/4" high, U shaped footing.
Ungemach Pottery, closely connected
with American Bisque,
(many variations available).
Value: $250-300

Deer at Stump with Log Finial
9" high, Ungemach Pottery marked "USA".
Value: $225-250

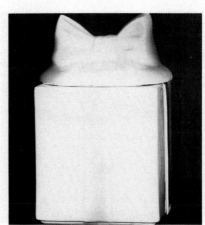

Gift Box
9 1/2" high, marked "U.S.A."
Value: $160-200

Mohawk Indian
12" high, commonly referred to as "Little Mo",
promotional item for Mohawk Carpet Company.
Very difficult to find, being reproduced.
Value: $3,500-4,200

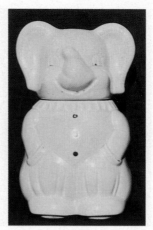

Elephant
combination bank in lid, marked "U.S.A. ABC".
Value: $195-225

Flower Jar
11 3/4" high, marked "U.S.A."
Value: $40-45

Cookies out of this World Spaceship
10 1/4" high, marked "U.S.A."
(spaceman coming out of lid, difficult to find).
Value: $1,500-1,800

Seal on Igloo
11" high, marked "U.S.A."
Value: $350-400

Cookie Tray
6 3/4" high, marked "USA 602",
lid to be used as a tray for cookies,
this is not a common jar.
Value: $200-250

Carousel
9 1/4" high, marked "U.S.A.", cold painted.
(Two different versions of this jar,
this is the more common one.)
Value: $150-175

Kittens on a Ball of Yarn Cookie Jar
9 1/2" high, marked "U.S.A."
Value: $125-150

Kittens on Ball of Yarn Cookie Jar
10 1/2" high, also found in dark pink.
Their are many matching pieces to this jar.
Sometimes referred to as (Figaro) although it
was never commissioned by Disney.
Value: $600-625

Kittens on a Ball of Yarn Figurines
Value: $125 ea.

Kittens on a Ball of Yarn Milk Pitcher
Value: $400-450

Toothache Dog
13 1/2" high, marked "U.S.A."
Value: $750-825

Lamb with Flower Hat
13" high, marked "U.S.A."
Value: $295-350

Little Girl Lamb
10 1/2" high, marked "U.S.A."
Value: $175-200

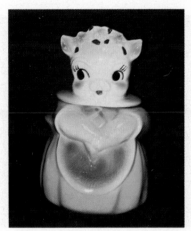

Lady Pig
11 1/2" high, unmarked,
also available with gold trim.
Value: $150-175

Spool of Thread with Thumble Finial
10 3/4" high, marked "U.S.A."
Value: $175-225

Sailor Elephant
10 1/4" high, brown tones,
marked "USA".
Value: $195-225

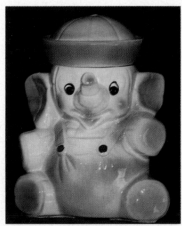

Sailor Elephant
10 1/4" high, marked "U.S.A."
Value: $150

Pinky Lee Clown
10 1/2" high, marked "USA".
Also known as Clown Bust, comes with two
different color hats. Ungemach Pottery,
U-Shaped Footing.
Value: $550-625

Mrs. Rabbit
11 3/4" high, marked "U.S.A."
Value: $275-300

Mr. Rabbit
11 3/4" high, marked "U.S.A."
Value: $275-300

Sad Iron
11 1/2" high, marked "U.S.A."
Value: $150-195

Cat with Hands in Pocket
11 1/2" high, marked "U.S.A.", multi-color.
Value: $150-175

Cookie Girl
9" high, marked "U.S.A. 202",
trimmed in gold.
Value: $150-165

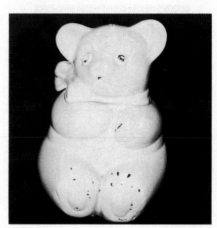

Bear
11" high, unmarked,
blank, all the paint is worn off.
Value: $25-30

Alice in Wonderland Bank
6 1/4" high, marked on front of skirt
"Alice in Wonderland", and
marked on back "WD Productions".
Value: $275-300

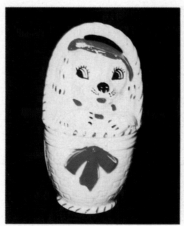

Dog in Basket
13" high, unmarked,
early American Bisque.
Value: $65-75

Rudolph the Red Nosed Reindeer
9 1/4" high, marked "Copyright RLM for
Robert L. May, Creator of the Children's Classic,
Rudolph the Red Nosed Reindeer". (Hard to find jar).
Value: $675-800

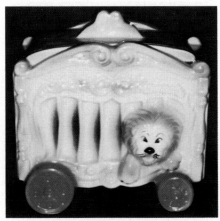

Circus Wagon with Lion
(really cute). This jar looks like American Bisque
but probably isn't, it is unmarked.
Value: $300-325

Cross Eyed Chick
very rare jar, marked "U.S.A."
Value: $700-750

Cookie Basket
6 3/4" high, marked "601 U.S.A."
Basket is a tray for cookies.
Value: $175-195

Milk Can
bell in lid, marked "U.S.A."
Value: $125

Clown
12" high, marked "U.S.A.", made in 1959.
Value: $95-150

Clown
12" high, no paint,
marked "U.S.A.", made in 1959.
Value: $35-40

Coffee Pot
9 1/2" high, stamped in gold
"American Bisque Company", hard to find.
(Speckled with 24kt Gold).
Value: $85-95

Diaper Pin Pig Bank
9" high, marked "USA", heavily
trimmed in gold.
Value: $250-325

Diaper Pin Pig Bank
9" high, marked "USA".
Value: $250-325

Smokey the Bear Bank
5 3/4" high, top reads "Save for the Future -
Save Forests from Fire", marked "USA".
Made by Apco.
Value: $200-250

Smokey the Bear Bank
2 1/2" high, (smaller version
then pictured at the left).
Value: $175-200

Happy Clown
11" high, marked "U.S.A."
This jar is being reproduced,
various colors are available.
Value: $150-165

Feed Sack
9 1/2" high, marked "U.S.A.",
(hard to locate this jar), made in 1958.
Value: $125

Poodle
10 1/2" high, many different color
variations, marked "U.S.A."
Value: $125-150

Poodle
10 1/2" high, marked "U.S.A.",
trimmed in gold.
Value: $225-250

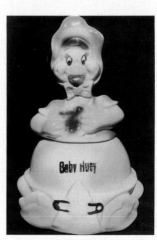

Dog on Quilted Base
marked "USA", made in 1959.
Value: $250-295

Cat on Quilted Base
marked "USA", made in 1959.
Value: $250-295

Baby Huey
13 1/2" high, (hard jar to find),
this jar is being reproduced.
Value: $3,000-3,200

Pig with Hands in Pocket
marked "U.S.A.", (difference in color variations)
Value: $150-175 ea.

Cow/Lamb Turnabout

as shown below in next 3 pictures

Cow/Lamb Turnabout
(four different views),
marked "Copyright Reg. Turnabout 4 in 1".
Value: $150-175

Pig Turnabout
10 3/4" high, produced by American Pottery.
(two different views).
Value: $150-175

Elephant with Hands in Pocket
stands 10 1/2" high, marked "USA",
all paint is under glaze.
Value: $150-175

Pup on Pot
rare color.
Value: $250-300

Peasant Girl
unmarked.
Value: $700-900

Peasant Girl
Value: $700-900

(Two different color variations)

Cookie Cylinder
10" high, stamped in gold, "American Bisque
Company USA", decorated with 24kt. gold.
Value: $85-95

Little Lulu

same as pictured in next 4 pictures.

Little Lulu

same as pictured in next 4 pictures.

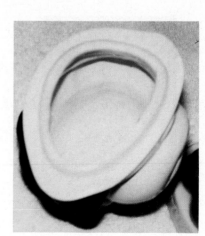

Little Lulu
13 3/8" high, wedges on bottom like typical
American Bisque, bottom is marked
"Western Publishing", back of base is marked "USA", incised in head marked "55" with
"Little Lu Lu USA" stamped, this jar is being reproduced.
Value: $4,000+

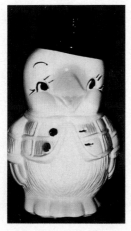

Chick
This jar's tam lifts off instead of
the entire head as other jars do.
This is very rare.
Value: $300-350

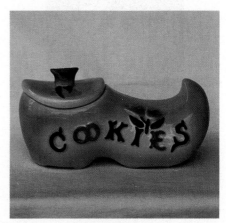

Dutch Shoe
Extremely rare, unmarked.
Value: $1,000+

Doug Anderson

Doug Anderson of San Francisco, California, was born in Salt Lake City, Utah in 1957. His family relocated to California in 1963. Doug attended San Jose State University where he acquired the skills and self discipline of a ceramic artist. He received his Bachelor of Arts Degree in 1980 with a strong concentration in Ceramics and Glass. Focusing primarily on chess sets, and his sculptural form, he explored many different glaze techniques, while developing his style. Most recently, his whimsical caricatures have found themselves on top of colorful vessels including teapots and cookie jars.

Clown
Hand designed and created
by Doug Anderson, limited edition.
Value: $395-425

Chef
Blond Hair, marked Doug Anderson.
Value: $395-425

Chef
Brown Hair, marked Doug Anderson.
Value: $395-425

Court Jester
marked "Doug Anderson"
(slightly different color variations).
Value: $395-425

Policeman
marked "Doug Anderson".
Value: $395-425

Cow with Gold Bell
marked "Doug Anderson", (two different views).
Value: $395-425

Fat Lady on Stool
marked "Doug Anderson".
Value: $395-425

Orangutan
marked "Doug Anderson", (two different color variations).
Value: $395-425

Elephant
marked "Doug Anderson".
Value: $395-425

Clown
marked "Doug Anderson".
Value: $395-425

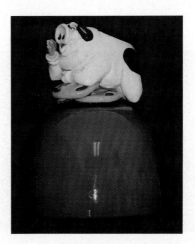

Pig
marked "Doug Anderson".
Value: $395-425

Brandi Supnick
especially for Mark and Ellen Supnick
of their dog Brandi,
marked "Doug Anderson".
Value: $395-425

Dalmatian
marked "Doug Anderson".
Value: $395-425

Glenn Appleman

Glenn Appleman was born in New York City in 1949. Glenn attended and graduated from the City University of New York in 1971 with a Fine Arts Degree. Glenn began creating sculptures by hand in 1970. In the late 1970's Glenn designed a line of cookie jars that are extremely collectible today. His cookie jars were produced from 1978 until 1987 with one reissue in 1992.

Buick Convertible
created in 1981, marked "Glenn Appleman".
Value: $750-900

Red Buick Sedan
big heavy jar, 1980, marked in
black letters "Glenn Appleman"
Value: $750-900

Phantazoom
16" long, big heavy jar, marked in
black letters, "Glenn Appleman".
Value: $750-900

Blue Buick Sedan
(all of Glenn's Jars are very
large and very heavy), 1980.
Value: $750-900

White Buick Sedan
15 1/2" long, modeled after the Roadmaster Series.
(two views, the front view showing luster trimmed grill)
Value: $750-900

Phantazoom with Cat on Bumper
marked "Glenn Appleman".
Value: $950-1,100

Sid's Taxi
created in 1978, 14 1/2" long
(two views).
Value: $750-900

Sid's Taxi
(another variation), also shown is bottom of jar showing markings.
Value: $750-900

Benjamin & Medwin, Inc.

Benjamin & Medwin, Inc., a New York City based importer and distributor. All of their cookie jars are made in Taiwan.

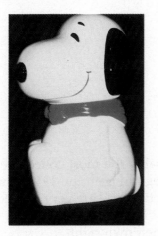 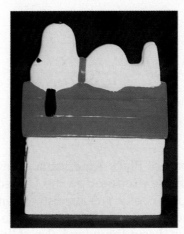 

Snoopy
marked "United Features Syndicate".
Value: $45

Snoopy on Doghouse
marked "United Features Syndicate".
Value: $45

Lambchop
licensed by Shari Lewis.
Value: $39-45

Woodstock
marked "United Features Syndicate".
Value: $39-45

Lucy
made in Taiwan.
Value: $45

Charlie Brown
made in Taiwan.
Value: $45

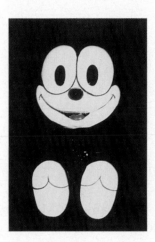

Felix the Cat
made in Taiwan.
Value: $45

Black Americana

Many different companies are a part of Black Americana. They are probably the most collectible of all cookie jars. The most collectible jars are those produced in the United States beginning in the 1940's through present. Many foreign made Black Americana cookie jars are also extremely collectible and are very hard to find. Prices on the older Black Americana cookie jars and older foreign made cookie jars have been climbing for years. Newer Black Americana jars that have been discontinued are also collectible in their own right.

Japan Basket Handled Mammy
stamped "Japan".
Value: $800

Japan Basket Handled Butler
marked "Made in Japan".
Value: $1,000

Mammy & Butler Salt and Pepper Shakers
marked "Made in Japan".
Value: $95-125/set

Basket Handled Mammy
elongated body with feet, this is a
mate to the Butler, marked "Japan",
under glaze, 9" high.
Value: $1,200+

Basket Handled Mammy
marked "Japan",
(this one is a darker skin color).
Value: $1,200+

Basket Handled Mammy
made in Japan, brown faced.
Value: $1,100-1,400

Basket Handled Mammy
with black face and maroon head scarf.
Value: $1,100-1,200

Plaid Basket Handled Mammy
with an orange scarf, decorated with
brown and blue stripes, and with
blue and brown polka-dots, glazed bottoms,
hard to find, marked "Made in Japan".
Value: $1,500

Plaid Mammy Shakers
marked "Made in Japan", hard to find.
Value: $350

Plaid Basket Handled Mammy
this is a back view of the previous picture.
Value: $350

Mammy
with red scarf.
Value: $1,100-1,200

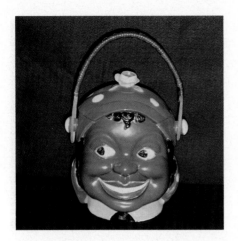

Basket Handled Mammy
marked "Maruhon Ware (k)
Handpainted in Japan".
Value: $1,250-1,400

Plaid Apron Mammy
Made in Japan.
Value: $650-900

Little Girl
marked "Copyright Sears Roebuck
& Co., 1978 Japan".
Value: $550-650

Basket Handled Mammy
with big bow on dress and
light skin color.
Value: $1,150

Polka Dot Mammy Utility Jar
7 1/2" high, not a basket handle jar,
marked"Made in Japan". This jar is extremely
rare, only two are known to exist.
Value: $1,800+

Basket Handled Mammy
with red checkered apron.
Value: $1,200

Basket Handled Mammy
Weller Lookalike, Maruhon Turban.
Value: $2,800

Syrup Pitcher Mammy
5" high, stamped "Marukonware", with a
"K" in a circle. Made in Japan,
very rare, Weller Lookalike.
Value: $800+

Basket Handled Butler
smaller jar, marked "Japan".
Value: $1,250

Basket Handled Butler
Value: $1,000

Mandy set with paper label "OCI", impressed "Omnibus".

Mandy Cookie Jar –Value: $400-450
Mandy Milk Pitcher – Value: $225
Mandy Teapot – Value: $225
Mandy Syrup Pitcher – Value: $150
Mandy Sugar & Creamer – Value: $165/set

Mann Mammy
9 3/4" high, impressed into
the pottery "Copyright Mann",
(rare colors).
Value: $1,500

Mandy set

Mandy Covered Butter – Value: $225

Mandy Chip Bowl
(Very Rare) – Value: $400-425

Mandy Cracker Tray
(Very Rare) – Value: $300-350

Mandy Salt & Pepper – Value: $125/set

Basket Handled Mammy Head
(different color skin), some paint wear.
Value: $1,500

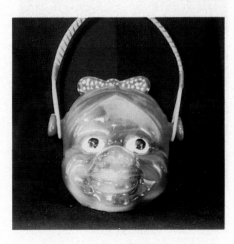

Basket Handled Mammy Head
biscuit jar, (still another variation).
Value: $950

Basket Handled Mammy Head
unmarked, (great paint).
Value: $1,200-1,400

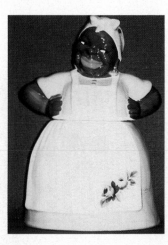

Italian Mammy
marked "Made in Italy 7780",
impressed in pottery "BECARA" in blue,
very rare, 11" high.
Value: $1,700

Mann Mammy
9 3/4" high, impressed in pottery
"Copyright Mann", rare colors.
Value: $1,500

MJ's Married Mammy
12 1/4" high, one is yellow in color, the other is green.
Produced by Mary Jane Giacomini.
Value: $175-225

Googly-Eyed Teapot
unmarked and hard to find.
Value: $550

Googly-Eyed Shakers
each shaker is stamped "Japan",
very hard to find.
Value: $325

MJ's Married Mammy
12 1/4" high, reproduction of Brayton
Cookie Jar, Total Ltd Ed. of 104.
Produced by Mary Jane Giacomini.
Incised in Lid "1991".
Value: $175-225

MJ's Married Mammy
blue color, produced by Mary Jane Giacomini.
Value: $175-225

Mammy with Spoon
with red and white turban.
Value: $4,500+

Brayton Laguna Mammy
12 5/8" high, with a blue plaid dress,
marked "Brayton Laguna Potteries, CA".
Value: $1,500-1,600

Brayton Laguna Mammy
12 5/8" high, marked "Brayton Laguna"
initial inside lid.
Value: $1,200-1,400

Brayton Laguna Mammy
with a green plaid dress and yellow turban.
Marked "Brayton Laguna" artist initial inside lid.
Value: $1,400-1,600

Brayton Laguna Green Plaid Mammy
with a green turban, marked "Brayton Laguna",
artitst initial inside lid.
Value: $1,500-1,700

Brayton Laguna Salt & Pepper Shakers
Value: $700/set

Mammy Planter
marked "Brayton Laguna".
Value: $450-500

Mammy & Chef Salt and Pepper Shakers
marked "Brayton Laguna".
Value: $165-195/set

Mammy & Chef Salt and Peppers
marked "Brayton", unusual colors.
Value: $195-250

Brayton Laguna Mammy
(zig-zag design in dress),
marked "Brayton Laguna CA",
artist description in lid, cold red paint.
Value: $1,200-1,400

Brayton Laguna Mammy
smaller candy jar, unusual, hard to find,
marked "Brayton".
Value: $900-1,000

Brayton Laguna Mammy
blue plaid design, artist initials in lid,
marked "Brayton Laguna Potteries".
Value: $1,500-1,600

Brayton Laguna Mammy
red bottom, striped top.
Value: $1,500-1,600

Brayton Laguna large Shakers
Notice greater detail in faces of large shakers
versus little detail in smaller shakers. Extremely
rare, chef is 7" high, mammy is 6 1/2" high,
marked "Brayton California USA 40-70".
Value: $1,000/set

Brayton Mammy small Shakers
marked "Brayton California USA 40-70" incised.
Value: $195-250/set

Brayton Mammy & Chef Shakers
blue striped dress, Mammy is 5 1/4" high, Chef is 5 1/2" high, very rare. Mammy has
an inked "R" and an incised "IV". The chef has an inked "#7", incised "II".
(front and back views)
Value: $375/set

Mustard Colored Brayton Mammy
incised in script on unglazed bottom "Brayton Copyright #5".
Value: $2,500

Mammy
Japan.
Value: $650-700

Brayton Laguna Mammy
yellow dress, zig-zag pattern, marked
"Brayton Laguna" artist initials in lid.
Value: $900-1,100

Mammy Scrub Woman
(also known as Washtub Mammy), made in
late 1940's by Metlox Pottery, unmarked.
Value: $2,400-2,600

Brayton Maid (extremely rare)
sought after by many black memorabilia
collectors. Marked "Brayton Laguna Potteries".
Value: $3,500+

Brayton Maid
blue, marked "Copyright Brayton Laguna Pottery",
inked "R", incised "#3". – **Value: $8,500**

Provencial Lady
13" high, unique finish, (some feel it's Black Americana,
others don't). Marked "Brayton Laguna CA 927".
Value: $1,100

Brayton Maid & Butler Salt and Peppers
marked "Brayton". – **Value: $700-900**

Brayton Maid & Butler Salt & Peppers
Maid Shaker incised "#3", Butler Shaker inked "R".
Value: $2,500/set

Provencial Lady Salt & Pepper Shakers
marked "Brayton". – **Value: $175-250**

Mammy Scrub Woman
(also known as Washtub Mammy),
very black skin, very rare coloring,
made by Metlox Potteries.
Value: $2,400-2,600

Mosaic Tile Mammy
13 1/4" high, basic yellow dress, unmarked.
Value: $550-650

Mosaic Tile Mammy
with blue dress.
Value: $700-800

Mosaic Tile Mammy
unmarked, very rare, shown here in different color variations.
Value: $1,800+

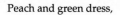

Peach and green dress,

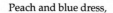

Peach and blue dress,

Blue and yellow dress

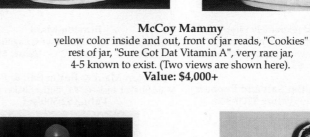

McCoy Lookalike Mammy
by Mann.
Value: $1,200

McCoy Mammy
yellow color inside and out, front of jar reads, "Cookies"
rest of jar, "Sure Got Dat Vitamin A", very rare jar,
4-5 known to exist. (Two views are shown here).
Value: $4,000+

McCoy Mammy
unusual color, harder to find.
Value: $750-850

McCoy Mammy
11" high, marked "McCoy",
made in the late 40's to Late 50's.
Value: $150-250

Rockingham Mammy
unmarked, made in early 1980's,
paper label reads "Sarsaparilla Deco Designs
NYC NY Copyright 1980 Japan".
Value: $400-450

Rockingham Mammy
unusual designs and coloring,
"Sarsaparilla Copyright 1980 Made in Japan".
Value: $600-750

Dinah
unmarked.
Value: $175

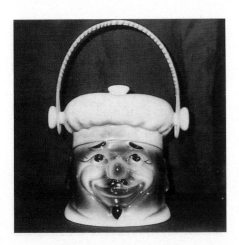

Basket Handled Chef
one of a kind, made in Japan.
Value: $2,500+

Butler Head Dresser Jar
marked "Butler Head" in relief off of head,
stamped "Made in Japan".
This is very hard to find, 4" high.
Value: $425-500

Chef Cookie Jar
made in Taiwan.
Value: $50-60

Cauliflower Mammy
11 3/4" high, marked "McCoy USA 1939".
Value: $750-900

Mammy
(This is not pottery, it is porcelain).
Made in Taiwan, unmarked.
Value: $100-150

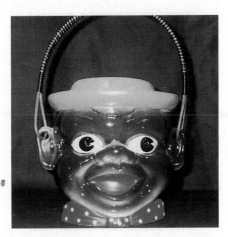

Googly-Eyed Man
(yellow hat, red polka-dot bow tie)
marked "Japan", 6 1/2" wide x 8" high at ears.
Value: $3,500+

Mammy and Cookie Chef
(one of a kind), this jar resides in the
Pottery Museum in Crooksville, Ohio.
Value: Too Rare to place a value on

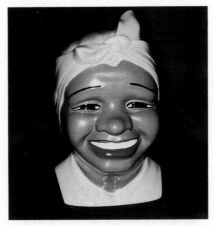

Gilner Mammy
11" high, unmarked, with yellow turban.
Value: $1,750+

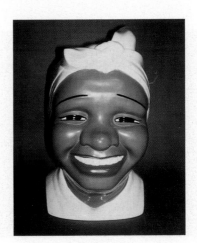

Gilner Mammy
unmarked, with white turban.
Value: $1,550+

Gilner Mammy
(slightly different color of face)
Value: $1,500+

Gilner Mammy Shaker
Value $225-250

Gilner Mammy Head Shaker & Spoon Rest
shaker is unmarked, spoon rest is marked
"Spoon Rest" on top side, and "Gilner CA"
on bottom side. This is very hard to find.
Value: $500

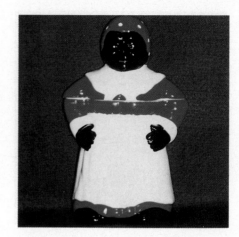

Mammy
smaller jar, marked "Made in Taiwan".
Value: $40-50

Mammy
larger jar, marked "Made in Taiwan".
Value: $75-85

Japan Mammy
unmarked, (two different variations).
Value: $300-350 ea.

Aunt Susan
marked "School of Minds", very, very rare.
Value: $4,000+

Luzianne Mammy
marked "U.S.A.", this jar is being reproduced.
Value: $800-900

Luzianne Mammy
with original paint.
Value: $900-1,100

Lady Holding Kid Crock
(only two known to exist), very rare.
Value: $4,000+

Aunt Jemima
unmarked, premium offer by
Quaker Oats, soft molded plastic.
Value: $325-400

Aunt Jemima
F & F Mold & Die Works, Dayton, Ohio,
hard plastic.
Value: $290-325

Aunt Jemima
green, F & F, probably one of a kind,
(shown with a previous Mammy).
Value: $3,000+

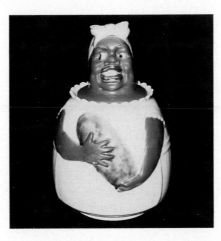

Weller Mammy
11" high, hard to find jar,
beautiful pottery, made in 1935.
Value: $1,800-2,000

Weller Mammy Teapot – Value: $1,000+

Weller Mammy Creamer – Value: $800+

Weller Mammy Covered Sugar
Value: $1,000+

Weller Mammy Batter Bowl
Value: $1,200-1,500

Weller Mammy Syrup Pitcher
Value: $750-900

National Silver Lookalikes – Man
reproductions of National Silver jars,
made in Japan.
Value: $300

National Silver Lookalikes – Woman
reproductions of National Silver jars,
made in Japan.
Value: $350

Abingdon Mammy
10" high, cold painted, bottom of jar
stamped "Abingdon USA 471", rare.
Value: $800-850

Chef
Enesco imports, Japan.
Value: $1,200-1,500

Mammy
Enesco imports, Japan.
Value: $1,500-1,800

Little Black Angel
produced by Mary Jane Giaomini, 1992, Ltd. Ed.
(two different color variations).
Value: $225-275 ea.

Watermelon Mammy
unmarked, made by Pearl China.
Value: $5,500-6,200

Indian Lady
13" high, unmarked,
(two different color variations).
Value: $300-375 ea.

Pearl China Mammy
10 1/2" high, gold stamp "Pearl China".
Value: $800-850

Pearl China Chef
10 3/4" high, marked "Pearl China Co.
Hand Decorated", gold label.
Value: $600-700

Pearl China Salt & Peppers
large salt & pepper shakers
Value: $400+

Pearl China Salt & Peppers
small salt & pepper shakers
Value: $200-225

Pearl China Salt & Peppers
large, made by Pearl China,
Chef is 7 3/8" high, Mammy is 7" high,
very rare, unmarked.
Value: $400+

Mammy
Japan
Value: $650-700

National Silver Chef
10 1/4" high, marked "NSCO".
Value: $350-425

Mammy
stamped "Made in Japan".
Value: $650-800

National Silver Chef
10 1/4" high, marked "NSCO"
Value: $350-425

Chef Shaker
Value: $125-200

National Silver Chef
10 1/4" high, marked "NSCO".
Value: $350-425

Mammy
McCoy look-a-like, unmarked.
Value: $1,500-1,800

Grandpa Butler
Japan.
Value: $1,250

Lady with Iron Humidor
Majolica Pottery, very rare.
Value: $2,000+

Man with Ball Cap Humidor
unmarked
Value: $400-500

Man with Green Hat Humidor
unmarked.
Value: $1,000+

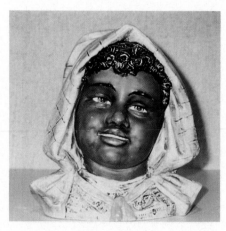

Woman with Green Scarf Humidor
unmarked.
Value: $1,000+

Man with Hat Humidor
unmarked.
Value: $1,000+

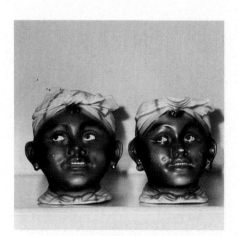

Woman with a Turban Humidor
unmarked.
Value: $300

Man with a Turban Humidor
unmarked.
Value: $300

Man with a Hat Humidor
unmarked.
Value: $1,200+

Cream of Wheat Chef
stamped "Japan".
Value: $900-1,100

Cream of Wheat Chef
8" high, stamped "Japan". – **Value: $900-1,100**

Cream of Wheat Chef
real white face, biscuit jar,
stamped "Japan", hard to find.
Value: $650-700

Cream of Wheat Chef
(different color variation)
paint under glaze, stamped "Japan".
Value: $1,200-1,500

Mammy
10" high, marked "'Little Lady' Abingdon
USA 471 Decoration 'C' 1942".
Value: $700-750

Wooden Jar
unmarked, black chef on front.
Value: $50-60

Black Santa
"Twin Winton 1993", Ltd. Ed. Designed
by Don Winton, produced by Craig Winton.
Value: $450+

Chef Head
unmarked.
Value: $150-200

Jug
marked "Canuck Pottery, St. John, NB Canada",
impressed, comes in a few designs.
Value: $1,100-1,500+

Mammy Candy Jar
laughing mammy, unmarked.
Value: $600-800

Basket Handled Fireman
made in Japan.
Value: $450

Bell Captain
in the heart on the bottom marked, "McMe
Copyright 92 USA", produced by
Gerald Meyer Simi Valley CA"
Value: $125-150

Crawling Clown
basket handled, marked "Japan".
Value: $150-200

Luzianne Mammy Reproduction
unmarked.
Value: $125-150

Mammy with Spoon
Japan, one of a kind.
Value: $2,500+

Someone's in the Kitchen Mammy
hand painted, "Japan Copyright Dept. 56".
Value: $225-325

Washtub Mammy
made in Taiwan.
Value: $40-50

Chef
unmarked.
Value: $150-175

Luzianne Mammy Reproduction
unmarked.
Value: $125-150

Sum-Mo Cylinder
made in Taiwan, Holmes Company, Louisiana.
Value: $300-400

Spice
marked "Treasure Craft USA".
Value: $75-85

Sugar Man
Value: $75-85

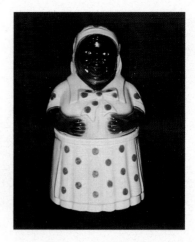

Polka-Dot Mammy
unknown origin, unmarked.
Value: $1,200-1,500

Artistic Pottery Mammy
very rare color, marked
"Artistic Potteries", Japan.
Value: $800+

Artistic Pottery Mammy
Artistic Potteries.
Value: $1,000-1,300

Artistic Pottery Chef
Artistic Potteries.
Value: $1,000-1,300

**Artistic Pottery
White Decorated Mammy**
(Mammy jar alone.)
Value: $1,200+

Metlox Mammy
with red polk-dots, marked
"Metlox CA USA", rare.
Value: $850

Metlox Mammy
light pink, marked "Metlox CA USA"
in script "By Vincent Copyright", rare.
Value: $2,000

Artistic Pottery White Chef
impressed "Artistic Potteries Inc. CA"
Value: $600+

McCoy Mammy Reproduction
issued by George Williams, Ill., marked "Dem Cookies Shor Am Good",
(different variations).
Value: $175-225 ea.

Artistic Pottery White Decorated Mammy
of all of the colors made by Artistic Pottery, i.e.
red, pink, green, blue, aqua, brown, white, etc.
Only the White Mammy was decorated.
But not all white mammies were marked,
"Artistic Potteries Inc CA USA 31".
Value: $1,200+

Brayton Laguna

Brayton Laguna, of Laguna Beach, California, was originally started in a garage prior to becoming a big pottery company. Their cookie jars are highly collectible as well as all of their other pottery items they have produced.

Lady with Squeezebox
extremely rare, possibly one of a kind,
incised "Brayton Laguna".
Value: $3,000+

Matilda
incised "Brayton".
Value: $600-700

Matilda
incised "Brayton Laguna CA".
Value: $600-700

Matilda
incised "Brayton Laguna",
(two different variations).
Value: $600-700

Ringmaster
marked "Gepetto Pottery from Walt Disney,
Pinnochio Trademark Reg. U.S. Pat. Office",
A Brayton Laguna Production.
Value: $2,500+

Goose Woman
marked "Brayton Laguna, Laguna Beach, CA"
(different color variations).
Value: $2,000+

Plaid Dog
unmarked.
Value: $400-475

Plaid Dog Toothbrush Holder
unmarked.
Value: $125-150

Wedding Ring Granny
incised "Brayton Laguna Potteries".
(All different color variations).
Value: $750-900

Circus Tent
stamped, "Brayton Laguna".
Value: $350-425

Pedro & Rosita Figurines
Value: $125 each

Francine Planter
marked "Brayton Laguna".
Value: $165-195

Sambo & Petunia Figurines
marked "Brayton".
Value: $350/pair

Mandy Planter
marked "Brayton".
Value: $450

Gypsy Woman
marked "Brayton Laguna Pottery".
Value: $450

Black Children Figurines
marked "Brayton Laguna".
Value: $150/each

Brush Pottery Company

Brush Pottery Company began in 1925 when the McCoy family withdrew from the Brush-McCoy Pottery Company. Brush Pottery was in business until 1982. Ross and Don Winton, from Twin Winton Ceramics designed many of the Brush cookie jars that are marked on the bottom with a "W" and a number. Brush Jars are highly sought after and extremely beautiful.

Clown Bust
unmarked, 11" high, 1970.
Value: $475-575

Humpty Dumpty
10" high, with yellow beanie,
produced from 1956-1961, marked
"Brush W18 USA".
Value: $300-325

Humpty Dumpty with Cowboy Hat
11 1/4" high, 1962, marked
"W29 Brush USA".
Value: $350-375

Lantern
9 1/2" high, "K1 Brush USA".
Value: $65-75

Pumpkin with Lock on Door
marked "W24 USA", discontinued in 1962.
Value: $425-500

Davy Crockett
gold trim, dark jacket, marked "USA",
10 1/4" high, 1956.
Value: $900-1,100

Davy Crockett
gold trim, light jacket, marked "USA",
10 1/4" high, 1956.
Value: $900-1,100

Davy Crockett
different gold trim, light jacket,
10 1/4" high, 1956.
Value: $900-1,100

Davy Crockett
no gold, unmarked,
10 1/4" high, 1956.
Value: $300-350

Davy Crockett
different color, unmarked,
10 1/4" high, 1956.
Value: $300-350

Davy Crockett
different color variation,
10 1/4" high, 1956.
Value: $300-350

Squirrel on Log
10 3/4" high, 1961, marked "USA".
Value: $75-95

Squirrel on Log
10 3/4" high, 1965, gray color,
(a light brown color was introduced in 1969).
Value: $95-150

Cookie House
10 3/4" high, 1962, marked "W31 Brush USA".
Value: $150-175

Cookie House
10 3/4" high, 1962, marked "W31".
Value: $175-195

Old Clock
10" high, 1956, marked "W20 Brush USA".
(A delightful poem engraved on the sides).
Value: $400-475

Stylized Owl
1967, marked "W42".
Value: $600-650

Stylized Siamese
1967, "W41".
Value: $600-625

Crock with Cat Finial
10 3/4" high, 1956, marked "K26 USA".
Value: $65-75

Crock with Girl Praying Finial
10 3/4" high, 1956, marked "K26 USA".
Value: $65-75

Crock with Duck Finial
10 1/4" high, 1956, marked "K26 USA".
Value: $65-75

Smiling Bear
unmarked, sits on wedges.
Value: $500-550

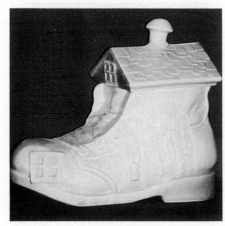

The Old Shoe
10 1/4" high, 1959, marked "W23 Brush USA".
Value: $150-175

Dog with Basket
12" high, 1971, paper label reads
"Brush Ware W54 Brush Pottery
Company, Zanesville, OH".
Value: $600-700

Granny
11" high, 1957, marked "W19 Brush USA".
(Notice the glaze skips on apron,
very common in Brush Pottery).
Value: $375-425

Clown
12 1/2" high, with yellow pants, 1965,
marked "W22 Brush USA".
Value: $425-475

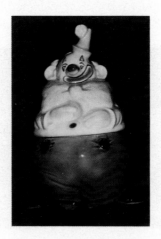

Clown
12 1/2" high, with brown pants, 1965,
marked "W22 Brush USA".
Value: $375-400

Covered Wagon
11 3/4" high, 1962,
marked "W30 Brush USA".
Value: $700-750

Treasure Chest
marked "W28", 1962.
Value: $325-350

Cinderella's Pumpkin Coach
9 3/4" high, 1962, marked
"W32 Brush USA".
Value: $350-375

Little Girl
11 3/4" high, marked "0-17 USA Brush".
Value: $750-800

Little Angel
12" high, 1956,
marked "Brush USA".
Value: $1,100-1,200

Little Angel
12" high, 1956,
marked "Brush USA".
Value: $850-950

Little Angel
12" high, 1956,
marked "Brush USA".
Value: $1,100-1,200

Elephant with Ice Cream Cone
13" high, with a yellow jacket,
made in early 1950's, marked "W8 USA".
Value: $650-700

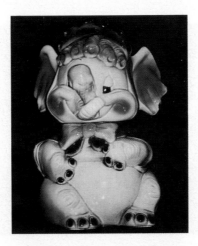

Elephant with Ice Cream Cone
13" high, with a gray jacket,
extremely hard-to-find,
made in early 1950's, marked "W8 USA".
Value: $850-925

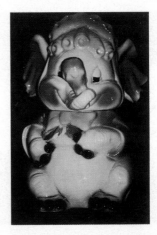

Elephant with Ice Cream Cone
13" high, with a blue jacket,
made in early 1950's, marked "W8 USA".
Value: $600-650

Elephant with Ice Cream Cone
13" high, made in early 1950's,
marked "W8 USA".
Value: $700-725

Elephant with Ice Cream Cone
13" high, gray in color, heavy gold trim,
made in early 1950's, marked "W8 USA".
Value: $1,500-1,800

Hen on Basket
10 1/4" high, unmarked, 1969.
Value: $125-150

Cow with Cat Finial
8 1/2" high, made in the early 1950's,
came in many different color combinations,
marked "W10 Brush USA".
Value: $1,200-1,400

Brown Cow with Cat Finial
8 1/2" high, made in the early 1950's,
marked "W10 Brush USA".
Value: $125-150

Brown Cow with Cat Finial
8 1/2" high, made in the early 1950's,
(back view of different jar,
showing the available advertising,
Value: $400-450

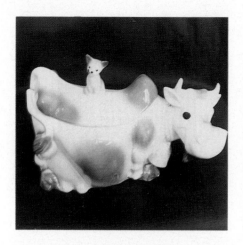

Cow with Cat Finial
8 1/2" high, made in the early 1950's,
(purple and white), marked "W10 Brush USA".
Value: $1,200-1,500

Cow with Cat Finial
8 1/2" high, made in the early 1950's,
(blue and white with gold trim),
marked "W10 Brush USA".
Value: $1,500-1,800

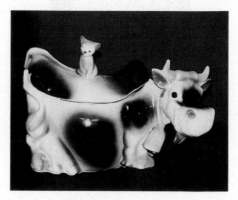

Cow with Cat Finial
8 1/2" high, made in the early 1950's,
(different color variation).
Value: $1,200-1,400

Cow with Cat Finial
8 1/2" high, made in the early 1950's,
(tan color), marked "W10 Brush USA".
Value: $125-150

Cow with Cat Finial
8 1/2" high, made in the early 1950's,
(blue and white), marked "W10 Brush USA".
Value: $1,200-1,500

Nite Owl
10 3/4" high, 1967,
marked "W40" gloss glaze.
Value: $90-125

Nite Owl
10 3/4" high, 1967, marked "W40".
with matte glaze.
Value: $90-125

Panda
10 3/4" high, marked "W21 Brush USA".
(two different color variations).
Value: $300-350

Little Boy Blue
10 1/4" high (small size), 1956,
marked "K25 USA".
Value: $725-800

Little Boy Blue
12 1/4" high (large size), 1956,
marked "K24 USA".
Value: $725-800

Little Boy Blue
10 1/4" high (small size),
with gold trim, marked "K25 USA".
Value: $900-975

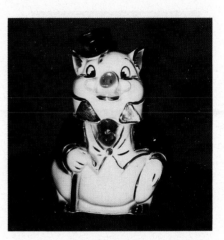

Happy Bunny
12 3/4" high, 1960, gray color,
marked "W25 Brush USA".
Value: $325-375

Happy Bunny
12 3/4" high, 1965,
marked "W25 Brush USA".
Value: $300-325

Formal Pig
11 1/4" high, with gold trim,
marked "W7 USA".
Value: $475-525

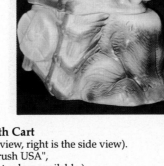

Donkey with Cart
10 1/2" high, 1962, (left is the front view, right is the side view).
Marked "W33 Brush USA",
(There are many different colors available.)
Value: $575-650

Formal Pig
11 1/4" high, marked "W7 USA".
Value: $300-325

This is a harder to find color.

Formal Pig
11 1/4" high, with green coat,
marked "W7 USA".
Value: $475-500

Formal Pig
11 1/4" high, different color variation,
marked "W7 USA".
Value: $300-375

Sitting Piggy Bank
11" high, 1966,
marked "837 USA Brush".
Value: $475-550

Sitting Piggy Cookie Jar
1966, marked "837 USA Brush".
Value: $550-600

Sitting Hippo
11" high, 1969, unmarked.
Value: $550-600

Touring Car
6 3/4", 1971, unmarked,
(this car is very hard to find).
Value: $1,200-1,400

Fish
(hard to find jar),
unmarked, 1971.
Value: $475-525

Teddy Bear
10 1/2" high, 1957, with a green apron
and the feet together. Marked "W14 USA".
Value: $400-425

Teddy Bear
10 1/2" high, 1957, with a brown apron
and the feet together. Marked "W14 USA".
Value: $175-200

Teddy Bear
10 1/2" high, made in the early 1950's,
with a green apron and gold trim,
and the feet are apart. Marked "W14 USA".
Value: $475-525

Teddy Bear
10 1/2" high, made in the early 1950's,
with a green apron and the feet are apart.
Marked "W14 USA".
Value: $175-225

Circus Horse (pink & white)
9 1/2" high, made in the
early 1950's. Unmarked.
Value: $900-1,100

Circus Horse (green & white)
9 1/2" high, made in the
early 1950's. Unmarked.
Value: $825-900

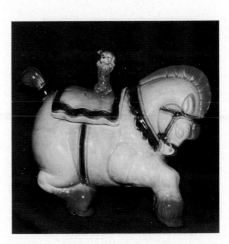

Circus Horse (brown)
9 1/2" high, made in the early 1950's.
Unmarked, hard to find.
Value: $1,100-1,400

Three Bears
9 3/4" high, 1962, marked "K-2 Brush USA".
Value: $125-150

Laughing Hippo
9" high, 1961, marked "W27 Brush USA".
Value: $850-975

Chick on Nest
11 3/4" high, 1966, marked "W38 Brush USA".
Value: $600-650

Cylinder with Clover Blossom
9 1/2" high, marked "Brush".
Matching salt & peppers also available.
Value: $65-75

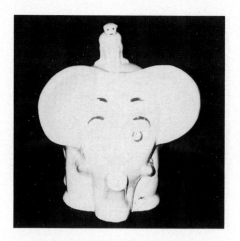

Elephant with Monkey Finial
unmarked, (very rare jar).
Value: $2,000+

Puppy Police
9 1/4" high, 1966, marked "W39 Brush USA".
Value: $600-650

Balloon Boy
11" high, paper label marked "W56".
Hard to find, (one of Brush Pottery's
last jars, made in 1971).
Value: $1,200-1,400

Raggedy Ann
11 1/2" high, 1956, marked "W16 USA".
(Hard to find color combination).
Value: $1,100-1,200

Raggedy Ann
11 1/2" high, 1956, marked "W16 USA".
Value: $750-800

Little Red Riding Hood
11 1/2" high (large size), 1956,
marked "K24 Brush USA",
also available in 9 1/2" size.
Value: $800-850

Little Red Riding Hood
unmarked, but impressed in front
of dress, "Littl Red Ridding Hood".
(Notice the incorrect spelling).
Value: $950-1,000

Little Red Riding Hood
with gold trim, marked "K24 Brush USA".
Value: $1,000-1,100

Hillbilly Frog
1969, unmarked.
This jar has been reproduced by a few different ceramicists. (The jars shown in this book under Brush are all original) "43D".
Value: $4,000+

Hillbilly Frog
unusual color and larger in size, very rare.
Value: $5,000+

Hillbilly Frog
unmarked, original, shown in previous picture.
Value: $4,000+

Hillbilly Frog
unusual color and large size,
shown in previous picture.
Value: $5,000+

Hobby Horse
unmarked, 10" high, 1971, (very hard to find).
Value: $1,200-1,400

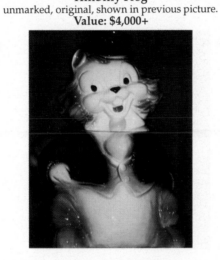

Squirrel with Top Hat
12" high, marked "W15 USA",
made in the early 1950's.
Value: $575-650

Squirrel with Top Hat
12" high, gold trim, marked "W15 USA",
made in the early 1950's.
Value: $675-800

Peter Pan
10 3/4" high (small size),
marked "USA", 1956.
Value: $550-625

Peter Pan
12 3/4" high (large size),
marked "K23 Brush USA", 1959.
Value: $625-725

Granny
11" high, with a green dress,
marked "W19 Brush USA", made in 1957.
Value: $375-425

Formal Pig
green coat with gold trim,
marked "W7 USA".
Value: $550-625

Clown
12 1/2" high, with pink pants, made
in 1965, marked "W22 Brush USA".
Value: $425-475

Squirrel with Top Hat
Value: $450-500

Donkey with Cart
beautiful high gloss finish,
marked "W33 Brush USA".
Value: $575-650

Humpty Dumpty
marked "W29 Brush USA",
very rare and hard to find color.
Value: $550-600

Tulip Cylinder
marked "#137 USA".
Value: $125-150

Crock with Duck Finial
10 1/4" high made in 1956,
marked "K26 USA".
Value: $65-75

California Cleminsons

California Cleminsons began in 1941 in El Monte, California in a garage before expanding to a larger factory. These jars are highly sought after by collectors.

Gingerbread House
marked "The California Cleminsons,
Copyright, handpainted".
Value: $150-175

Cookie House
marked "The California Cleminsons,
Copyright, handpainted".
Value: $150-175

Cookie Box
marked "The California Cleminsons,
Copyright, handpainted".
Value: $525-650

Potbellied Stove
marked "The California Cleminsons,
Copyright, handpainted".
Value: $250-300

Card King
marked "The California Cleminsons,
Copyright, handpainted".
Value: $900-1,100

California Originals

California Originals was established in 1940 in Torrence, California by William D. Bailey. In 1979, Harold Roman purchased the company. California Originals closed in 1982.

Superman in Phone Booth
13" high x 5 ¹/₄" square,
marked "California Originals USA 846
Copyright DC Comics 1978".
Value: $450-525

Superman in Phone Booth
13" high x 5 ¹/₄" square, aluminum color.
Marked "California Originals USA 846
Copyright DC Comics 1978".
Value: $850-975

Superman in Phone Booth
13" high x 5 ¹/₄" square, Antique finish,
marked "CAL. ORIG. USA #846
Copyright DC Comics Inc., 1978".
Value: $525-575

Wonder Woman
marked "USA 847 Copyright
DC Comics Inc. 1978".
Value: $1,100-1,200

Elf School House
12 ¹/₄" high, paper label "California Originals
USA", also available with different color roofs.
Value: $125-150

Cookie Bakery
9" high, marked "863 USA",
various colors available.
Value: $85-95

Christmas Tree
12 1/4" high, marked "873".
Value: $750-900

Snowman
12" high, marked "872 USA".
Value: $500-525

Victrola
12" high, marked "891 USA".
Value: $350-450

Oscar the Grouch
12" high, marked "Copyright
Muppets, Inc. 972".
Value: $95-125

Ernie
12" high, marked "Copyright
Muppets, Inc. 973".
Value: $95-125

Big Bird
13 3/4" high, marked "USA Copyright
Muppets, Inc. 971".
Value: $110-150

Ernie & Bert Fine Cookies
11" high x 8" wide x 6" deep.
Marked "977 Copyright 1971,
1978 Muppets, Inc."
Value: $475-525

Cookie Monster
12" high, from Sesame Street,
marked "Copyright Muppets Inc. 970".
Value: $90-125

The Count
11 3/4" high, marked "975".
Value: $1,000-1,200

Schnauzer
marked "905" in lid, and impressed
in bottom "905 USA".
Value: $150-195

Scarecrow
12 1/4" high, marked "871 USA".
Value: $250-300

Sheriff with Hole in Hat
12" high, marked "726".
Value: $50-60

Sheriff
13" high, marked "USA".
Value: $70-75

Keystone Cop
marked "GKI USA", also known as Bobby.
Value: $50-60

Pelican
unmarked
Value: $95-110

Scarecrow Turnabout
(Happy Side & Sad Side Shown)
marked "858" on lid and base.
Value: $250-275

Sitting Turtle
13" high, marked "2635 USA".
Value: $40-50

Mickey & Pluto Cylinder
marked "Walt Disney Productions 505 USA".
Value: $125-150

Cookie Monster, Ernie & Bert
from Sesame Street, marked "505 USA".
Value: $125-150

Cookie Monster Cylinder
from Sesame Street, marked "505 USA".
Value: $125-150

Mickey Down on the Farm
marked "Walt Disney Productions Made
by California Originals".
Value: $125-150

Grandma
unmarked.
Value: $150-175

Apple
(this jar was part of a canister set),
marked "8214 USA", 10 3/4" high.
Value: $75-90

Pack Mule
marked "2633" on lid, and "2633 USA" on base.
This jar is hard-to-find and a beautiful CA Originals Design.
Value: $325-375

Panda with a Leaf
marked "USA".
Value: $225-250

Indian with Lollypop
unmarked, 12 1/2" high
Value: $90-95

Gumball Machine
12" high, marked "890 USA",
(two different variations).
Value: $150-165

Red Baron in Plane
marked "2629 USA".
Value: $625-695

Platypus Duck
marked "790 USA".
Value: $150-195

Humpty Dumpty
marked "882 USA" on lid and base, 13" high.
Value: $125-150

Reclining Frog
10 1/4" high, marked "877 USA"
(also available in brown).
Value: $125-150

Koala Bear
unmarked, (many accessories
are also available).
Value: $225-250

Spacecadet
unmarked, 12 1/2" high.
Value: $150-175

Big Dumb Clown
marked "213",
(two different color variations).
Value: $50-55

Rabbit
unmarked, (definitely California Originals).
Value: $175-190

Wind-up Car
7" high, marked "California Originals".
Value: $250-275

Little Red Riding Hood
13 1/2" high, marked "320 USA".
Value: $450-500

California Originals Display Sign
marked "California Originals
Stoneware by Suzi".
Value: $150-175

Woody Woodpecker
marked "Copyright Walter Lantz 980 USA".
Value: $1,200-1,300

Woody Woodpecker
Antique Finish, marked "Walter Lantz 980 USA".
Value: $700-800

Smiling Tiger
8 3/4" high, marked "USA".
Value: $125-150

Octapus on Treasure Chest
11" high, marked "878" on lid and
"878" on base.
Value: $225-250

Hare on Cookies Safe
15" high, marked 2630 USA"
Value: $110-125

Cat on a Safe
marked "2630-1-2".
Value: $110-125

Cat on a Safe
marked "2630-1-2".
Value: $150

Full Figured Clown
incised in the lid and base "862 USA".
Pictured in 1974 catalog.
Value: $125-175

Clown Bust
12 1/2" high, incised in
lid and base "859 USA".
Value: $175-250

Duck
incised in lid and base "857 USA".
Value: $75-95

Raggedy Andy
incised in lid and base
"860 USA".
Value: $250-300

Raggedy Ann
13 3/4" high, incised in
lid and base "859 USA".
Value: $250-300

Little Girl
incised in lid and base "872 USA",
shown in 1974 catalog.
Value: $275-400

Crocogater
12 1/2" high, incised in lid and base
"862 USA".
Value: $250-325

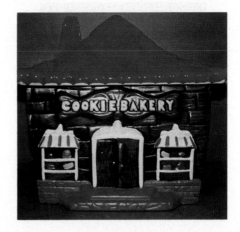

Cookie Bakery
9" high x 8 3/4" long x 5 3/4" wide,
incised in lid and base, marked "863 USA".
(different variation)
Value: $85-95

Caterpillar
10 1/4" high, incised in lid and base
"853 USA".
Value: $300-350

Lil O'le School House
11 1/4" high, incised in
lid and base "869 USA"
Value: $200-225

Squirrel on Stump
incised in lid and base "863 USA".
Value: $150-175

Koala Bear
unusual color, marked "885 USA",
incised in the lid and base.
Value: $300-375

Elf
yellow hat, paper label
"California Originals Manhattan Beach CA".
Value: $125-175

Poodle in Chair
unmarked
Value: $125-150

Girl with Flowers
incised in lid and base "2636 USA".
Value: $350-425

Santa
11 1/2" high, incised in lid and base
"871 USA".
Value: $650-750

Telephone
8" high, incised in lid and base
"853 USA".
Value: $400-500

Frog
8" high, incised in lid and base
"884 USA".
Value: $125-150

Turtle
12 1/2" high, incised in lid and
base "2635 USA".
Value: $125-150

Turtle
12 1/2" high, (different version).
Value: $40-50

Owl on Stump
14" high, incised on lid and base
"2620-1-2-3 USA".
Value: $60-75

Squirrel on Stump
12 1/2" high, marked "2620",
(small size).
Value: $60-75

Squirrel on Stump
14" high, marked "2620-1-2-3 USA"
(large size).
Value: $125-150

Rabbit on Stump
14" high, marked "2620-1-2-3 USA".
Value: $75-95

Bear on Stump
15" high marked "2648 USA".
Value: $75-95

Puppy on Stump
14" high, marked "2620-1-2-3 USA".
Value: $75-85

Puppy on Stump Salt and Peppers
Value: $25-35

Mouse on Stump
marked "891-892 FS USA"
Value: $75-85

Snail
marked "878 USA".
Value: $125-150

Holly Hobby
marked "505".
Value: $175-250

Cookie Monster
marked "505 USA".
Value: $125-150

Cookie Monster Chef
marked "505 USA".
Value: $125-150

Cylinder with Strawberries
marked "899 Copyright USA".
Value: $90-95

Christmas House
11 1/2" high, marked "857".
Value: $150-175

Tiger Salt and Peppers
marked "883".
Value: $50-65/set

Hippo
14" high, marked "883 USA".
Value: $250-275

Taxi
7 1/4" high x 10 3/4" long x 5 3/4" wide,
marked "501".
Value: $200-250

Red Van
10" high, marked "843 Copyright USA".
Value: $200-250

School Bus
unmarked.
Value: $250-300

Red House
marked "741" on lid and base.
Value: $125

Shoe House
12" high, paint under glaze,
marked "874 USA".
Value: $65-75

Shoe House
12 1/2" high x 11 1/2" long x 6" wide,
incised in lid and on base "874 USA".
Value: $75-85

Kitten with Ball of Yarn
marked "321".
Value: $85-95

Turtle
11 1/2" high, glaze and cold paint,
marked "842 Copyright".
Value: $85-95

Elephant
marked "826 USA",
A Marsh Industries Jar.
Value: $85-95

Tea Kettle
12" high, marked "737 USA".
Value: $65-70

Rooster
9" high, marked "California Originals
USA 1127" in lid and base.
Value: $55-60

Puppy
11 3/4" high, marked "458 USA".
Value: $55-60

Bear
12" high, unmarked.
Value: $60-65

Hobo in Barrel
marked "873 USA".
Value: $225-275

Rabbit in Bucket
marked "703 USA".
Value: $150-195

Potbellied Stove
marked "743 USA".
Value: $95-100

Penguin
12" high, marked "459 USA".
Value: $95-125

Orange
11" high, marked "8718 USA".
Value: $95-125

Pear
marked "8217 USA".
Value: $50-55

Lemon
marked "8496-84-97-1-8499".
Value: $65-75

Green Apple
10 3/4" high, marked "8214 USA".
Value: $65-75

Have a Happy Day Cylinder
marked "505".
Value: $35-50

Clown
white, marked "213 USA".
Value: $95-100

Rabbit with Cookie
unmarked.
Value: $75-95

Liberty Bell
10" high, marked "883 USA".
Value: $65-75

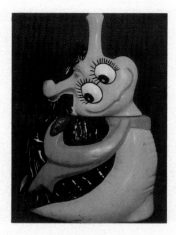

Snail
pink and yellow, 13" high,
marked "854 USA".
Value: $200-250

Owl
blue eyes, (markings are hard to read).
Value: $50-55

House
marked "2754",
shown in 1974 catalog.
Value: $65-85

Circus Tent
marked "226".
Value: $125-140

Vegetable Basket
marked "2650-650-654-1 USA".
Value: $125

Lion
large head, unmarked.
Value: $125-150

Lion
marked "866 USA".
Value: $125-150

Tortoise and Hare
12 1/2" high, marked "728 USA".
Value: $75-85

Shoe
12 1/4" high, marked "2637 USA".
Value: $65-75

Clock House
9 1/2" high, marked "840 USA".
Value: $350-400

Scottie Dog
marked "937".
Value: $75-95

Noah's Ark
12" high, marked "881 USA".
Value: $225-250

Cookie Time Clock
13 1/2" high, marked "860 USA".
Value: $125-140

Big Bird on Nest
13" high, incised in lid and base,
marked "Copyright Muppets Inc. 971".
Value: $55-65

Humpty Dumpty
marked "882 USA".
Value: $200-250

Circus Elephant
marked "896 USA".
Value: $95-125

Monkey
13" high, marked "884 USA".
Value: $175-190

Owl
12 3/4" high, marked 856 USA".
(three different variations)
Value: $65-75 ea.

Juggler
13" high, marked "876 USA".
Value: $175-200

Juggler
13" high, marked "876 USA".
Value: $150-175

Baseball Boy
12" high, marked "875 USA".
Value: $6570

Ferdinand the Bull
12" high, marked "870 USA".
Value: $65-70

Ferdinand the Bull
12" high, marked "#870".
Value: $175-200

Coffee Grinder
11 1/2" high, marked "861 USA".
Value: $95-125

Paddle Boat
14 1/4" high, marked "868".
Value: $400-450

Circus Wagon
marked "2631".
Value: $125-150

Choo Choo Train
7" high, marked "2628 USA".
Value: $125-165

Bear
11 1/2" high, marked "2648 USA".
Value: $95-140

Bear
larger jar, paint under glaze,
marked "2648 USA".
Value: $175-225

Frog
10 1/2" high, marked "2645 USA".
Value: $95-110

Turtle on a Rock
10" high, marked "2637 USA".
Value: $150-175

Telephone
marked "741 USA".
Value: $125-150

Mouse
12 1/2" high, marked "2630 USA".
Value: $95-110

Chipmunk
11 1/4" high, marked "2625 USA".
Value: $95-110

Tree Stump
10" high, marked "2956 F".
Value: $50-55

Lion with Lamb
marked "928 USA".
Value: $150-195

Rabbit on Turtle
13" high, marked "2728 USA".
Value: $75

Cookie Shoppe
12" high, marked "2856 USA".
Value: $150-175

Elephant
10" high, marked "2643 USA".
Value: $55-65

Lion
12" high, marked "739 USA".
Value: $75-95

Fire Truck
11 1/4" high, marked "841 Copyright USA".
Value: $195-250

Old Radio
12" high, marked "888 USA".
Value: $95-110

Owl
10" high, unmarked.
Value: $50-55

Owl
10" high, marked "2751 USA".
Value: $65-70

Elephant
10" high, unmarked.
Value: $150-165

The Cardinal China Company

The Cardinal China Company was a distributor in Carteret, New Jersey. Connected with the American Bisque Corporation in Williamstown, West Virginia, they did not produce cookie jars at the Cardinal factory.

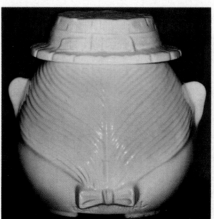

Little Girl
8" high, marked "Cardinal USA 301",
(two views).
Value: $150-175

Parking Garage
6 1/2" high, marked "Cardinal USA 306".
Value: $75-95

Pig
7 1/2" high, marked "Cardinal USA 304".
Value: $85-110

Cookie Sack
10" high, marked "USA #4200".
Value: $75-95

French Chef
9" high, marked "Copyright Cardinal USA".
Value: $150-175

Clown
9 1/2" high, "Copyright Cardinal USA".
Value: $125-150

Cookieville Bus
marked "Cardinal Copyright USA"
(two views)
Value: $325-375

Castle
11 1/2" high, marked "Cardinal
301 Copyright USA".
Value: $525-575

Soldier
12 3/4" high, marked "Cardinal USA 312".
(Also available with bank in head).
Value: $500-550

Henry Cavanagh

Henry Cavanagh was born in 1946 in Brooklyn New York, and now resides with wife, Laura, in Kingston, New York. Henry graduated from New York State University at Newpaltz, studying Art Appreciation, Painting, Sculpture, and Goldsmithing. Traveling into Germany, he worked for two years in bronze foundry in Dusseldorf, Germany. Upon returning to the United States, Henry turned his skill to ceramics, producing porcelain hippos. One of a kind, they were put on display at the Smithsonian Institute and other galleries over a 17 year period. In 1992, he began his line of automobile cookie jars under the name of Ceramicar. They are all fantasy cars lavishly painted and detailed. Each piece is a Limited Edition and of top quality. Henry makes all of his own molds and all cookie jars are totally lead free in clays, colors, and glazes.

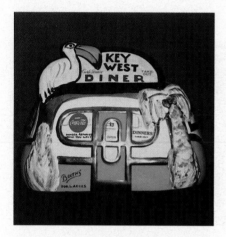

Key West Diner
marked "H Cavanagh Copyright",
limited edition of 200, custom designed
for Mark and Ellen Supnick.
Value: $250-300

Supnick's Diner
marked "H Cavanagh Copyright",
custom designed for Mark and Ellen Supnick.
Value: $250-300

Mom's Diner
marked "H Cavanagh Copyright",
limited edition of 200, 1992.
Value: $250-300

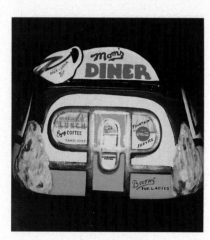

Mom's Diner
marked "H Cavanagh Copyright",
limited edition, (slightly different design).
Value: $250-300

Empire Diner
marked "H Cavanagh Copyright",
very few of these produced, large jar,
beautiful quality.
Value: $375-450

Empire Diner
marked "H Cavanagh Copyright",
smaller versions, limited edition.
Value: $175-250

Blimpmobile
limited edition of 200,
marked "H Cavanagh Copyright".
Value: $300+

Convertible
marked "H Cavanagh Copyright",
limited edtion of 200.
Value: $300+

Panel Delivery Truck
for Empire Deli,
marked "H Cavanagh Copyright".
Value: $400+

Panel Delivery Truck
for Empire Meats & Vegetables,
marked "H Cavanagh Copyright".
Value: $400+

Fire Chief's Car
marked "H Cavanagh Copyright",
limited edtion of 200.
Value: $300-350

Fire Chief's Car
Number 1 Engine, Post Company #6,
limited edition of 200,
marked "H Cavanagh Copyright".
Value: $450

Police Car
marked "H Cavanagh Copyright",
limited edtion of 200.
Value: $300+

Police Paddy Wagon
marked "H Cavanagh Copyright",
limited edtion of 200, (different design).
Value: $300+

Police Car
marked "H Cavanagh Copyright",
limited edtion of 200, (different design),
all jars can be customized.
Value: $300

Royal Oak Police Department
marked "H Cavanagh Copyright",
limited edtion of 200.
Value: $300+

Police Car
marked "H Cavanagh Copyright",
limited edtion, customized to order.
Value: $300+

Metro Cab Company
marked "H Cavanagh Copyright",
limited edtion of 200.
Value: $350

Empire Cab Company Taxi
marked "H Cavanagh Copyright",
limited edtion of 200.
Value: $300+

Empire Taxi Company
marked "H Cavanagh Copyright",
limited edtion of 200.
Value: $300+

Empire Taxi Cab
marked "H Cavanagh Copyright",
limited edtion of 200, (different design).
Value: $300+

Good Humor Truck
marked "H Cavanagh Copyright",
prototype, limited edition.
Value: $300+

Good Humor Truck
limited edition of 200 pieces,
marked "H Cavanagh Copyright Ceramicar",
Value: $425

Pick-up Truck
marked "H Cavanagh Copyright",
limited edtion of 200.
Value: $300

Elliott's Speed & Custom
marked "H Cavanagh Copyright",
(one of a kind, this was given to Henry
Cavanagh's Auto Mechanic for a
Christmas gift in 1994).
Value: $400

Clay Art

Clay Art is located in San Francisco, California.

Stacked Animals
hand painted, paper label reads
"Clay Art, San Francisco, CA".
Value: $50-60

Sunday Cow
marked "Clay Art, San Francisco".
Value: $75-95

Cow with Bell
paper label reads "Clay Art".
Value: $50-60

Midnight Snack
marked "Clay Art, San Francisco".
Value: $75-110

Wizard of Oz
hand painted, sticker reads
"Clay Art, San Francisco, CA".
Value: $95-110

Humpty Dumpty
with a paper label.
This jar had a lot of production problems
and was discontinued.
Value: $125-150

Cat in the Primroses
with a paper label.
Value: $55-65

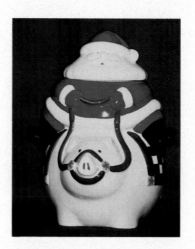

Barnyard Santa
with a paper label.
Value: $75-85

Watermelon Pig
marked "4401".
Value: $55-65

Pig Racer
marked "8808".
Value: $55-65

Toaster
marked "8811".
Value: $55-65

Cat Racer
marked "8810".
Value: $55-65

Cow Cookie Jar
with a paper label.
Value: $55-60

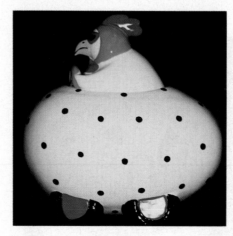

Chicken Racer
marked "8807".
Value: $55-60

Merlin
with a paper label.
Value: $150-175

Cow in the Corn
with a paper label, marked "8601".
Value: $50-65

Cow
with a paper label.
Value: $40-50

Corl Pottery Company

Shirley Corl is the owner of the Corl Pottery Company of Caro, Michigan. Shirley is a talented artist and ceramist who designs and produces Limited Edition cookie jars. She works along with husband, Bill, and daughter, Darcy. Shirley is very well known across the country and other parts of the world for her beautiful original designs. Shirley's jars are made with the finest materials available and each jar is decorated solely by hand. Shirley and Bill Corl are also avid cookie jar collectors.

Fanny Turnabout / Manny Turnabout
(one side is Fanny the other is Manny, both views shown here),
marked "Limited Edition 1993 Copyright SA Corl".
Value: $300-350

Little Black Sambo
made exclusively for Mark & Ellen Supnick,
designed and created by Shirley Corl,
this is a limited edition of 100, 1994.
(Picture shows both sides of jar).
Value: Issue Price $195

Fanny Turnabout / Manny Turnabout
(one side is Fanny the other is Manny, both views shown here),
with red polka dots, test patterns. Limited edition of 100.
Value: $300-350

Fanny Turnabout / Manny Turnabout
(one side is Fanny the other is Manny, both views shown here),
in yellow, limited edition of 100.
Value: $300-350

Tar Baby
with a blue coat, original design,
limited edition of 100.
Value: $325-375

 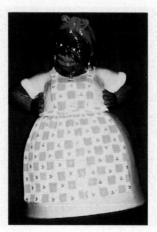 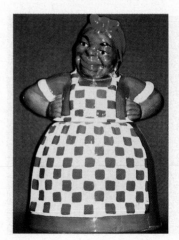

Tar Baby
with a red coat, original design,
limited edition of 100.
Value: $325-375

Brayton Mammy Reproduction
limited edition of 50.
Value: $225-275 ea.

Brayton Mammy Reproduction
limited edition of 50, 1992.
Value: $225-275

Victorian Santa
(Santa's hat is gilded in solid gold),
original design by Shirley Corl,
limited edition of 100.
Value: $400-475

Victorian Santa
black face, limited edition of 100,
marked "S Corl".
Value: $250-295

Victorian Santa
white face, limited edition of 100,
marked "S Corl".
Value: $250-295

Porky Pig in Chair
limited edition of 50,
from a Duncan Mold.
Value: $150-195

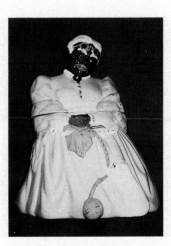

Napping Della
limited edition.
Value: $450-575

Ugly Pumpkin Witch
limited edition of 25,
made for Mark and Ellen Supnick,
(this is a very heavy jar), marked "S Corl".
Value: $175-225

Trick or Treat
(turnabout showing both sides)
limited edition of 100.
Value: $175-225

Witch with Jack-O-Lantern
limited edition of 50,
marked "S Corl".
Value: $200-250

Skull with Spider Finial
limited edition of 50, (notice big gold tooth).
Value: $160-195

Christmas Tree with Snow Babies
limited edition of 100, 1994.
Value: $195

Mr. Snowman
with ear muffs (shown here, one pictures has red and the other blue).
Limited edition of 100.
Value: $150-175 ea.

Newfoundland Dogs
limited edition.
Value: $150-175 ea.

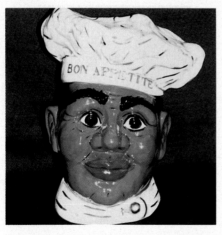

Bon Appetite
limited edition of 100.
Value: $195-225

Popeye in Spinach Can
limited edition, Popeye has a plastic pipe,
made for George Williams III of North Carolina.
Value: $150-195

Popeye in Spinach Can
limited edition of 35, first of the Popeyes,
the back of this jar has other Popeye Characters.
Value: $450-575

Mosaic Tile Mammy Reproduction
limited edition of 50, (shown in two different color dresses,
teal and purple). Marked "S Corl".
Value: $250 ea.

Humpty Dumpty
limited edition of 100.
Value: $175

Indian Head Reproduction
only 10 produced, marked "S A Corl".
Value: $150

Cumberland Ware

Cumberland Ware, also known as Roman Ceramics, is owned by Harold Roman, of Mayfield, Kentucky. It closed its doors in 1982.

Stan Laurel
marked "C-W", Cumberland Ware is closely connected
to Roman Ceramics and California Originals
Value: $900-950

W. C. Fields
marked "Cumberland Ware C-W USA".
Value: $1,100

Oliver Hardy
marked "C-W USA".
Value: $1,400-1,800

Stan Laurel
marked "C-W".
Value: $900-950

W. C. Fields
marked "Cumberland Ware C-W".
Value: $1,100

Oliver Hardy
marked "C-W USA".
Value: $1,400-1.800

R2D2
(actually made by Roman Ceramics)
12 1/2" high, marked "Star Wars TM Copyright
1977 20th Century Fox Film Corporation".
Value: $150-225

Clown
marked "Cumberland Ware".
Value: $175-200

Transformers
marked "Roman Ceramics".
Value: $175-225

Elephant with Baseball Cap
marked "C-W".
Value: $125-150

Ranger Bear
marked "C-W".
Value: $125-150

Monk
marked "C-W".
Value: $150-175

DeForest of California

DeForest of California is another family owned California business. Started by Margaret DeForest in 1950, with Jack DeForest serving as President. The company closed in 1970.

Bear
marked "G-405".
Value: $40-45

Smiling Bear
marked "De-Forest of CA".
Value: $125-150

Poodle
marked "DeForest of CA".
Value: $175-250

Snappy Gingerbread Boy
marked "DeForest of CA Copyright #6,
Made in USA".
Value: $225-250

Gingerbread House
marked "DeForest of CA, Hand Painted".
Value: $150-195

Frog
marked "DeForest of CA, Hand Painted".
Value: $145-175

Nun
12 1/2" high, "Thanks for Our Daily Cookies".
(This jar was also available with various sayings.)
Marked "DeForest of CA USA".
Value: $500-550

Chipmunk
marked "DeForest 514".
Value: $110-150

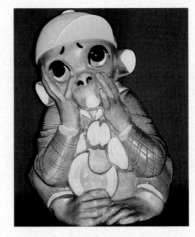

Monkey
marked "DeForest of CA 5516".
Value: $110-150

Halo Boy / Holy Devil
marked "DeForest of CA, Copyright 1956".
Value: $900-1,100

Ponytail Girl
marked "DeForest of CA".
(front and back view).
Value: $1,200-1,400

Parrot
marked "DeForest of CA".
Value: $175-195

Happy Budda
marked "USA DeForest of CA #527"
Value: $150-165

Clown
unmarked.
Value: $50-60

Clown
paint under glaze, marked
"DeForest of CA USA" in script.
Value: $550-595

Clown
unusual finish, marked "DeForest of CA
Copyright USA".
Value: $225-250

Clown
marked "DeForest of CA Copyright USA".
Value: $75-95

Clown
unmarked.
Value: $110-150

Pig Goodies Jar
marked "DeForest of CA USA".
Value: $250-275

Pig Bank
"Go Ahead - Make a Pig of Yourself",
marked "DeForest of CA".
Value: $75-95

Pig
"Go Ahead - Make a Pig of Yourself",
marked "DeForest of California Hand Painted".
Value: $175-225

Pig Head Jar
marked "DeForest of CA Hand Painted",
(different color variation).
Value: $175-225

Pig Head Jar
"Go Ahead - Make a Pig of Yourself",
marked "DeForest of CA Hand Painted".
Value: $150-175

Pig Candy Jar
marked "DeForest"
Value: $125-140

Pig Goody Bank
full figured cookie jar and bank head,
marked "DeForest of CA Hand Painted",
(two different color variations shown here).
Value: $600-625

Pig Bank Head
"For My Swimming Pool".
Value: $125-145

Cookie King
marked "DeForest of CA Hand Painted".
Value: $1,800-2,000

Coffee Pot
marked "DeForest of CA Hand Painted".
Value: $75-85

Rabbit
marked "DeForest of CA Copyright 58".
Value: $145-165

Monk
marked "DeForest of CA Copyright USA".
Value: $150-195

Nun
marked "DeForest of CA Copyright USA".
Value: $350-395

Monk
marked "DeForest of CA Copyright USA".
Value: $150-195

Soup Ladle
Value: $65-75

Rooster
unmarked
Value: $400-450

Rooster
marked "DeForest of CA".
Value: $175-200

Parrot
marked "DeForest".
Value: $200-225

Turtle
Value: $250-275

Mrs. Rabbit Salt & Peppers
marked "DeForest USA".
Value: $65-75

Department 56

Dept. 56 is an importer/distributor based in Eden Prairie, Minnesota.

Cantaloupe
paper label "Hand Painted".
Value: $65-75

Car with Luggage on Top
paper label "Hand Painted".
Value: $65-75

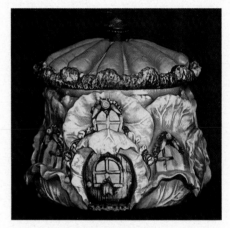

Carrot House
(beautiful quality pottery)
marked "Dept. 56".
Value: $175-195

McNutts Chicken Coop
marked "McNutts Dept. 56 Japan Copyright
1988 Schialfer Nance & Co., Inc."
Value: $150-175

McNutts Chicken Coop Salt & Peppers
paper label read "Dept. 56".
Value: $55-60 a set

McNutts Chicken
marked "Dept. 56".
Value: $150-160

McNutts Salt & Pepper Shakers
Value: $45-55 a set

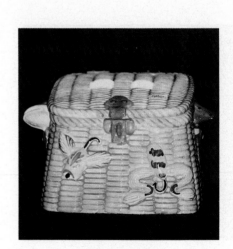

Fishing Creel
paper label "Dept. 56".
Value: $55-60

Witch
paper label "Dept. 56".
Value: $225-250

McNutts Chicken with Egg
paper label "Dept. 56".
Value: $210-240

Doranne of California

Doranne of California was established in 1951 in Los Angeles by Irving Deitz.

Elephant
12 1/2" high, marked "16 USA".
(Many different varieties available).
Value: $100-125

Elephant
12 1/2" high, marked "16 USA".
Value: $65-75

Cow Over The Moon
13 1/2" high, marked "J2 USA",
made in the late 1950's.
Value: $250-300

Monkey in Barrel
marked "CJ43 USA".
Value: $125-145

Lion
markings are hard to read.
Value: $50-60

Graduate Owl
marked "J4 USA".
Value: $55-65

Pineapple
marked "USA".
Value: $55-65

Cow with Can of Milk
marked "CJ107", 1984.
Value: $125-135

Noah's Ark
unmarked.
Value: $325-350

Dragon
marked "USA".
Value: $325-350

Cookie
10 1/2" high, marked "USA J55".
Value: $75-80

Lunch Box
unmarked, (this is now discontinued).
Value: $50-60

Sheep Dog
marked "USA".
Value: $125-150

Bread with Butter
marked "USA".
Value: $125-150

Squash
marked "CJ Copyright USA".
Value: $75-80

Fish
10 $^{1/2}$" high, marked "J 9 USA".
Value: $75-80

Camel
9 $^{1/4}$" high, marked "J8 USA".
Value: $225-250

Hen
marked "CJ 100".
Value: $125-150

Donkey with Cape
marked "USA".
Value: $225-275

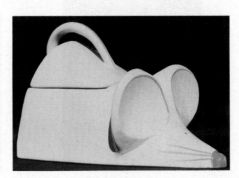

Mouse
marked "M-450 USA".
Value: $95-110

Mouse
marked "California USA".
Value: $110-125

Peanut
marked "CJ 18 USA".
Value: $50-55

Cookie Cola
marked "CJ 67 USA",
(this has been discontinued).
Value: $55-65

Owl
marked "Copyright USA J 62"".
Value: $75-85

Dapper Cat
13 1/2" high, marked "J5 USA".
(two different color variations shown).
Value: $110-125

Elephant
marked "California".
Value: $125-150

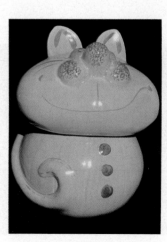

Lion
marked "USA".
Value: $110-125

Bear
marked "USA".
Value: $50-55

Hippo
marked "California USA 18".
Value: $95-110

Mailbox
10 1/2" high, marked "CJ52 USA".
Value: $95-110

Hound Dog
12 1/4" high, marked "J1 USA".
Value: $95-110

Happy Dog
13" high, marked "California USA MM 600".
Value: $75-80

Leprechaun
marked "J42 USA".
Value: $325-375

Rabbit
marked "California USA".
Value: $75-95

Van
marked "118 CJ USA Copyright".
Value: $150-175

Monkey
12" high, marked "CJ 21".
Value: $110-150

Frog
10 1/2" high, unmarked.
Value: $110-150

Brown Bagger
10 3/4" high, marked "J71 B".
Value: $75-85

Pinnochio/Court Jester
11" high, marked "CJ 46 Copyright USA".
Value: $250-300

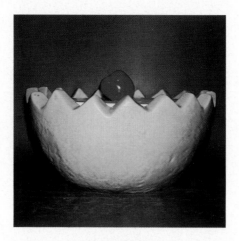

Grapefruit
marked "California USA".
Value: $225-250

Snowman
marked "J52 USA".
Value: $425-450

Rabbit in Hat
16" high, marked "C4 74".
Value: $140-160

Rocking Horse
unmarked.
Value: $125-150

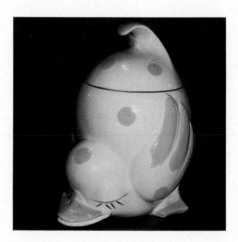

Duck
marked "USA".
Value: $125-150

Hippo
marked "USA".
Value: $175-200

Deer
marked "Copyright USA CJ #8".
Value: $125-150

4 x 4 Jeep
marked "Doranne CA CJ 115 Copyright USA".
Value: $175-200

Hound Dog
marked "USA".
Value: $95-110

Mother Goose
marked "USA CJ 16".
Value: $125-150

Doctor
marked "CJ 130 Copyright USA Doranne CA".
Value: $165-185

Beer Mug
marked "USA Copyright USA 12".
Value: $65-75

Keywee Bird
marked "USA CJ 41".
Value: $65-75

1971 Chianti Bottle
marked "USA CJ 76".
Value: $125-140

School Bus
marked "Doranne CA".
Value: $140-160

Dice
marked "J70 Copyright USA".
Value: $40-50

Cow over the Moon
(gold color).
Value: $250-300

Hippo
(green) marked "USA".
Value: $175-200

Clown
marked "Doranne USA".
Value: $95-125

Humpty Dumpty
marked "USA CJ 47".
Value: $400-450

Wide Mouth Jar
marked "CJ 54W USA".
Value: $50-55

Globe
marked "RC #60".
Value: $300-350

Pure Cane Sugar
unmarked.
Value: $150-195

Chef
(white).
Value: $75-95

Fitz & Floyd of Dallas, Texas

Fitz & Floyd of Dallas, Texas was founded in 1960 and is still in business today. Fitz & Floyd produces fine china, dinnerware, and giftware. Their cookie jars have been very collectible over the past 25 years. Their designs are of the highest quality. All of their cookie jars are produced overseas in either Taiwan or Japan. Fitz & Floyd also owns Omnibus Corporation.

Sugar Plum Castle
part of the Nutcracker Series,
paper label, marked "Fitz & Floyd".
Value: $200

Rio Rita
10 3/4" high, designed by Vicki Balcou,
paper label "F & F Taiwan".
Value: $150-225

Victorian House
paper label "F & F ".
Value: $175-225

Santa on Sled
stamped on bottom, (hard to read).
Value: $75-95

Santa on Motorcycle
9 3/4" high x 10 3/4" wide x 13 3/4" long,
incised "Copyright FF", paper label reads
"FF Taiwan", "Robert C. Floyd" in script.
Value: $450-500

Santa in Chair
original paper label "Fitz & Floyd 1993 ".
Value: $125-150

Spirit of St. Nicholas
9 3/4" high x 15 3/4" wide x 15 1/2" long,
incised "Copyright FF", paper label reads
"FF Taiwan", "Robert C. Floyd" in script.
Value: $1,100-1,500

Rolls Royce Santa
from the Robert C. Floyd Signature Collection,
paper label reads "FF Japan",
8" high x 8 1/2" wide x 15 3/8" long.
Value: $1,100-1,500

Rolls Royce Candy Jar
6" high, incised into pottery "Copyright FF 1987",
paper label reads "FF Japan".
Value: $200-225

Rolls Royce Santa
8" high x 8 1/2" wide x 15 3/8" long,
paper label reads "FF Japan" (cookie jar alone).
Value: $1,100-1,500

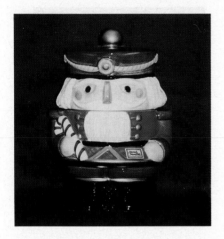

Nutcracker Soldier Candy Jar
original paper label "F & F ".
Value: $65-75

Queen of Hearts
original paper label, marked "Made in Japan",
from Wonderland Series, 1993, "Fitz & Floyd".
Value: $150-175

Woodland Santa
original paper label,
marked "F & F Made In Japan".
Value: $350-400

Quilted Stocking
original paper label "Fitz & Floyd ".
Value: $90-95

Southwest Santa
marked "Copyright F & F 1989".
Value: $600-650

Plaid Teddy Christmas Tree
original paper label "F & F ".
Value: $165-225

Kittens of Knightbridge
marked "F & F".
Value: $125-150

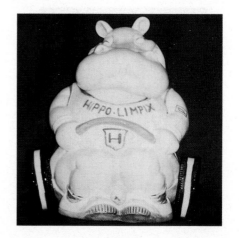

Hippo-Limpix
10" high, marked "F & F 1989".
Value: $125-150

Hoedown Witch
impressed "Fitz & Floyd Copyright F & F 1992",
original paper label "Made in Korea F & F".
Value: $125

Bunny Bonnet Hill
original paper label "F & F ".
Value: $125

Dracula Candy Jar
original paper label "Fitz & Floyd ".
Value: $50-60

Clown
marked "Fitz & Floyd".
Value: $125

Haunted House
original paper label "Fitz & Floyd
Copyright FF 1987 ".
Value: $150-175

Halloween Witch
paper label reads "F & F Korea",
impressed "F & F 1987".
Value: $120-150

Santa with Bag of Toys
original paper label "F & F ".
Value: $145-165

Mr. Snowman
10" high, original paper label "Copyright
Fitz & Floyd 1987 ", impressed "FF",
"Robert Floyd" in script.
Value: $125-150

Petting Zoo
original paper label "F & F Copyright".
Value: $175-195

Hydrangea Bear
original paper label "F & F 1993".
Value: $135-150

Mother Rabbit
original paper label "Copyright Fitz & Floyd ".
Value: $135-150

Prunella Pig
original paper label "Copyright Fitz & Floyd".
Value: $135-150

Dinosaur
original paper label "Copyright F & F ".
Value: $150-160

Harvest Piggly Wiggly
paper label "Copyright F & F 1993".
Value: $130-150

Scarlet O'Hare
original paper label "Copyright Fitz & Floyd ".
Value: $150-175

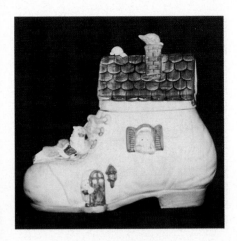

Old Woman in the Shoe
incised in jar, "Fitz & Floyd Copyright 1986",
paper label reads "FF Japan".
Value: $135-150

Christmas Carolers
original paper label "Fitz & Floyd ".
Value: $150-195

Kitchen Cousins
original paper label "F & F Copyright".
Value: $110-120

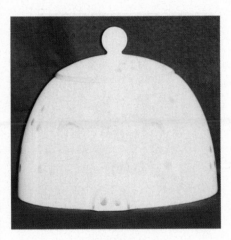

Pig Head
original paper label "Fitz & Floyd ",
(older jar).
Value: $125-150

Clown
stamped under glaze "Fitz & Floyd Inc.
Copyright MCMLXXIX FF".
Value: $150-175

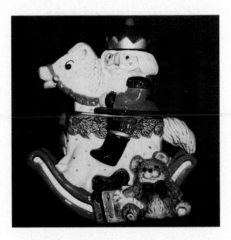

Nutcracker Soldier on Rocking Horse
marked "F & F Copyright 1993 ",
original paper sticker.
Value: $95-110

Night Before Christmas Candy Jar
original paper label "F & F Copyright 1993 ".
Value: $65-75

Quilted Santa
paper label "F & F Copyright 1993".
Value: $125

Hampshire Hog
original paper label
"Copyright F & F 1992" incised.
Value: $165-175

Santa in Sleigh
original paper label.
Value: $95-110

Night Before Christmas
1994 original paper label "F & F Copyright".
Value: $275-325

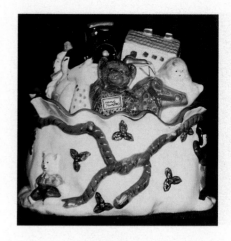

Toy Bag
original paper label "1988 Copyright F & F".
Value: $125-140

Night Before Christmas Santa Candy Jar
1994, original paper label "F & F Copyright".
Value: $75-95

Reindeer
unknown, paper label is missing.
Value: $95-110

Bloomers
original paper label "F & F ", "Copyright incised.
Value: $175-225

Car with Flat Tire
marked "Fitz & Floyd ".
Value: $175-225

Rolls Royce
marked "Fitz & Floyd ".
Value: $225-300

Mixing Bowl Duck
marked Fitz & Floyd".
Value: $125-150

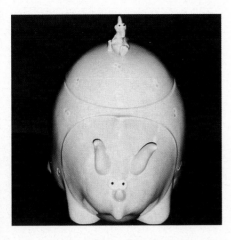

Triceratops
marked "Fitz & Floyd ".
Value: $195-200

Mother Goose
marked "Fitz & Floyd".
Value: $195

Foreign Jars

The Foreign Jars Category contain jars that are produced in many overseas countries such as Taiwan, Japan, China, Portugal, Italy, England, Holland, and Germany. Some of these jars are extremely sought after and collectible.

Cookie Guard Fire Hydrant
stamped "Japan".
Value: $65-95

Graduate Owl
marked "Japan".
Value: $40-50

Cookie Box
marked "Japan".
Value: $40-45

Fire Chief Dog
marked "Japan", unknown.
Value: $85-95

Rabbi
marked "Designed in America by TSVI 384792",
made in Japan.
Value: $800-900

Chipmunk
marked "Japan 2863".
Value: $50-60

Chef Nerd
marked "Made in Taiwan 1984 Willie Wonka
Brands, United Silver & Cutlery Co.".
Value: $125-150

Baseball Nerd
marked "Made in Taiwan 1984 Willie Wonka
Brands, United Silver & Cutlery Co.".
Value: $125-150

Skateboard Nerd
marked "Made in Taiwan 1984 Willie Wonka
Brands, United Silver & Cutlery Co.".
Value: $125-150

Baseball Nerd
marked "Made in Taiwan 1984 Willie Wonka
Brands, United Silver & Cutlery Co.".
Value: $125-150

Christmas Nerd
marked "Made in Taiwan 1984 Willie Wonka
Brands, United Silver & Cutlery Co.".
Value: $175-210

Santa Nerd
marked "Made in Taiwan 1984 Willie Wonka
Brands, United Silver & Cutlery Co.".
Value: $175-210

Reindeer Nerd
marked "Made in Taiwan 1984 Willie Wonka
Brands, United Silver & Cutlery Co.".
Value: $175-210

Troll Bank
marked "International Silver, Taiwan".
Value: $65-75

Troll Cookie Jar
marked "International Silver, Taiwan".
Value: $125-150

Cantalope House
marked "Made in Japan".
Value: $75-85

Marching Soldiers
marked "Ballonoff".
Value: $25-30

Mrs. Humpty Dumpty
unmarked.
Value: $225-250

Emmett Kelly Jr. on Barrel
(three different views), lid has signature,
marked "Emmett Kelly Jr. Collection, Exclusively from Flambro".
Value: $650-750

Feeding Time
marked "MI Hummell, Made exclusively for the
Danbury Mint 1993", trimmed in 24kt.
Value: $250-300

Chef
marked "Made in Japan".
Value: $150-175

Bull
marked "Poubelle De Trole" candy jar,
made in Japan.
Value: $40-50

Volkswagen Beetle
Certified International.
Value: $60-75

Chevy Belair
Certified International.
Value: $60-75

Ford Thunderbird
Certified International.
Value: $60-75

Raggedy Ann & Andy Salt & Peppers
Certified International.
Value: $65-75 a set

Raggedy Andy
Certified International.
Value: $110-130

Raggedy Ann
Certified International.
Value: $110-130

Raggedy Andy
unmarked.
Value: $50-60

Precious Moments Teddy Bear
Enesco, first jar to be made, heavy,
signature jar, only sold to signature stores.
Value: $140-160

Precious Moments Bake Shop
incredible jar.
Value: $100-120

Precious Moments Coffee Canister
(part of the Canister Set).
Value: $60-70

Precious Moments Tea Time
(part of the Canister Set).
Value: $60-70

Pinnochio Lollypop Jar
paper label "Devar Japan".
Value: $225-300

You're a Devil

You're an Angel

Cookie Telephone
made in Japan.
Value: $125-150

7" high, unmarked, reversible lid sucker jar, (two sides of the lid shown)
Value: $325-350

Alligator
marked "Sweet Pickles", related to
Children's Story Books.
Value: $225-250

Girl Holding Fruit
marked "Vcago, Japan".
Value: $150-175

Betsy Ross
made by Enesco.
Value: $285-300

Koo Kee Chef
unknown
Value: $375-400

Cow
made in China.
Value: $50-60

Chef
marked "Poubella de Table", made in Italy.
Value: $150-160

Girl with Grapes
with a Bluebird finial, marked "Arcadia #C6672".
(all three pictures are same jar just different views).
Value: $150-160

Penguin with Top Hat
unmarked.
Value: $35-45

Chef
made in Japan.
Value: $125-150

Ye Olde Outhouse
"Copyright I.E. Ely & Co. 1959",
ink stamped in base and lid.
Value: $125-150

Here Comes Trouble/Girl
marked "Enesco Imports Japan".
Value: $150-175

Here Comes Trouble/Boy
marked "Enesco Imports Japan".
Value: $150-175

Monk
made in Mexico by a Priest.
Value: $350-450

Little Cheeser Mouse
made by Ganz Canada
Value: $150-175

Little Cheeser Mouse
musical, made by Ganz Canada
Value: $175-200

Cookie Teepee
Japan.
Value: $95-110

Soldier Bear
unknown.
Value: $50-60

Little Lamb Head
paper sticker "Brinnoo made in Japan BN-432".
Value: $50-60

Dutch Lady
unmarked, Japan.
Value: $75-95

Pirate
marked "Japan".
Value: $75-95

Lion
17 1/2" high, unmarked.
Value: $150-165

Frog with Cowboy Hat
marked "Sears Roebuck & Co. 1981 made in Japan".
Value: $95-125

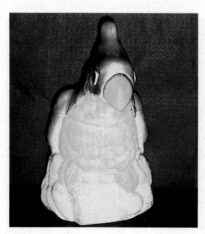

Parrot
unmarked.
Value: $75-85

Tortoise with Top Hat
made in Japan.
Value: $85-95

Treasure Chest
marked "Japan".
Value: $95-125

Dragon
unmarked, made in Japan.
Value: $75-95

Porky Pig
unmarked.
Value: $50-60

Standing Pig
unmarked.
Value: $125-150

Fruit Basket
marked "Japan".
Value: $65-75

Rooster
basket handled, marked"Japan".
Value: $125-150

Clown
basket handled, unmarked.
Value: $85-95

Robot
paper label reads "Fred Roberts Co. San
Francisco, Made in Japan".
Value: $225-250

Robot
paper label, "Designed by Taylor & Ng
San Francisco, Made in Japan".
Value: $175-200

Leprechaun
dressed as a clown, basket handled.
Value: $125-150

Tugboat
unmarked, made in Japan.
Value: $125-150

Elephant
marked "Noleas" on paper sticker, Japan.
Value: $95-110

Robot
marked "Designed by Taylor & Ng,
San Francisco, Japan".
Value: $175-200

Chick with Hat
embossed on bottom "Made in Italy RH2636".
Value: $45-55

Pig
marked "Japan".
Value: $25-30

Hamburger
embossed on bottom, "1979
Cara Creations Made in Japan".
Value: $150-175

Hip Cat
made in Italy, marked "PQ 22-78" hand painted.
Value: $200-225

Scarecrow
paper label, "Royal Sealy Japan".
(two different colors).
Value: $125-150

Bell
marked "Copyright Sittre Ceramics 1977".
Value: $45-55

Sleigh
marked "Christmas 1977", possibly homemade.
Value: $40-50

Dicken's Christmas Tree
sold thru The Home Shopping Channel, 1993.
Value: $75-95

Santa with Gift
Taiwan.
Value: $50-60

Mr. & Mrs. Claus Salt and Peppers
Taiwan.
Value: $30-40 a set

Christmas Tree
Taiwan.
Value: $50-60

Santa Claus at Desk
Alberta Mold
Value: $65-75

Santa Claus
Taiwan.
Value: $50-60

Santa in Club Chair
(probably homemade).
Value: $50-60

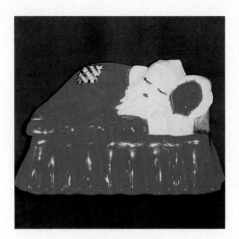

Santa in Bed
Alberta molds.
Value: $65-75

Santa in Chimney
marked "Homco Copyright 1990 Home Interiors".
Value: $175-195

Dicken's House
made by Applause 1990.
Value: $95-110

Snowman with Wreath
marked "Taiwan", sold in Kitchenware Stores.
Value: 75-85

Snowman
made in China.
Value: $65-75

Snowman
made in Japan, found in Alaska by a collector.
Value: 75-85

Snowman
made in Japan, large jar.
Value: 75-85

Snowman
sold in Bon Marche Dept. Stores 1993, made in Taiwan.
(two different color scarfs shown).
Value: $65-70

Cat Santa Claus
made by O.G.G.I.
Value: $85-90

Santa Bear with Christmas Tree
made in Japan, wind-up music box in lid.
Value: $95-110

Santa Dog in Christmas Stocking
paper label "Made in Mexico".
Value: $65-75

Leprechaun
made in Japan.
Value: $95-110

Pinnochio
made for Dayton Hudson Dept. Stores
1991, Made in Taiwan.
Value: $175-195

Mr. Red Pepper
marked "Made in Japan".
Value: $75-85

Indian Tee Pee
unmarked, made in Italy.
Value: $65-70

Radio
marked "Made by Enesco #978, E-1034".
Value: $75-80

Radio
marked "Essentials Japan".
Value: $60-75

Flower Cylinder
basket handled, marked "MIK DRI Ware,
Hand Painted, Made in Japan".
Value: $30-40

Doghouse
made in Japan.
Value: $125-150

Car with Puppy Finial
marked "Japan".
Value: $125-150

Three Little Kittens
basket handled, ink stamped "Japan".
Value: $125-150

Three Little Pigs
unmarked.
Value: $85-110

Three Little Kittens
unmarked, probably Lipper Mann Creations, Japan. (Two middle jars).
Value: $140-150

Three Little Kittens
marked "Lipper Mann".
Value: $140-150

Three Little Puppies
unmarked.
Value: $85-110

Three Little Pigs
unmarked.
Value: $85-110

Lady with Glasses
basket handled marked "Japan".
Value: $95-125

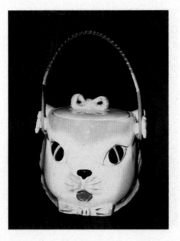

Pink Cat
basket handled marked "Relco Japan".
Value: $125-150

Chef
basket handled, marked "Made in Japan".
Value: $125-150

Little Boy
basket handled, marked "Japan".
Value: $125-150

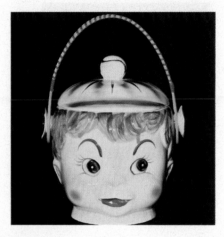

Baseball Boy
basket handled, made in Japan,
(two jars shown here with different lid variations).
Value: $95-110

Elephant
basket handled, made in Japan.
Value: $110-125

Woman with Bird on Hat
basket handled, Japan.
Value: $110-125

Happy Clown
basket handled, Japan.
Value: $125-150

Sad Clown
basket handled, marked "10052",
ink stamped "Japan" on paper label.
Value: $110-125

Cat
basket handled, paper label reads "Japan".
Value: $110-125

Basket Handled Chef
made in Japan.
Value: $100-125

Queen
made in Italy.
Value: $125-150

Green Embossed Jar
made in Germany.
Value: $45-55

Basset Hound
made by Enesco.
Value: $75-85

Bear
marked "Boston Mfg.".
Value: $45-55

Cowboy Pig
marked "Boston Mfg.".
Value: $45-55

Fire Truck
marked "Himark".
Value: $125-150

Clown Head
marked "60-153 Japan".
Value: $50-60

Rabbit with Babies
Japan.
Value: $65-75

Happy Clown
A McCoy lookalike reproduction,
unmarked, foreign made.
Value: $30-35

Pig
unmarked, (two jars shown).
Value: $45-50

Fish
marked "Japan".
Value: $65-75

Christmas Tree
marked "R.H. Macy & Company".
Value: $85-95

Pumpkin with Fruit
marked "Russ", sold in Publix
Supermarkets, South Florida.
Value: $80-85

Snail
made in Italy for Lord & Taylor.
Value: $225-300

Floral Basket Handled Jar
embossed, Japan.
Value: $45-55

Oriental Gardens Basket Handled Jar
with matching small jar, made in Japan.
Value: $110 a set

Clowns on Balls
basket handled jar, Japan.
Value: $125-150

Pup with Floppy Ears
basket handled, Japan.
Value: $140-150

Embossed Flowers
basket handled, Japan.
Value: $55-65

Cookie Shop
basket handled, Japan.
Value: $150-165

Chef Monkey
made in Japan.
Value: $55-65

Cat Biscuit Jar
basket handled, Japan.
Value: $140-150

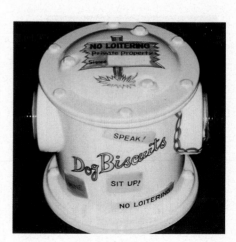

Dog Biscuit Jar
made in Japan.
Value: $165-175

Cat
made in Taiwan.
Value: $45-55

Humpty Dumpty
made in Italy.
Value: $450-550

Blue Colonial Cylinder
made in Japan.
Value: $30-40

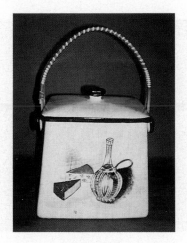

Square Jar
basket handled.
Value: $45-55

Fish
basket handled, Japan.
Value: $85-95

Flowers
basket handled, Japan.
Value: $45-55

Dragon Design
basket handled, Japan.
Value: $55-65

Fruit Design
basket handled, Japan.
Value: $40-50

Garden of Eden
basket handled, Japan.
Value: $140-150

Fruit Design
basket handled, Japan.
Value: $45-55

Cherries
basket handled, Japan.
Value: $45-55

Flowers
basket handled, Japan.
Value: $45-55

Petticoat Kitty
made in Japan.
Value: $65-70

Cat with Derby
unknown, unmarked.
Value: $75-85

Flowers
basket handled, unmarked.
Value: $40-50

Ghost with Pumpkin
marked "Boston Mfg.", made in Taiwan.
Value: $65-70

Cat with Straw Hat
made in Taiwan.
Value: $65-70

Christmas Cat
unmarked.
Value: $65-70

Emily Cat
sticker, marked "Made in Japan".
Value: $125-150

Monk Boy
ink stamped "A 3438".
Value: $175-250

Cat in Basket
made in Japan.
Value: $95-110

Cats on Basket
unmarked.
Value: $55-65

Cat in High Chair
made in China.
Value: $55-60

Cat Driving Car
marked "Cooks Bazaar".
Value: $110-125

Bunny Rabbit House
10 1/2" high, marked "Made in Japan".
Value: $95-110

Cat
unmarked.
Value: $25-30

Indian
made in Japan.
Value: $95-110

Diner
marked "O.G.G.I.", Taiwan.
Value: $50-60

Juke Box
marked "O.G.G.I.", Taiwan.
Value: $50-60

Sandwich
marked "O.G.G.I.", Taiwan.
Value: $50-60

Hamburger
marked "O.G.G.I.", Taiwan.
Value: $50-60

Alice's Adventures in Wonderland
made in Japan.
Value: $225-250

Humpty Dumpty
made in Japan.
Value: $250-300

Dog with Santa Hat
made in China.
Value: $40-50

Winking Kitty
paper label reads "Made by Enesco".
Value: $350-450

Queen on Throne
most likely Japan made, (older jar).
Value: $125-150

Elephant Sitting on Car
unmarked.
Value: $75-95

Christmas Tree Cookie Jar
paper label reads "Copyright RPCP MCMXCI
Made in Taiwan ROC", Royal China Porcelain,
Moorestown, NJ
Value: $200-250

Christmas Tree Salt & Peppers
Value: $35-40 a set

Christmas Tree Teapot
Value: $50-55

Christmas Tree Sugar Bowl
Value: $40-45

Christmas Tree Creamer
Value: $40-45

Christmas Tree Cookie Jar
Value: $200-250

Love Birds
marked "H 7525".
Value: $90-110

Holstein Cow
marked "Copyright Otagiri".
Value: $50-55

Chimney Sweep
Goebel #8351624
West Germany in 1974.
Value: $350-450

Chimney Sweep Bank
marked "5000214" Goebel paper label, West Germany.
Value: $125-150

Chimney Sweep Salt & Pepper Shakers
marked "7323308 A Goebel Paper Label".
Value: $75-80

Raggedy Ann
marked "C/88241972, The Bobbs Merrill Co., Inc."
Value: $175-200

Raggedy Andy
marked "C/88241972, The Bobbs Merrill Co., Inc."
Value: $175-200

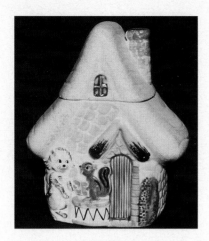

House with Pink Roof
marked "G 1907".
Value: $65-75

Old King Cole
marked "Japan".
Value: $225-250

Girl Hummel
marked "Japan".
Value: $165-200

Boy Hummel
marked "Japan".
Value: $165-200

German Jar
with boy finial, made in Germany.
Value: $150-200

Peasant Man
marked "Made in Germany".
Value: $150-200

Clown
marked "George Good Trademark", Taiwan.
Value: $140-155

Man Head
7" high, marked "PY Japan".
Value: $150-175

Lady Head
7" high, marked "PY Japan".
Value: $150-175

Santa Head
9" high, paper label,
marked "PSM Made in Japan".
Value: $150-175

Cat
made in Japan for Mervyns, paper label.
Value: $140-150

Bear
made in Japan for Mervyns, paper label.
Value: $140-150

Bunny
made in Japan for Mervyns, paper label.
Value: $140-150

Little Girl with Cat
made in Japan.
Value: $125-150

Little Girl with Cat
paper label.
Value: $125-150

Cat
Value: $75-80

Pumpkin Shelf Sitter
unmarked.
Value: $150-200

Witch Shelf Sitter
unmarked.
Value: $150-200

Rag Doll
paper label reads "Royal Sealy Japan".
Value: $200-225

Dutch Girl
paper label reads "Royal Sealy Japan".
Value: $125

Horse Doctor
marked "Japan".
Value: $125-150

Pig Chef
marked "Japan".
Value: $125

Hippo Fisherman
marked "Japan".
Value: $95-110

Bear Ranger
marked "Japan".
Value: $125

Hound Dog Hunter
marked "Japan".
Value: $125

Cow Bell Farmer
marked "Japan".
Value: $125

Humpty Dumpty
marked "Japan".
Value: $200-250

Spaceship
marked "Copyright Fres-O-Lone".
Value: $150

Covered Wagon
marked "Japan".
Value: $125-150

Humpty Dumpty
unmarked, (two different variations).
Value: $300-350

Monk
unmarked.
Value: $50-55

Dinosaur
unmarked.
Value: $50-55

Monk
unmarked.
Value: $75-80

Pig
unmarked.
Value: $55-60

Monk Salt and Peppers
unmarked.
Value: $20-25 a set

Irish Boy
unmarked.
Value: $95-110

Card King
unmarked.
Value: $125-150

Penguin with Cane
unmarked.
Value: $95-110

Penguin with Bow Tie
unmarked.
Value: $65-75

Southwest Horse
unmarked.
Value: $150-195

Cat with Apron
marked "Made in Taiwan".
Value: $65-75

Cat with Apron Shakers
marked "Made in Taiwan".
Value: $25-30 a set

Boy on Stump
unmarked.
Value: $75-85

Chef
unmarked.
Value: $125-155

Bear in Overalls
marked "Made in Brazil".
Value: $125-150

Chipmunk
marked "Made in Japan".
Value: $75-85

Rabbit
marked "Made in Japan".
Value: $75-85

Duck with Glass Bowl
unmarked.
Value: $45-50

Pencil
12 1/2" high, marked "M. Kamenstein Inc.
Copyright MCMLXXXIV Made in Portugal".
Value: $65-75

Light Bulb
12 1/2" high, marked "M. Kamenstein Inc.
Copyright MCMLXXXIV Made in Portugal".
Value: $50-60

Cookie Major
made in Italy.
Value: $150-175

Chef
made in Italy.
Value: $95-110

Pinnochio
made in Italy.
Value: $300-350

Granny
unknown.
Value: $175-225

Grandpa
unknown, (two different variations).
Value: $175-225

Elephant
made in Japan.
Value: $40-50

Jemima Duck
made in Japan.
Value: $125-150

Beulah the Calf
smaller than the Metlox jar, made in Mexico.
Value: $200-250

Clown
unknown.
Value: $75-125

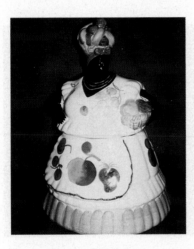

Mammy Miranda
made in Indonesia.
Value: $60

Mandy
made in Indonesia,
reproduction of OCI Jar.
Value: $60

Whiskers the Cat
made in Japan, includes Cookie Jar, Teapot,
Covered Sugar, Covered Creamer, and Mug.
Value: $225 a set

Pinnochio
made in Italy.
Value: $400-500

Humpty Dumpty
biscuit jar, made in England.
Value: $160-195

Cookie House
made in Italy.
Value: $150-165

Peter Gemmi

Artist Peter Gemmi owns and operates Star Jars in Palm Beach, Florida. He recently began a special edition of five jars commemorating the Wizard of Oz movie, which debuted in 1939. The Cowardly Lion and Scarecrow jars are in the final stages of production. Other jars to come in the series include the Tin Man, Dorothy and Toto, The Wicked Witch, Glinda the Good Witch, The Wizard of Oz, The Ruby Slippers, Munchkin Mayor, Lollypop Guild, and Lullabye League. All these jars are licensed from Turner Entertainment Licensing. These jars are also made by Treasure Craft, Compton, California. Upcoming editions include jars from Star Wars movies as well as other well known characters.

Cowardly Lion
Special Edition Commemorating Wizard of Oz
Movie, 1939, 1st in Series of 5 jars, Ltd. Ed. of
1939, with 139 Artist Proofs, prototype jar,
(finished product wasn't completed at publishing).
Value: $200-225

Scarecrow
Special Edition Commemorating Wizard of Oz
Movie, 1939, 2nd in Series of 5 jars, Ltd. Ed. of
1939, with 139 Artist Proofs, prototype jar,
(finished product wasn't completed at publishing).
Value: $200-225

Bob & Gale Gerds

Bob & Gale Gerds of West Alice, Wisconsin. Bob and Gale started in approximately 1991, making reproduction cookie jars in their home. Their jars are of a very high quality and are all Limited Editions. All of Gale's cookie jars are marked with her name on the bottom and each piece is numbered. Their newest Edition is of their own design, and called Willie and Butler. I'm sure we'll see many more original designs from Bob & Gale in the future.

Sears Girl Reproduction
1991, limited edition.
Value: $150-175

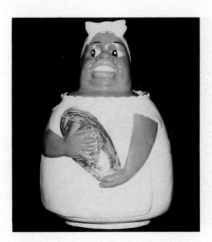

Weller Mammy Reproduction
1991, limited edition.
Value: $195

Black Granny Reproduction
yellow dress, limited edition.
Value: $150

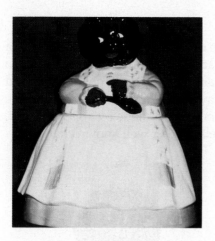

Black Granny Reproduction
blue dress, limited edition.
Value: $150

Cauliflower Mammy Reproduction
1991, no gold, limited edition.
Value: $175-225

Cauliflower Mammy Reproduction
(different color then previous picture)
with gold trim.
Value: $275-300

Cream of Wheat Chef Reproduction
1991, brown face, limited edition.
Value: $125-150

Cream of Wheat Chef Reproduction
1991, black face, limited edition.
Value: $125-150

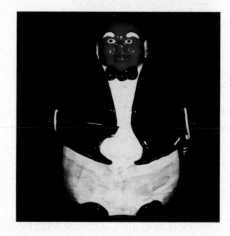

Japan Basket Handled Butler Reproduction
limited edition.
Value: $175-200

Mammy Head Reproduction Cookie Jar
basket handled, limited edition.
Value: $200

Mammy Head Reproduction Biscuit Jar
basket handled, limited edition.
Value: $200

Mammy Reproduction
basket handled.
Value: $150-195

Willie the Butler
limited edition, original design by Bob Gerds.
(Great jar, expect to find more originals by the Gerds).
Value: $200-225

Japan Mammy
reproduction, limited edition.
Value: $150

Mammy Reproduction Biscuit Jar
beautiful quality, limited edition.
Value: $150-175

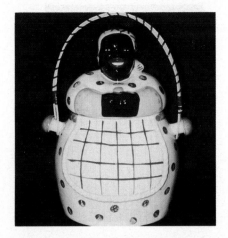

Mammy Reproduction Cookie Jar
beautiful quality, limited edition.
Value: $150-175

Black Mammy Candy Jar Reproduction
limited edition.
Value: $100-150

Maruhon Ware Reproduction
basket handled, limited edition.
Value: $150-195

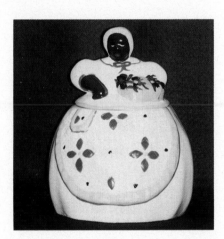

Old Lady Reproduction
1991, limited edition.
Value: $150

Artistic Pottery Mammy Reproduction
limited edition.
Value: $125-150

Artistic Pottery Chef Reproduction
limited edition.
Value: $125-150

Chef Reproduction
limited edition.
Value: $125-150

Olive Oyl
reproduction from American Bisque,
limited edition.
Value: $150

Popeye
reproduction from American Bisque,
limited edition.
Value: $150

Swee Pea
reproduction from American Bisque,
limited edition.
Value: $50

Little Lulu Reproduction
limited edition, (original jar possibly
made by American Bisque).
Value: $150-195

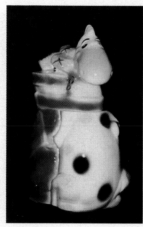

Dino and Golf Clubs
limited edition, reproduction, original made by American Bisque.
(two views of jar shown here, on the right is the bottom showing the markings)
Value: $150

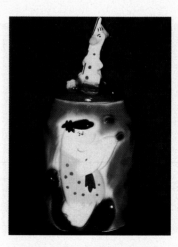

Rubbles House
limited edition, reproduction,
original made by American Bisque.
Value: $150

Wilma on the Telephone
limited edition, reproduction,
original made by American Bisque.
Value: $150

Fred with Dino Finial
limited edition, reproduction,
original made by American Bisque.
Value: $150

Wonder Woman
limited edition, reproduction.
Value: $150

Polka Dot Mammy
reproduction from original jar of
unknown origin, limited edition.
Value: $150

Davy Crocket in Woods
reproduction from Sirera Vista,
beautiful quality, limited edition.
Value: $175-200

Mammy with Watermelon
original design, limited edition, (three different color variations).
Value: $150

Carol Gifford-McCalip Originals

Carol was born and raised in Eureka, California. Carol's mother gave her a McCoy Aunt Jemima jar that she cherished for many years. She fell in love with Black Americana and quickly became a major collector. After collecting and filling up her kitchen of nothing but Black Collectibles, Carol was encouraged to do her own design of a Mammy cookie jar. With many years of ceramics behind her, and the help of an Oklahoma City artist, Carol sculpted her first cookie jar, Watermelon Mammy. This jar was a tremendous success. She then set out to do more and decided to make a set of five jars, in an Edition of 250. She has grown in leaps and bounds and produces some of the finest Black Americana cookie jars in the United States. Her newest are the Picaninny Straw Hat Twins and the Picaninny Basket Handled Twins. I'm sure we will see many more original designs of Carol Gifford-McCalip in the future.

Watermelon Sammy
11" high, marked "Copyright 1987 Carol Gifford". This jar is #1 of 5 and is a limited edition of 250. Value set of 5 jars $1,000+.
Value: $350-425

Watermelon Mammy
11" high, marked "Copyright 1986 Carol Gifford". This jar is #2 of 5 and is a limited edition of 250.
Value: $250-300

Pancake Mammy
9 1/2" high, marked "Copyright 1987 Carol Gifford". This jar is #3 of 5 and is a limted edition of 250.
Value: $300-325

Rocking Chair Granny
9 1/2" high, marked "Copyright 1987 Carol Gifford". This jar is #4 of 5 and is a limited edition of 250.
Value: $300-325

The Butler
9 1/2" high, marked "Copyright 1987 Carol Gifford". This jar is #5 of 5 and is a limited edition of 250.
Value: $300-325

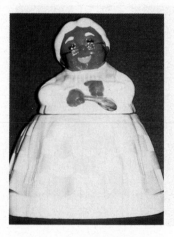

Granny with Spoon
9 1/2" high, marked "1987 Carol Gifford". From a Public Mold.
Value: $250-275

Watermelon Granny
9 3/4" high, marked "Carol Gifford 1987". From a Public Mold, hand painted Watermelons.
Value: $300

Granny with Spoon
9 1/2" high, black and white dress.
Value: $250-275

Christmas Granny
marked "Carol Gifford 1987", a Christmas present to Mark Supnick from Ellen Supnick 1991.
Value: $300-350

Granny with Spoon
green dress, marked "Carol Gifford 1987".
Value: $250-275

Luzianne Mammy Reproduction
12 1/2" high, incised "Carol Gifford".
Value: $275-325

Luzianne Mammy Salt & Peppers
reproduction, incised "Carol Gifford".
Value: $60-75 per set

Mosaic Tile Mammy
12" high, trimmed in gold,
incised "Carol Gifford".
Value: $275-300

Mosaic Tile Mammy
12" high, Daffodil Yellow, trimmed in gold,
incised "Carol Gifford".
Value: $275-300

Mosaic Tile Mammy
12" high, Primrose Pink, trimmed in gold,
incised "Carol Gifford".
Value: $275-300

Santa Head Jar
11" high, trimmed in gold,
incised "Carol Gifford".
Value: $300-350

Santa in Club Chair
11 1/2" high, very heavy jar,
incised "Carol Gifford".
Value: $350-395

Pickaninny Straw Hat Twins
Roses on girl are handmade by Carol McCalip,
Carol's newest editions in her line of jars.
Value: $425-500 ea.

Pickaninny Basket Handled Twins
Roses on girl are handmade by Carol McCalip,
Carol's newest editions in her line of jars.
Value: $425-500 ea.

Little Keith Lytle
designed for Keith Lytle,
marked "Carol Gifford Originals, Made
Exclusively for Cookie Jar Antiques,
Don Wirfs Assoc. 1990".
Value: $150+

Keitha
Keith Lytle in Drag, made as a gift to
Keith from Carol, Candy Wayne was
commissioned to do a limited edition
of 50 jars in this design.
Value: $250-300

Pickaninny Girl with Braids
one of a kind, made as a Christmas Gift
from Carol for Mark and Ellen Supnick.
Value: No Established Value

Gilner Pottery

Gilner Pottery is a California based company.

Peter Pumpkin Eater
8 1/4" high, marked "Gilner Potteries Design
Patent Copyright". All different color
variations available. This same jar can also
be found with Vallona Starr on bottom.
Value: $325-350

Mother Goose
11" x 9" x 7 1/2", marked "Gilner USA G-720".
Value: $300-350

Gonder Pottery

Gonder Pottery produced jars in Zanesville, Ohio, from 1941 until 1955.

Sheriff Bank
marked "Gonder Original 950".
Value: $400-450

Sheriff
marked "Gonder Original 950",
(shown here in two different color variations).
Value: $1,200-1,400

Pirate Bank
unmarked.
Value: $600-650

Helen Hutula

Helen Hutula ceramics plant was located on Old San Fernando Road in Burbank, California. Most of Helen's Wares were designed by her alone. She created the Mary Had A Little Lamb figurine lamps, while Bob Allen did Little Boy Blue Asleep in The Hay. Also working for Helen was Mel Shaw. Bob Allen and Mel Shaw worked for Helen's Ware before leaving to work at Metlox Potteries.

Helen's pottery was very unusual, very beautiful, and is highly sought after by all collectors. Helen's Ware was forced to close because of rough financial times.

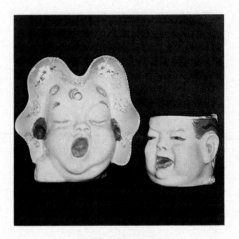

Tat-L-Tale
marked "Copyright Helen's Tat-L-Tale, Helen Hutula Original",
(shown here in different color variations).
Value: $900-1,100

Baby Mug
marked "Helen's Ware".
Value: $185-200

Milk Pitcher
marked "Helen's Ware".
Value: $400-450

Tat-L-Tale
(another color combination, like shown above)
Value: $900-1,100

Gim-Me Jar
marked "Gim-Me Helen's House",
extremely hard-to-find.
Value: $1,200-1,600

Tat-L-Tale
smaller in size,
highly decorated.
Value: $1,200-1,500

Tat-L-Tale
Value: $900-1,100

Tat-L-Tale
highly decorated, beautiful colors.
Value: $1,000-1,200

Tat-L-Tale
smaller size, original paper label,
very unusual design.
Value: $1,200-1,500

Tat-L-Tale
larger design, yet even different than the rest.
Value: $900-1,100

Boy Tat-L-Tale
original paper label reads "Helen Hutula's
Tat-L-Tale". Extremely rare, only
a few are known to exist.
Value: $2,000-2,500

Gim-Me Jar
marked "Helen Hutula Originals".
Value: $1,200-1,600

Boy Tat-L-Tale
another design, (two views shown).
Value: $2,000-2,500

Jewelry Jar
with felt on base.
Value: $1,200-1,350

William S. Hirsch

William S. Hirsch was a jobber that carried most of the Twin Winton products in the 1950's. Not much else is known about William Hirsch.

Monk
12 1/4" high, marked "Wm H Hirsch Mfg
Co LA Calif USA Copyright 1958".
Value: $125-150

Happy Budda
marked "William Hirsch CA USA".
Value: $150-175

Nun
marked "Hirsch Manufacturing CA USA",
very hard to find jar.
Value: $450-525

Monk
marked "Hirsch Manufacturing Co. CA USA".
Value: $125-150

J. D. James

JD James of Buckeye Lake, Ohio, is a talented artist and ceramist who works with his wife, Pat. JD started around 1991 with the reissue of the Brush Hillbilly Frog, from the original Brush Pottery mold. For the most part, JD has been into making very fine reproductions of some very beautiful cookie jars. He is now entering into the new field of his own original designs and licensed products. I'm sure we will see many more wonderful designs to come.

Freddy the Gleep
a McCoy reproduction, marked "JD James".
Value: $150

Mr. Weller-Be
Value: $250-350

Leprechaun
multicolor.
Value: $300-350

Little Lulu
Value: $150-250

Wilma on Telephone
American Bisque reproduction,
marked "JD James".
Value: $150-195

Barney & Bamm Bamm
original design, marked "JD 1992".
Value: $375-425

Fred Flintstone Reproduction
from the American Bisque original,
marked "JD James".
Value: $150

Dino with Golf Clubs
a reproduction from the American Bisque
original, marked "JD James".
Value: $150

Rubbles House
a reproduction from the American Bisque
Original, marked "JD James".
Value: $150

Fred Flintstone
original design, marked "JD 1992".
Value: $375-425

Indian
Lane reproduction, marked "JD James".
Value: $150

Sheriff
Lane reproduction, marked "JD James".
Value: $150

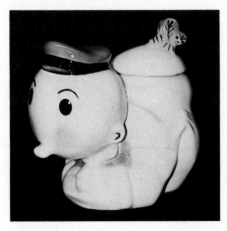

Swee Pea
American Bisque reproduction,
marked "JD James".
Value: $150

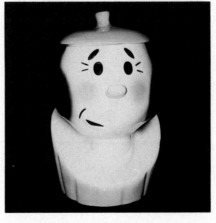

Olive Oyl
American Bisque reproduction,
marked "JD James".
Value: $150

Popeye
American Bisque reproduction,
marked "JD James".
Value: $225-250

Wimpy
original design, marked "JD James".
Value: $195

Tuffy
original design, marked "JD James".
Value: $195

Casper the Ghost
American Bisque reproduction,
marked "JD James".
Value: $150

Little Angel
Brush jar reproduction,
marked "JD James".
Value: $150

Mohawk Indian
American Bisque reproduction,
marked "JD James".
Value: $195-225

Formal Pig
Brush jar reproduction,
marked "JD James".
Value: $125-150

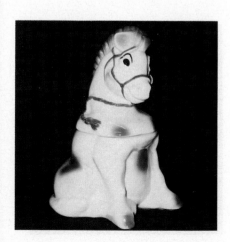

Sitting Horse
American Bisque reproduction,
marked "JD James".
Value: $195-250

Little Red Riding Hood
Brush Jar reproduction,
marked "JD James".
Value: $195-250

Cauliflower Mammy
McCoy reproduction, marked "JD James".
Value: $100-150

Peter Pan
Brush Jar reproduction,
marked "JD James".
Value: $150

Peek-A-Boo
Regal Jar reproduction,
marked "JD James".
Value: $250-325

Brush Hillbilly Frog
re-issue, marked "JD James".
Value: $450-600

George Zoltin Lefton Company

George Zoltin Lefton Company, a Chicago based importer, began operations in 1940. Lefton's marks often display a crown. Most pieces have a paper label, stamped with a number, and are marked, "Made in Japan."

Winking Santa
Value: $150-185

Scottish Girl
marked "1173 Lefton China".
Value: $200-275

Teddy Bear
original Lefton Sticker.
Value: $125-150

Lady with Hat Accessories, Jam Jar w/spoon marked "323" – **Value: $95-100**
Wall Pocket, 7" high, marked "50264-N". – **Value: $95-110**
Candy Dish, marked "1277". – **Value: $95-110**
Cookie Jar, 7 3/4" high, marked "George Z. Lefton 1957", marked "1277". – **Value: $150-195**
Tea Pot, marked "321". – **Value: $95-110**
Salt and Peppers, marked "439". – **Value: $40-45 a set**
Wall Pocket, marked "50264-N". – **Value: $95-110**
Cup & Saucer, marked "936", Lefton Sticker. – **Value: $75-95**

Tulip
paper label reads "Lefton, Exclusively,
Made in Japan".
Value: $125-150

Pixie Baby
marked with paper label.
Value: $150-175

Boy with Helmet
marked with paper label.
Value: $125-150

Cat Head Accessories Sugar, marked "1508". – **Value: $40-50**
Creamer, marked "1508". – **Value: $40-50**
Cat Head Cookie, 8" high, marked "1502". – **Value: $125-150**
Teapot, marked "1516". – **Value: $65-70**
Condiment w/Spoon, marked "1515". – **Value: $40-45**
Covered Bowl, marked "ESD". – **Value: $85-90**
Salt & Peppers, marked "1511". – **Value: $25-30**

Little Girl Head
8" high, marked "397" with Lefton sticker.
Value: $195-225

Dutch Girl Accessories, Sugar, marked "2698".
Value: $45-50

Creamer, marked "2698". – **Value: $45-50**

Butter Dish, marked "2822". – **Value: $75-80**

Cookie Jar, marked with paper label
"George Lefton Japan 2366". – **Value: $395-425**

Teapot, marked "2699". – **Value: $75-80**

Syrup, marked "2701". – **Value: $50-55**

Condiment, marked "2697". – **Value: $45-50**

Salt & Peppers, marked "2367". – **Value: $45-55 a set**

Bluebird Accessories
Sugar & Creamer, marked "290". – **Value: $40-45**

Planter, marked "288". – **Value: $40-45**

Bluebird Cookie Jar
7 1/2" high, Lefton sticker reads
"Copyright George Z. Lefton 289".
Value: $75-100

Salt & Peppers, large marked "282". – **Value: $40-45**

Salt & Peppers, small with
rhinestone eyes marked "239". – **Value: $40-45**

Wall Pocket, marked "283". – **Value: $65-70**

Butter Dish, marked "437". – **Value: $65-70**

Pixie Wall Pocket
"3972" Lefton Label, "Japan".
Value: $50-55

Salt & Pepper Shakers
"3968" Lefton Label, "Japan".
Value: $40-45

Pixie Teapot
"3973" Lefton Label, "Japan".
Value: $50-55

Pixie Sugar & Creamer
"3970" Lefton Label, "Japan".
Value: $45-50

Little Girl Wall Pocket, marked "744".
Value: $95-110

Little Boy Wall Pocket, marked "744".
Value: $95-110

Little Old Lady Cookie Jar
7 3/4" high, without lid, marked "Copyright
George Z. Lefton 1957 040".
Value: $175-200

Little Girl with Daisy Hat & Butterfly Finial
8" high, Lefton Sticker reads "1692".
Value: $125-150

Holly Cylinder
Value: $50-55

Louisville Stoneware Company

Louisville Stoneware Company originally called Louisville Pottery Company, opened its doors in 1905 and is still in business today. Their cookie jars are made out of stoneware, very unusual, one in particular is the Christmas House Cookie Jar. This company is located in Louisville, Kentucky.

The Night Before Christmas
side view, marked "Louisville Stoneware Company", very heavy jar,
(two different views shown here).
Value: $295-350

Troll
Precious Peepers Collection,
marked "Louisville Stoneware Company".
Value: $100-125

Rabbit
Precious Peepers Collection,
marked "Louisville Stoneware Company".
Value: $100-125

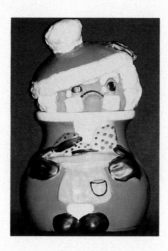

Mrs. Claus
Precious Peepers Collection,
marked "Louisville Stoneware Company".
Value: $100-125

Santa Claus
Precious Peepers Collection,
marked "Louisville Stoneware Company".
Value: $100-125

Little Girl
Precious Peepers Collection,
marked "Louisville Stoneware Company".
Value: $100-125

Little Boy
Precious Peepers Collection,
marked "Louisville Stoneware Company".
Value: $100-125

Belle of Louisville Steamship
marked "Louisville Stoneware".
Value: $125-195

Maddux of California

Maddux of California was established by William Maddux of Los Angeles in 1938. After some years, it was sold to Louis and Dave Warsaw. The pottery was no longer made after 1974, and Maddux of California went out of business in 1980.

Squirrel
13" high, marked "Maddux of California
Copyright Romanelli 2110".
Value: $200-225

Humpty Dumpty
11" high, marked "2113
Copyright Maddux of CA USA".
Value: $300-350

Humpty Dumpty
11" high, marked "2113 Copyright
Maddux of CA USA".
Value: $300-350

Cat
marked "Copyright Maddux of CA".
Value: $250-300

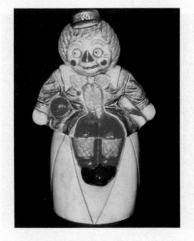

Clown
marked "Maddux of CA".
Value: $400-475

Paint under glaze, this is a hard jar to find.

Cold paint, another color variation.

Rabbit
marked "Copyright Maddux of
California Beatrix Potter".
Value: $450-575

Raggedy Andy
marked "Copyright Maddux of
California USA 2108".
Value: $200-300

Maurice of California

Maurice of California is located in Los Angeles, California, and run by Mr. Maurice Peckman. It began in 1967 and is still in business today.

Raggedy Ann
marked "Maurice of California USA WD 33".
Value: $150-175

Gigantic Clown
marked "Maurice of California USA JA 10".
Value: $250-300

Shoehouse
marked "Maurice of California ".
Value: $250-300

Rooster
marked "Maurice of California ".
Value: $85-95

Train
marked "Maurice of California USA JD 45".
Value: $200-225

Two Kittens in a Shoe
marked "Maurice of California USA ".
Value: $45-55

Chef
unusual design,
marked "Maurice of California ".
Value: $400-500

Hippo
marked "Maurice of California ".
Value: $150

McCoy Pottery

Original McCoy Pottery dates back to 1848 when W. Nelson McCoy went into the pottery business in Putnam, Ohio. The Nelson McCoy company was founded in 1910 in Roseville, Ohio. Many different books have been written on McCoy. It is extremely sought after by collectors across the country.

Green Pepper
10" high, marked "157 McCoy USA ".
Value: $60-75

Yellow Pepper
10" high, marked "McCoy USA ".
Value: $95-125

Pineapple
10 3/4" high, #52 marked "McCoy USA ".
Value: $75-80

White Strawberry
9 1/2" high, #263,
marked "McCoy LCC USA ".
Value: $65-75

Ear of Corn
12 1/2" high, #156, original paper label
reads "McCoy USA ".
Value: $225-250

Lemon
9" high, #262,
marked "McCoy USA ", 1972.
Value: $55-65

Bunch of Bananas
11" high, #33, marked "McCoy",
made in 1948-1952.
Value: $175-200

Basket of Eggs
9 1/2" high, marked "0274 McCoy USA ",
made in 1977-1979.
Value: $70-80

Apple
7 1/2" high, #20,
marked "McCoy USA ".
Value: $45-55

Pear
10" high, #18,
marked "McCoy USA ".
Value: $45-55

Engine
8 1/2" high, #207, marked "McCoy USA ",
made in 1962-1964.
Value: $195-225

Engine
8 1/2" high, #207, marked "McCoy USA ".
Value: $250-300

Caboose
7 1/2" high, #182, marked "McCoy USA ",
made in 1961, also available in all red.
Value: $200-250

Cookie House
6 1/2" high, #192, the lid is a bank,
marked "McCoy USA ", made in 1961.
Value: $90-110

Tea Kettle
9 1/2" high, #188, marked "McCoy USA ",
Value: $40-50

Raggedy Ann
11" high, marked "USA 741 ".
Value: $125-175

Touring Car
6 1/2" high, #139, marked "McCoy USA ".
Value: $95-110

Hot Air Balloon
9" high, marked "#353 USA ".
Value: $75-85

Hen on Nest
10 1/2" high, #139, marked "USA ".
Value: $65-75

Thinking Puppy
11" high, #272, marked "McCoy USA ",
made in 1977-1979.
Value: $35-40

Cookie Jug
11 1/4" high, #145, marked "USA ".
Value: $30-40

Christmas Tree
11 1/2" high, #174, marked "McCoy USA 1959".
Value: $1,200-1,400

Winking Pig
13 1/2" high, marked "#150 USA",
made in 1972.
Value: $400-450

Upside Down Panda
11 1/2" high, marked "#210 McCoy USA", made
in 1978-1979, also available with a clear glaze.
Value: $75-95

Traffic Light
10 1/2" high, marked "USA McCoy LCC".
Value: $75-85

Granny
11" high, with gold trim, marked "159 USA",
made in 1974-1975.
Value: $200-250

Granny
11" high, #159, marked "USA".
Value: $125-150

Indian Head
11 1/2" high, #50, light skin,
marked "McCoy USA", made in 1954-1956.
Value: $450-500

Coalby Cat
11 1/4" high, #207, marked "USA 207",
made in 1967-1968.
Value: $350+

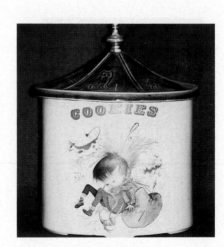

Little Boy Blue
8 3/4" high, finial is metal, unmarked,
(many more storybook characters are available).
Value: $150-195

Drum
9 1/2" high, #170, marked "McCoy USA",
made in 1960.
Value: $125-150

MacDog
11 1/2" high, marked "#208 USA",
made in 1967-1968.
Value: $95-125

Dalmatians in Rocking Chair
10" high, #189, marked "McCoy USA",
made in 1961.
Value: $550-600

Bear with Beehive
9" high, marked "#143 USA".
Value: $40-45

Stagecoach
unmarked.
Value: $1,100+

White Stagecoach
unmarked.
Value: $1,100+

Cookie House
8" high, #151, marked "McCoy USA",
made in 1958-1960.
Value: $110-125

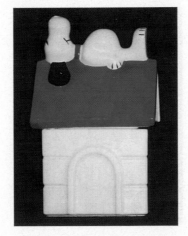

Snoopy on Doghouse
11 1/4" high, marked "USA", ink stamped
"Copyright United Features Syndicate Inc. 1970
Sears Roebuck & Company".
Value: $300-350

Chipmunk
10 3/4" high, marked "McCoy USA",
made in 1960-1961.
Value: $125-150

Barnums Animal Crackers
11 1/2" high, marked "#152 USA",
(front is a transfer), made in 1972-1973.
Value: $475-500

Fireplace
9 1/2" high, #209, marked "USA",
made in 1967-1968.
Value: $125-150

Black Cook Stove
10" high, marked "McCoy USA",
made in 1961-1969.
Value: $15-20

Boy on Baseball
13 1/2" high, marked "#221 McCoy USA LCC".
Value: $325-395

Boy on Football
11" high, marked "#222 McCoy USA".
Value: $350-425

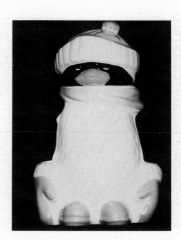

Chilly Willy
12" high, marked "#155 USA".
Value: $95-110

Cookie Cylinder
8 1/2" high, #7024, marked "McCoy USA ",
made in 1968-1969.
Value: $20-25

Doghouse
13" high, marked "206 McCoy
LCC USA", made in 1983.
Value: $275-300

Doghouse
13" high, marked "206 McCoy LCC USA",
different color variation, made in 1983.
Value: $350-400

Chairman of the Board
10 1/2" high, marked "#162 USA",
made in 1985, (has burgundy pants).
Value: $850-950

Chairman of the Board
10 1/2" high, marked "#162 USA",
made in 1985, (has brown pants).
Value: $700-800

Lunchbox
7" high, #357, marked "McCoy".
Value: $75-80

Davy Crocket
10" high, #140, marked "USA", 1957.
Value: $850-950

World Globe
10" high, #173 marked "McCoy USA", 1960.
Value: $450-525

W.C. Fields
11" high, marked "#153 USA",
made in 1972-1974.
Value: $350-400

Turkey
11 1/2" high, #23 marked "McCoy USA".
Value: $500-550

Tee Pee
11 1/4" high, marked "McCoy USA 137".
Value: $425-475

Tee Pee
11 1/4" high, with slant top,
marked "McCoy USA 137".
Value: $550-600

Jack-O-Lantern
marked "McCoy USA".
Value: $700-750

Jack-O-Lantern
with a green lid, marked "McCoy USA".
Value: $1,100-1,200

Chef Head
11" high, #206 marked "McCoy USA",
made in 1962-1964.
Value: $125-150

Picnic Basket
7 3/8" high, #191 marked "USA",
made in 1961-1963.
Value: $75-80

Hobby Horse
10 1/4" high, #36 marked "McCoy USA",
made in 1948-1953.
Value: $200-250

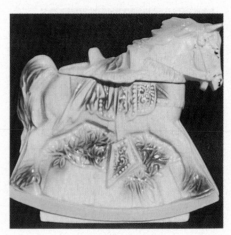

Hobby Horse
10 1/4" high, #36 marked "McCoy USA",
made in 1948-1953,
(this cookie jar has better paint).
Value: $300-350

Kangaroo
11 1/2" high, #234, marked
"McCoy USA", original design.
Value: $400-450

Blue Kangaroo
shown with previous jar,
produced after 1965, unmarked.
Value: $300-325

Circus Horse
9 1/2" high, #193, marked
"McCoy USA", 1961.
Value: $150-195

Sack of Cookies
gold trim.
Value: $150-175

Kitten on Coal Bucket
10" high, marked
"#218 McCoy LCC USA".
Value: $350-395

Kitten on Coal Bucket
10" high, marked
"#218 McCoy LCC USA".
Value: $200-250

Liberty Bell
7 3/4" high, #264, marked
"McCoy LCC USA", 1975.
Value: $65-85

Coffee Cup
9 1/4" high, #232, marked "USA"
on the handle, made in 1963-1966.
Value: $95-125

Clown Bust
10 1/2" high, #79, marked
"McCoy", made in 1945-1947.
Value: $65-75

Two Kittens in Low Basket
marked "McCoy USA".
Value: $750-800

Woodsy Owl
12 1/2" high, #201, marked
"USA", made in 1973-1974.
Value: $300-325

Mr. & Mrs. Owl
10 3/4" high, #38, marked
"McCoy USA", made in 1952-1955.
Value: $95-110

Owl
marked "204 McCoy USA", made in 1978-1979,
(two different color variations).
Value: $10-15

Mother Goose
10 ³/⁴" high, #34, marked
"McCoy USA", made in 1948-1952.
Value: $100-125

Sweet Notes
unmarked, possibly McCoy.
Value: $900-1,100

Market Lady
marked "Leslie Cope Galleries 1991".
Value: $450-500

Cylinder
marked "McCoy".
Value: $10-15

Panda with Swirl Lollypop
11" high, #741, marked
"McCoy USA", 1978.
Value: $500-550

Leprechaun
12 ¹/²" high, #169, unmarked.
Value: $2,000+

Red Leprechaun
12 ¹/²" high, #169, unmarked,
(various colors available).
Value: $3,000+

Pig Bank/Cookie Jar
10 ¹/²" high, marked "224 USA", 1985.
Value: $225-250

Strawberry Cylinder
marked "McCoy USA".
Value: $25-30

Frontier Family Cylinder
9 ¹/²" high, #213, unmarked, made in 1964-1971.
(Also available with an eagle finial.)
Value: $50-60

Thinking Puppy
11" high, #272, marked "McCoy USA",
made in 1977-1979.
Value: $30-35

Timmy Tortoise
10 ¹/²" high, marked "271 McCoy USA",
made in 1977-1980.
Value: $40-50

Milk Can
10" high, #7019, marked "McCoy USA",
made in 1972-1977.
Value: $30-40

Puppy with Sign
marked "McCoy USA".
Value: $65-95

Have a Happy Day
marked "McCoy USA".
Value: $65-70

Cookie Time Clock
13 ¹/²" high, #848, marked "McCoy",
made in 1968-1973.
Value: $35-45

Duck
11 1/2" high, unmarked, 1964.
Value: $65-75

Crock
unmarked.
Value: $30-35

Honey Bear
9" high, #37, marked "McCoy USA",
made in 1953-1957.
Value: $110-125

Whole Trunk Elephant
#41, unmarked, 1953.
Value: $200-225

Chiffonnier
11 1/2" high, #245, marked "McCoy USA".
Value: $95-125

Flower Cylinder
marked "McCoy".
Value: $15-20

Freddy the Gleep
marked "#189 McCoy USA".
This jar is being reproduced.
Value: $550-650

Freddy the Gleep
(green).
Value: $600-700

School Bus
8 1/4" high, marked "#352 USA".
Value: $95-125

Soccer Ball
unmarked, made in 1978.
Value: $1,500-1,800

Covered Wagon
7 1/4" high, #148, made in 1961-1967,
(two views shown here).
Value: $95-125

Snow Bear
11" high, #235, marked "McCoy USA", 1965.
Value: $95-125

Rabbit on Stump
marked "McCoy USA".
(Also available in other animal-on-stump styles).
Value: $75-85

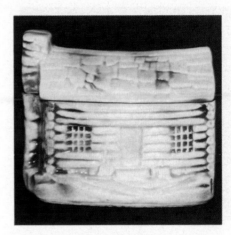

Cookie Cabin
7" high, marked "McCoy USA".
Value: $95-110

Apollo
13" high, marked "#260 McCoy Copyright USA",
made in 1970-1971.
Value: $1,000-1,200

Astronauts
11" high, marked "USA #226", 1963.
Value: $1,000-1,200

Friendship Seven
11 1/2" high, #204, unmarked,
made in 1962-1963.
Value: $125-135

Popeye Cylinder
10 1/2" high, #222, unmarked,
made in 1971-1972.
Value: $250-300

Bugs Bunny Cylinder
10 1/2" high, unmarked, made in 1971-1972.
Value: $250-300

Yosemite Sam Cylinder
10 1/2" high, unmarked, made in 1971-1972.
Value: $250-300

The Wren House
9 1/2" high, #153, marked "McCoy USA".
Value: $175-200

Fox Squirrel
very rare jar, marked "McCoy",
(two different views shown).
Value: $2,000+

Duck
unmarked.
Value: $30-40

Sad Clown
9 1/2" high, marked "255 McCoy USA",
made in 1970-1971.
Value: $125-150

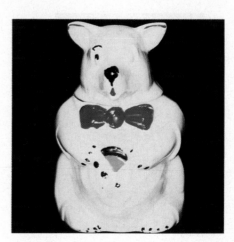

Bear with Cookie in Vest
10 3/4" high, #22, marked "McCoy made in 1945".
Value: $75-95

Bobby Baker
10 3/4" high, marked "#183 McCoy".
Value: $50-75

Betsy Baker
10 3/4" high, marked "McCoy USA 184",
(some of these jars are unmarked, three
different styles of hats are available), 1974.
Value: $400-450

Cat on Basket Weave
10 1/4" high, #126 marked "McCoy USA",
made in 1958-1959.
Value: $65-75

Lamb on Basket Weave
10 1/4" high, #127 marked "McCoy USA".
Value: $65-75

Cat
marked "McCoy USA".
Value: $85

Metlox Pottery

Metlox Pottery was founded in Manhattan Beac h, California in 1927. Cookie jars began to be produced in 1947 when the plant was purchased by Evan K. Shaw. Metlox cookie jars can also be found marked with the tradename, "Poppytrail of California". This was a division of Metlox. Metlox closed its doors on June 1, 1989. Metlox Pottery, mostly cookie jars, are extremely sough after by many cookie jar collectors all over the United States.

Calf Head with Crier in Lid
11" high, marked "Made in California -
Poppytrail Pottery by Metlox".
Value: $400-450

Sitting Piggy
marked "Made in Poppytrail, CA USA",
Bisque in Color.
Value: $350-400

Sitting Piggy
marked "Made in Poppytrail, CA USA".
Value: $400-450

Gingham Dog
marked "Metlox CA USA".
Value: $200-250

Gingham Dog
marked "Metlox CA USA".
(same jar as pictured at left just a different color).
Value: $350-400

Parrot
marked "Made in Poppytrail, CA USA".
Value: $350-400

Puddles the Duck
11 1/4" high, white sticker read "Metlox".
Value: $100-150

Santa Standing
marked "Original CA Pottery by Metlox Copyright".
Value: $700-750

Standing Santa
marked "Metlox CA USA".
Value: $750-800

Squirrel on Barrel of Nuts
unmarked.
Value: $475

Schoolhouse
unmarked, paper label.
Value: $1,200-1,400

Squash
all white, paper label.
Value: $225-250

Squash
full color, marked "Poppytrail CA, USA".
Value: $250-300

Basket of Apples
paper labels
Value: $100-150

Barrel of Apples
10 3/4" high, hoopes are made of copper,
with paper label.
Value: $100-150

Ballerina Bear
marked "Metlox Made in USA".
Value: $150-200

Slenderella Pig
marked "Metlox CA USA".
Value: $165-225

Walrus
beige, smaller jar,
marked "Metlox CA USA".
Value: $350-375

Walrus
marked "Made in Poppytrail CA".
Value: $525-575

Raggedy Andy
11" high, marked "Made in Poppytrail CA".
Value: $200-250

Raggedy Ann
11" high, marked "Made in Poppytrail CA".
Value: $200-250

Pretty Ann
11" high, marked "Poppytrail, CA".
Value: $350-400

Panda with Lollypop
marked "Made in Poppytrail CA USA".
Value: $950-1,000

Panda
marked "Metlox".
Value: $125-175

Francine Duck
marked "Metlox".
Value: $275-325

Sir Francis Drake
unmarked.
Value: $100-150

Squirrel on Pine Cone
12" high, marked "Metlox".
Value: $125-175

Bluebird on Pine Cone
marked "Metlox".
Value: $200-250

Children on Drum
with bisque finish,
marked "Metlox Poppytrail USA".
Value: $300-350

Children on Drum
underglazed finish, marked
"Metlox Poppytrail USA".
Value: $350-400

Bear with Red Sweater
marked "Metlox USA", designed by Helen McIntosh.
(This bear is the oldest character jar Metlox made.)
Value: $175-225

Metlox Box
original box that the Teddy Bear came in.
Value: No Value

Bear with Blue Sweater
marked "Metlox CA USA".
Value: $100-125

Bear with Blue Sweater Holding a Heart
marked "Metlox in USA".
Value: $400-450

Bear with Yellow Sweater
marked "Metlox in USA".
Value: $150-200

Bear with Blue Sweater
stoneware finish,
marked "Made in Poppytrail CA".
Value: $150-175

Bear with Blue Sweater
stoneware finish,
marked "Made in Poppytrail CA".
Value: $150-175

Corn
(harvest gold kernels of corn)
marked "Made in Poppytrail CA".
Value: $400-450

Corn
with a common finish.
Value: $250-300

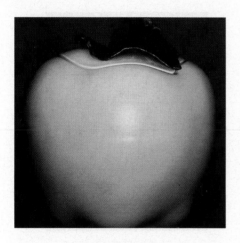

Yellow Apple
marked "Metlox".
Value: $250-300

Grapes
8 1/2" high, marked "Made in USA".
Value: $325-350

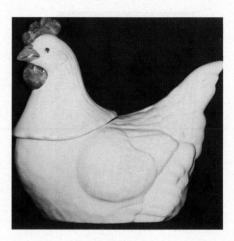

Mother Hen
marked "Metlox".
Value: $350-400

Uncle Sam Bear
marked "Metlox CA USA".
Value: $1,600-1,800

Pineapple
marked "Made in USA".
Value: $150-195

(Very deep rich harvest squash color).

(Regular production color).

218

Cinderella
blond hair, possibly Metlox.
Value If Metlox: $400-450

Cinderella
red hair, possibly Metlox.
Value If Metlox: $400-450

Koala Bear
12 1/2" high, light green leaf, marked "Metlox CA USA".
Value: $250-300

Koala Bear
12 1/2" high, dark green leaf, marked "Metlox CA USA".
Value: $350-400

Crowing Rooster
marked "Made in Poppytrail, CA".
Value: $550-600

Hen
marked "Made in Poppytrail, CA".
Value: $500-550

Beaver
marked "Metlox, Made in USA".
Value: $250-300

Blue and White Clown
marked "Metlox Made in USA".
Value: $450-500

Yellow Clown
13 1/2" high,
marked "Made in Poppytrail, CA".
Value: $125-150

Black and White Clown
13 1/2" high, marked "Metlox".
Value: $200-250

Watermelon
paper label, marked "Made in Poppytrail, CA".
Value: $850-925

Cow Bank
marked "Made in Poppytrail, CA".
Value: $150-200

Brownie Scout
three paper labels.
Value: $1,900-2,000

Owl
gold trim, marked "Made in Poppytrial CA".
Value: $75-100

Owl
9" high, marked "Made in Poppytrial CA".
Value: $175-200

White Scottie Dog
marked "Metlox".
Value: $300-350

Black Scottie Dog
marked "Metlox".
Value: $125-175

Frosty Penguin
12" high, marked "Metlox CA USA".
Value: $175-200

Happy Time Children
marked "Poppytrail by Metlox CA".
Value: $250-300

Wheat
marked "Metlox".
Value: $250-300

Racoon Cookie Bandit
bisque finish,
marked "Made in Poppytrail CA USA"
Value: $175-250

Racoon Cookie Bandit
paint under glaze,
marked "Made in Poppytrail CA USA"
Value: $250-300

Rag Doll
bisque finish,
marked "Made in Poppytrail CA USA"
Value: $200-250

Rag Doll
under glaze,
marked "Made in Poppytrail CA USA"
Value: $350-400

Rag Doll
cold paint, unmarked.
Value: $225-250

Humpty Dumpty
white, marked "Metlox CA USA".
Value: $350-400

Humpty Dumpty
yellow and green lid and trim, unmarked.
Value: $1,400

Humpty Dumpty
common colors, unmarked.
Value: $1,000-1,100

Bassett Hound
marked "Metlox CA USA".
Value: $950-1,000

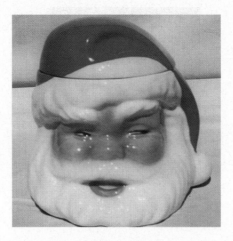

Santa Head
marked "Metlox CA USA".
Value: $900

Piano Candy Jar
gold trim, marked (Metlox Manufacturing Co.,
(also available without gold trim)
Value: $350-400

Happy the Clown
unmarked.
Value: $850-900

Cub Scout
three paper labels.
Value: $1,900-2,000

Metlox Box
another different version
of the boxes used by Metlox.
Value: No Value

Mother Goose
beautiful deep color scarf, paper label,
marked "made in Poppytrail CA".
Value: $450-550

Purple Cow
10 1/4" high, marked "Made in CA Poppytrail".
Value: $750-800

Yellow Cow
10 1/4" high, marked "made in CA Poppytrail".
Value: $600-650

Budweiser Wagon
trimmed in gold, made for Budweiser in
1950's, unmarked, but has been
found with paper label.
Value: $1,000-1,200

Spaceship
(shown on front cover of this book)
marked "Made in USA".
Value: $1,200-1,400

Lighthouse
marked "Metlox, Made in CA".
Value: $900-1,100

Scrub Woman
(also known as Washtub Mammy),
marked "R" under glaze, available in many
colors, made by Metlox Potteries. (Also in
Black Americana section of this book)
Value: $2,400-2,600

Woodpecker on Acorn
white chest with black dots, paper label.
Value: $950-1,000

Jolly Chef
unmarked, paper label,
marked "Made in CA; Poppytrail Pottery".
Value: $1,100-1,200

Mrs. Rabbit
marked "Metlox CA USA",
(two different variations shown here).
Value: $250-300

Wells Fargo Stagecoach
paint under glaze, paper label, marked "Made in CA".
Value: $1,800-2,000

Wells Fargo Stagecoach
bisque finish, paper label, marked "Made in CA".
Value: $1,800-2,000

Bluebird on Stump
marked "Made in USA".
Value: $500-600

Squirrel on Stump
marked "Made in USA".
Value: $500-600

Santa Claus Candy Bowl
white, stamped "Original CA Pottery by Metlox".
Value: $100-125

Cookies with Heart Cylinder
unusual jar, marked "Metlox".
Value: $125-175

Circus Bear
marked "Metlox, Made in USA".
Value: $2,000-2,200

Nun
marked "Metlox CA".
Value: $2,000-2,200

Pelican – US Diving Team
10 1/2" high, marked "Made in Metlox CA USA".
Value: $200-250

Bubbles the Hippo
marked "USA".
Value: $850-900 ea.

(This jar had many production problems and was redesigned many times).

Lamb with Blue Collar
marked "Made in Poppytrail CA".
Value: $550-600

Lamb with Flowers
marked "Made in Poppytrail CA".
Value: $425-475

Poppytrail Sign
marked "Made in California",
available in two different sizes,
Large– 6" high, and Small – 5 1/2" high.
Value: $350/large $225/small

Red Pepper Candy Jar
marked "Poppytrail CA".
Value: $200-225

Bell Pepper Salt & Pepper Shakers
incredibly life-like, unmarked.
Value: $250-300 a set

Cylinder of Fruit
marked "Made in USA",
(looks to be hand painted).
Value: $300-350

Orange
8 3/4" high, marked "Metlox USA".
Value: $150-200

Fruit Basket
unmarked, paper label.
Value: $195-225

Rooster Cylinder
wooden lid, marked "Metlox".
Value: $195-225

Strawberry
9" high, marked "Metlox USA".
Value: $95-100

Lamb
9 1/4" high, Crier in Hat "Baas",
marked "Made in Poppytrail CA Metlox".
Value: $200-250

Cat
9" high, Crier in Hat "Meows",
marked "Made in Poppytrail CA Metlox".
Value: $200-250

Apple
marked "Made in USA",
(two different color variations)
Value: $195-250

Apple
marked "Made in USA",
red wine color, no grain.
Value: $245-295

Rabbit on Cabbage
11 1/2" high, unmarked.
Value: $300-325

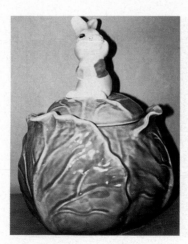

Rabbit on Cabbage
11 1/2" high, darker green and harder to find.
Value: $400-425

Daisy Time Cylinder
with wooden lid, marked "Metlox".
Value: $250-300

Birds with Flower Cylinder
paper label, marked "Metlox".
Value: $350-400

Metlox Rose
7 1/2" high, paper label, marked "made in USA".
Value: $400-450

Sammy the Seal
marked "Metlox Made in USA".
Value: $1,500-2,000

Sammy the Seal Salt & Peppers
marked "Metlox Made in USA".
Value: $350-400 a set

Beau Bear
11 1/2" high, Maroon Bow,
marked "Metlox CA USA
Value: $75-100

Beau Bear Canister Set
11 1/2" high, Maroon Bow,
marked "Metlox CA USA
Value: $350-425 a set

Rex
13" high, marked "Metlox CA USA
Copyright 87 by Vincent".
Value: $300-325

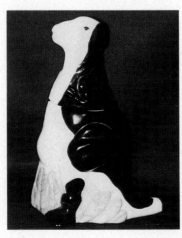

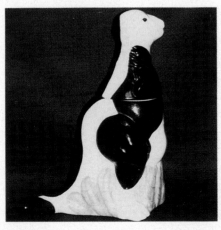

Cow Painted Rex
13" high, Tyrannosaurus Rex, made for the Tonight show, very rare jar, (two views shown here).
Marked "Metlox CA USA #87 by Vincent".
Value: $2,500+

Rex
13" high, marked "Metlox CA
USA by Vincent Copyright 1987".
Value: $300-325

Mona
marked "Metlox CA USA
Copyright 87 by Vincent".
Value: $300-325

Mona
(orange).
Value: $300-325

Mona
marked "Metlox CA USA
by Vincent Copyright 1987".
Value: $300-325

Dino
marked "Metlox CA USA Copyright
87 by Vincent".
Value: $300-325

Dino
marked "Metlox CA USA by Vincent
Copyright 1987", in pink.
Value: $300-325

Dino
marked "An Original Design by Metlox
Potteries" in beautiful black script. This jar
is lavendar, a rare color, and is hard to find.
Value: $400-450

Mammy
yellow and white polka-dots,
marked "Metlox CA USA".
Value: $500-550

Mammy Salt and Pepper Shakers
marked "Metlox CA USA",
shown with cookie jar.
Value: $350 a set

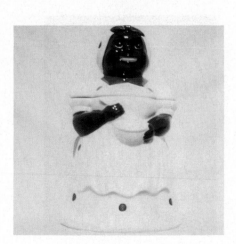

Mammy
blue and white polka-dots,
marked "Metlox CA USA".
Value: $500-550

Mammy Salt and Pepper Shakers
marked "Metlox CA USA".
Value: $400-450 a set

Topsy
blue and white polka-dots,
marked "Metlox CA USA".
Value: $500-550

Topsy
blue apron,
marked "Metlox CA USA".
Value: $650-700

Topsy
red and white polka-dots,
marked "Metlox CA USA".
Value: $750-800

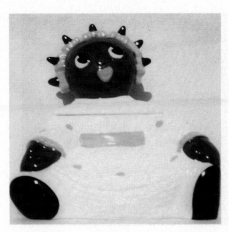

Topsy
yellow and white polka-dots,
marked "Metlox CA USA".
Value: $400-450

Lion
marked "Made in Poppytrail CA".
Value: $350-425

Laying Down Rabbit
marked "Metlox, Made in USA".
Value: $300-325

Green Pear
marked "Poppytrail CA, USA".
Value: $200-250

Yellow Pear
marked "Made in USA".
Value: $400-450

Noah's Ark
paper label, marked "Made in Poppytrail CA".
Value: $350-395

Rollerskating Bear
marked "Metlox USA".
Value: $150-200

Two Owls on Stump
bisque finish, paper label,
marked "Made in Poppytrail CA".
Value: $175-200

Little Red Riding Hood
marked "Made in Poppytrail CA".
Value: $1,500-1,800

Mouse Mobile
unmarked.
Value: $350-425

Squirrel Holding Acorn
marked "Made in USA".
Value: $1,000-1,100

Red Rooster Cookie Cylinder
marked "Poppytrail by Metlox CA".
Value: $250-300

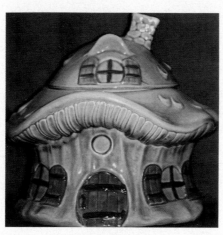

Mushroom House
marked "Poppytrail Made in USA".
Value: $450-500

Alley Cat
marked "Metlox USA".
Value: $450-500

Basket of Eggs
marked "Metlox Made in USA".
Value: $500-600

Calico Cat
marked "Made in Poppytrail CA USA".
Value: $425-475

Lucy Goose
14 1/4" high, marked "Metlox CA USA".
Value: $200-225

Grapefruit
with original paper sticker.
Value: $600-650

Pumpkin
with brown lettering marked "Original CA Pottery by Metlox",
(two views showns).
Value: $650-700

Debutante
with original paper Metlox label,
(shown in two different color variations).
Value: $800-950

Lady with Lace Dress
definitely Metlox, unmarked.
Value: $1,200-1,400

Flower Pot with Topiary Lid
with original paper label, marked "Poppytrail".
Value: $125-150

Tomato
7" high, marked "Made in USA".
Value: $475-550

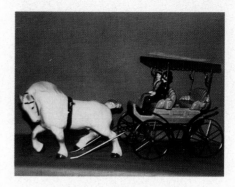

Surrey with Fringe on Top
marked "Metlox", not a cookie jar.
Value: $250-300

Barn
marked "Metlox CA USA".
Value: $500-550

Fido
marked "Metlox CA USA".
Value: $275-300

Hen with Bonnet & Chick Finial
marked "Metlox Potteries USA Copyright", very
rare, hard to find, paper label.
Value: $1,100-1,250

Carousel
marked "Poppytrail CA USA".
Value: $800-900

Granada Cookie Canister
marked "Made in Poppytrail CA".
Value: $75-100

Drummer Boy
10 3/4" high, paper label,
marked "Made in CA Poppytrail Pottery".
Value: $750-825

Tangerine Box
paper label reads "Metlox, Made in USA".
Value: $325-375

Pescado Fish
ink stamped, "Metlox, CA Pottery
Manhattan Bch. Est. 1927".
Value: $375-425

Pescado Fish Salt and Peppers
Value: $150-200 a set

Sun Face Jar
bisque finish, very rare jar, marked "Metlox".
Value: $1,000-1,100

Pierre Mouse
12" high, paper label, marked "Metlox
Manufacturing Company CA".
Value: $150-165

Dutch Girl
13 1/4" high, marked "Metlox CA USA".
Value: $375-425

Dutch Boy
marked "Metlox CA USA".
Value: $375-425

Sombrero Bear
marked "Metlox CA USA".
Value: $150-195

Pinnochio
paper label marked "Poppytrail".
Value: $450-500

Frog with Tie
marked "Metlox CA USA".
Value: $350-400

Red Cabbage
soup tureen, paper label.
Value: $150-200

White Cabbage
soup tureen, paper label.
Value: $150-200

Flashing Turtle
marked "Metlox Made in CA USA".
Value: $1,800-2,100

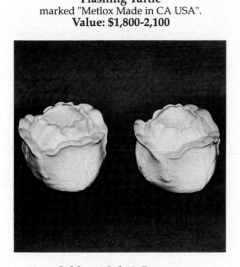

Cabbage Salt & Peppers
unmarked.
Value: $100-125 a set

Flamingo
marked "Metlox CA USA", Limited Production,
(two different color variations shown here).
Value: $1,000-1,200

J. C. Miller

Jerry and Clarice Miller of J.C. Miller, Wichita, Kansas, designs and produces cookie jars bearing similarities to individuals in Clarice's family, including her ancestors. All of these jars are done in Limited Editions.

Porsha
marked "Sculpted by Jerry P. Miller",
limited edition of 250.
Value: $100-125

Grandma Bell
limited edition of 250.
Value: $100-125

Grandpa Washington
limited edition of 250.
Value: $100-125

Baby Reese
marked "J.C. Miller Baby Reese",
limited edition of 250.
Value: $100-125

Joey
marked "J.C. Miller 1992",
limited edition of 250.
Value: $100-125

Sister Ruth
limited edition of 250.
Value: $100-125

Cora & George
marked "Cora & George limited edition of 250".
Value: $100-125

Sarah
marked "15/250 J Miller".
Value: $100-125

Miscellaneous

Baking Angel
unknown.
Value: $550-700

Lamb
unmarked.
Value: $200-250

Schoolhouse with Bell
unmarked, House of Webster,
originally sold with jam inside.
Value: $125-150

Hen
7 1/4" high, marked "Fapco USA".
Value: $75-125

Grapes
marked "Made in Italy".
Value: $250-300

Pineapple
unmarked.
Value: $50-60

Pineapple
unknown, unmarked.
Value: $50-60

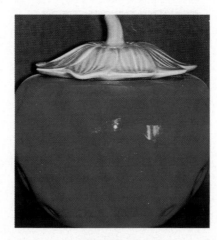

Strawberry
made for Sears, Roebuck & Co.
Value: $40-50

Grapefruit
jar on left is unknown, lightweight.
Value: $75-85

Grapefruit
jar on right is the real thing – See Metlox Section,
original Metlox paper label.
Value: $600-650

Tomato
8 1/4" high, unmarked.
Value: $50-75

Tomato
8 1/4" high, marked "Pantry Parade".
Value: $40-50

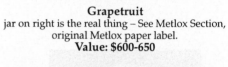

Peanut Face
unmarked, unknown.
Value: $100-125

Ear of Corn
marked "Standfordware".
Value: $150

Corn Cookie Jar
Cookie Jar, unusual color, hard to find.
Value: $175-200

Corn Sugar Bowl
Value: $85

Corn Creamer
Value: $65

Indian Woman
unmarked.
Value: $125-150

Indian Head
marked "Southeast Minnesota Potteries".
Value: $175-250

Pixie Boy
12 1/2" high, unmarked.
Value: $300-350

Beetle Boy
13 1/2" high, marked "H.M.",
marking number is hard to read.
Value: $250-300

Beetle Girl
13 1/2" high, marked "H.M.",
different marking number is hard to read.
Value: $250-300

Little Red Riding Hood
cold painted, unmarked.
Value: $75-125

Chef Elf
unmarked.
Value: $125-150

Chef Elf Salt & Pepper Shakers
unmarked.
Value: $50-60 a set

Cardinal
very rare jar, marked "Goebel".
Value: $2,000-2,200

Monk
common color, marked "Goebel".
Value: $250-350

Chef
unknown, marked "Cookies" on Hat.
Value: $125-175

Chef
large size, unknown, Italy.
Value: $75-95

Butler
unmarked.
Value: $110-125

Musical Sailor
music box in lid, made for Sears Roebuck & Co.
Value: $750-800

Neal the Frog
made for Sears Roebuck & Co.
Value: $75-125

Bulldog
unmarked, made of aluminum.
Value: $125-150

Carousel Horse
marked "Hearth & Home".
Value: $150-160

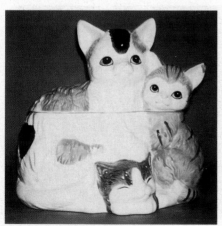

Three Little Kittens
marked "Hearth & Home".
Value: $50-60

The Box to
Man with Icebag on Head
(original).
No Value

Man with Icebag on Head
9" high, made by Nasco, unmarked.
Value: $275-300

Stagecoach
marked "Hearth & Home".
Value: $100-125

Pear China Teddy Bear
stamped "Pearl China",
heavy gold trim, hard to find color.
Value: $750-800

Pearl China Teddy Bear
matching bank.
Value: $200-250

Pearl China Teddy Bear
(cookie jar alone).
Value: $750-800

Pearl China Bear
paint under glaze, very rare and unusual.
Value: $600-700

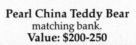

Pearl China Pig
with gold trim, marked "Pearl China", very rare.
Value: $700-750

Pearl China Teddy Bear Bank
unmarked.
Value: $125-175

Pearl China Teddy Bear
(another version).
Value: $600-700

Jack and the Beanstalk
marked "C-L Batlin & Son, Inc."
Value: $100-125

Jack and the Beanstalk Shakers
marked "C-L Batlin & Son, Inc."
Value: $40-50 a set

Mexican Head
unmarked, unknown.
Value: $75-100

Indian Chief
marked "Copyright 1950 Lane & Co.,
Los Angeles", artist signed, "R Nickerson".
Value: $1,200-1,500

Sheriff
reproduction.
Value: $125

Sheriff
marked "Copyright 1950
Lane & co. Los Angeles".
Value: $550-650

Mopsey
marked "Copyright Mopsey"
Value: $85-125

Raggedy Andy
unmarked.
Value: $75-85

Clown
marked "Copyright 1950 Lane & Co. Los Angeles".
Value: $700-750

Witch with Broom
this jar comes in all different sizes and
may have been a canister set, unmarked.
Value: $125-150

Mother in the Kitchen
blue, made by Enesco.
Value: $500-600

Mother in the Kitchen
made by Enesco.
Value: $400-450

Mother in the Kitchen
most common color, made by Enesco.
Value: $400-450

Mother in the Kitchen Canister Set
Value: $400-450 a set

Betsy Ross
made by N.S. Gustin.
Value: $50-75

Cookie House
heavy jar, unmarked.
Value: $150

**Holt Howard Red Rooster
Salt and Pepper Shakers**
(shown here with cookie jar).
Value: $65-75

Holt Howard Red Rooster

Cookie Jar
marked "Copyright 1961 Holt Howard".
Value: $150-165

Ketchup Jar – $65-75

Jam'n Jelly – $65-75

Mustard Jar – $65-75

Holt Howard Red Rooster

Coffee Pot – $165-175

Recipe Holder – $55-65

Mug – $15-20

Butter Dish – $65-75

Cigarette Holder – $125-140

Salt & Pepper Shakers (small) – $45-55

Candlestick Holders – $35-45

Egg Cups – $25-30

Hippo
nice and heavy jar, unmarked.
Value: $150-175

Ring for Cookies
made in USA.
Value: $65-95

Egg Shaped Cookie Jar
wooden face, marked
"Designed by TCACK Copyright 1958".
Value: $125-150

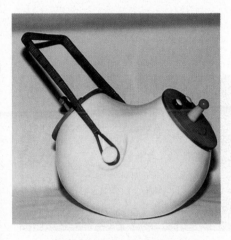

Double Sided Cookie Jar
wooden face, marked "Designed by
TCACK Copyright 1950".
Value: $125-150

Oval Shaped Cookie Jar
wooden face, marked "Designed by
TCACK Copyright 1950".
Value: $125-150

Amish Lady and Child at Fence
by Pennsbury Pottery.
Value: $150-195

Red Barn
Pennsbury Pottery.
Value: $195-225

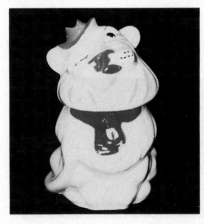

Belmont Lion
marked "Belmont" in script,
produced by Ludowici Celadon.
Value: $150-200

Huskies on Igloo
marked "Copyright M. Lagadda 1992".
Value: $125

Big Cat Head
marked "Artist Made USA",
beautifully designed.
Value: $200-250

Teddy Bear
marked "N. S. Gustin".
Value: $125-150

Cactus Cylinder
marked "USA".
Value: $75-95

Glenda Goose
North American Ceramics.
Value: $50-75

Glenda Goose Cookie Box
No Value

Woody Wagon
North American Ceramics.
Value: $250-300

Buick
unmarked.
Value: $125-150

Red Corvette
unmarked.
Value: $125-150

Strawberry Shortcake
8" high, unmarked.
Value: $150-175

Large Strawberry Cake
11" high, unmarked.
Value: $150-175

Barefoot Boy
14" high, produced by
Gem Refactories for Hull.
Value: $475-550

Panda
North American Ceramics.
Value: $75-85

Mercedes Benz
unmarked.
Value: $95-125

Fire Truck
marked "C.J. 31 1986 NAC USA".
Value: $400-450

Indian
unmarked.
Value: $195-250

Bulldog
unmarked.
Value: $95-100

Tree Trunk House
unmarked.
Value: $95-110

Red Corvette
unmarked, probably foreign made.
Value: $95-125

Bartender
10 1/4" high, marked "USA", Pan American Art,
(three different color variations).
Value: (left and middle pictures) $325-425 – (picture at right) $425-475

Sedan
unmarked, unknown.
Value: $95-125

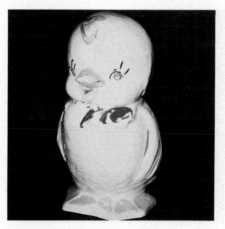

Baby Chick
marked "USA".
Value: $50-65

Tall Clown
marked "Yona Original Copyright 1956",
gold stamped.
Value: $200-225

Short Clown
marked "Yona Original Copyright 1956",
gold stamped.
Value: $150-175

Children on a Drum
marked "1957 Yona Original".
Value: $375-500

Happy Clown with Umbrella
marked "Copyright 1957 Yong Original
USA Northfork College".
Value: $350-400

Elephant with Clown
marked "Copyright 1957 Yona Original".
Value: $500-525

Cat with Fishbowl
this is a beautiful and heavy jar, very unusual, unknown.
Value: $225-250

Windmill
10" high, marked "Fapco", also available in red, gray, and yellow variations.
Value: $125-165

Jingle Bear
North American Ceramics.
Value: $195-250

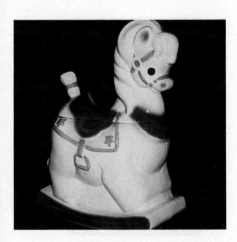

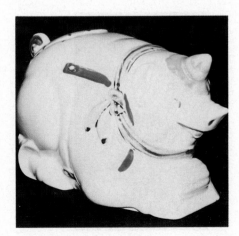

Rocking Horse
13" long, unmarked.
Value: $150-195

Pig Cowboy
unmarked, unknown.
Value: $50-60

Little Drummer Boy
marked "Enesco 1991".
Value: $75-95

Snowman
unknown.
Value: $75-85

Snowman
marked "Enesco 1994".
Value: $50-65

Santa Claus
unknown, maybe foreign made.
Value: $50-60

Santa in Chair
public mold, unmarked.
Value: $125-150

Christmas Tree Cylinder
marked "S. Claus Handmade & Created
by Sandra Claus Shoppe Columbus, Georgia".
Value: $100-125

Santa
unknown.
Value: $150

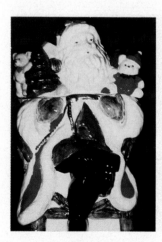

Santa in Club Chair
1994, marked "Marshall Fields Dayton Hudson".
Value: $150

Standing Santa
1992, marked "Marshall Fields Dayton Hudson".
Value: $150

Standing Santa
1991, marked "Dayton Hudson Marshall Fields".
Value: $150

Santa in Chimney
1989, marked "Hudson".
Value: $150

Santa Reading List
1990, marked "Dayton Hudson".
Value: $150

Santa with Bag of Toys
1987, marked "Hudson".
Value: $150

Santa with Bag of Toys
1984, marked "J.L. Hudson".
Value: $150

Santa with Bag of Toys
1982, marked "J.L. Hudson".
Value: $150

Santa
1983, marked "J.L. Hudson".
Value: $150

Snowman
Marcia Ceramics, very hard to find,
marked "Copyright 84".
Value: $300+

Santa Head
9" high, paper label,
marked "Luray Caverns, VA 50-286".
Value: $175-195

Santa
plastic, marked "USA Copyright Carolina
Ent. Tarborough NC 1973".
Value: $125

Santa
Jane Holland, California Pottery.
Value: $250-300

Santa
8 3/4" high, marked "Mallory Copyright Inc".
Value: $125-150

Santa with Bag of Fruit
unmarked.
Value: $150-165

Santa at Desk
unmarked.
Value: $175-200

Tillie the Hippo
marked "Richard Scarry's Goebel Int'l",
made in the mid 1980's.
Value: $250-300

First Factory Holiday Candy Jar
marked "Copyright 1992 Harley Davidson Inc.
Made in Taiwan".
Value: $250-325

Standing Santa
inside rim of lid, marked
"Alberta Molds Inc. 1980."
Value: $95-110

Roly Poly Santa
made by the Holt Howard Company,
paper label.
Value: $110-125

Red Sportscar
expressive design, Miami, Florida, first edition.
Value: $225-275

Pink Cadillac
Expressive Designs,
Miami, Florida, First Edition.
Value: $225-275

Police Car
blue Chevy, Expressive Designs,
Miami, FL, First Edition.
Value: $225-275

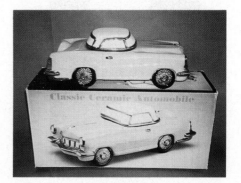

Blue Sportscar
Expressive Designs,
Miami, Florida, First Edition.
Value: $225-275

Yellow Taxi
Expressive Designs,
Miami, Florida, First Edition.
Value: $225-275

Blue Convertible
Expressive Designs,
Miami, Florida, First Edition.
Value: $225-275

Blue '57 Chevy
made by Applause, with plastic wheels.
Value: $125-175

Bobby Baker Cookie Jar
unmarked, unknown.
Value: $200-225

(close-up view)

Mary Had A Little Lamb
made for JC Penney's Home Collection.
Value: $150-175

Bobby Baker Salt & Pepper Shakers
Value: $50-65 a set

Humpty Dumpty
made for JC Penney's Home Collection.
Value: $150-175

Goldilocks and the Three Bears
made for JC Penney's Home Collection.
Value: $150-175

Old Woman in Shoe
made for JC Penney's Home Collection.
Value: $95-125

Three Little Kittens
made for JC Penney's Home Collection.
Value: $150-175

Plastic Diet Piggy Cookie Jar
battery operated Oinks.
Value: $45-65

Plastic Piggy Cookie Jar
maybe foreign made, battery operated Oinks.
Value: $45-65

Dog
marked "AMC New York",
has crier in lid.
Value: $75-95

Rooster
marked "AMC New York",
has crier in lid.
Value: $75-95

Lamb
marked "AMC New York",
has crier in lid.
Value: $75-95

Pig
marked "AMC New York",
has crier in lid.
Value: $75-95

Barn
marked "AMC New York",
has crier in lid.
Value: $75-95

Cookie Cab
made exclusively for RH Macy & Co.
Value: $75-95

Yellow Volkswagon
made exclusively for RH Macy & Co.
Value: $50-60

Radio
made exclusively for RH Macy & Co.
Value: $60-65

Covered Wagon
made exclusively for RH Macy & Co.
Value: $75-95

Cookie Time Clock
made exclusively for RH Macy & Co.
Value: $75-95

Commode
unmarked.
Value: $95-100

Harry
marked "Made by Jiri Bures 1991".
Value: $200-250

Harry
marked "Made by Jiri Bures 1991".
Value: $200-250

Lion
marked "Made by Weiss,
hand painted, Made in Brazil".
Value: $400-450

Rolling Pin
unmarked.
Value: $75-95

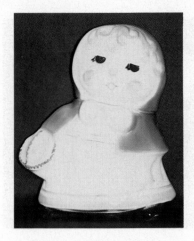

Little Red Riding Hood
marked "Weiss".
Value: $450-525

Mother Goose
marked "Weiss".
Value: $225-250

Bride Rabbit
marked "Made by Weiss,
hand painted, Made in Brazil".
Value: $475-525

Monkey
marked "Maurice of California USA".
Value: $75-85

Lady Holding Flowers
unmarked, unknown, lovely old jar.
Value: $175-225

Apple Cylinder
unknown.
Value: $50-60

German Gentlemen
marked "Made in Germany".
Value: $395-450

Soldier on a Drum
unmarked.
Value: $90-125

Clown
marked "Walmart Special 1991".
Value: $45-65

Elephant with Top Hat
paper label, National Silver Company, NY.
Value: $150-195

Man with Wheelbarrow
unmarked.
Value: $125-195

Curiosity Shop
unmarked.
Value: $250-350

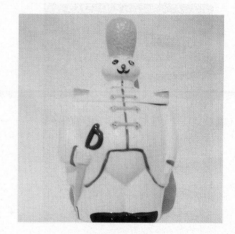

Toy Soldier
unmarked.
Value: $125-150

Cook with Spoon
made by Otagiri.
Value: $50-65

Dutch Girl
unmarked, unknown, very cute.
Value: $95-150

Albert Apple
marked "FKR 1942, Pitman Dreitzer & Company", signed "Albert Apple".
Value: $50-75

Albert Apple
fully painted.
Value: $50-75

Realty House
unknown.
Value: $125-150

Ozark Hillbilly
9 3/4" high, made by Morton Potteries.
Value: $65-95

Rooster
made by People Lovers Pacific
Stoneware Inc., artist signed Scarpino.
Value: $75-125

Captain Pig
unmarked, Unknown, fabulous jar.
Value: $200-250

Owl
unknown.
Value: $35-45

Russian Man
unknown.
Value: $125-150

Woodland Commune
marked "Made by Enesco".
Value: $150-195

Gingerbread Bakery
Schmid.
Value: $75-95

Shining Time Station Bank
Schmid.
Value: $30-50

Shining Time Station
Schmid.
Value: $65-75

Tiger
unknown.
Value: $65-75

Dutch Girl
stamped "Delft", made in Holland.
Value: $175-200

Kitty Cottage
unknown.
Value: $65-75

Bird Cage
marked "Hearth & Home".
Value: $75-95

Pig at Stove
unmarked.
Value: $150-195

Clown on Drum
unmarked.
Value: $150-175

Nun
jar reads "Thou Shall Not Get Fat",
unmarked, unknown.
Value: $65-75

French Poodle
unmarked, unknown.
Value: $95-125

Policeman
Watt Potteries, very rare, (two different variations shown here).
(Supposedly 12-14 were produced).
Value: $2,000-2,500

The King
marked "Hedi Schoop".
Value: $700-800

The Darner Doll
marked "#64 USA LA Potteries CA",
(two different color variations shown here).
Value: $350-395

Red Flower Cylinder
9 3/4" high, Ransburg Pottery,
extremely collectible by Ransburg collectors.
Value: $50-75

Red Flower Cylinder
Ransburg Pottery, extremely collectible by
Ransburg collectors.
Value: $50-75

Green Flower Cylinder
9 3/4" high, Ransburg Pottery, extremely
collectible by Ransburg collectors.
Value: $65-75

Coffee Canister
apple design, Purinton Pottery.
Value: $60-75

Cookie Canister
apple design, Purinton Pottery.
Value: $125-150

Howdy Doody
9 3/4" high, Purinton Pottery, unmarked.
Value: $750-900

Clown
unmarked.
Value: $700-750

Wheelbarrow
unmarked.
Value: $95-110

Cookie Time Clock
marked "Welcome".
Value: $65-70

Rabbit with Cookie
unmarked, A California Original look-alike.
Value: $125-150

Goodies Jar
Watt Pottery.
Value: $550-600

Clown Cylinder
unmarked.
Value: $125-150

Nun
Franciscan Pottery, unmarked.
Value: $225-250

Knight
stoneware, marked "Dakota Stoneware".
Value: $400-500

Choir Boy
incised, marked "Marcia Pottery of
CA Made in USA".
Value: $500-600

Dog
unmarked, very nice quality pottery.
Value: $125-150

Winky
marked "Vallona Star 302 Copyright 51".
Value: $1,200

Man with Chicken on Head
marked "1989 Animals & Co., by Allen Walter &
Jenny Lind 11SG5 192 USA".
Value: $650-800

Winky
(three different color variations shown).
Value: $700-850

Lady with Cat
"Copyright 1990 Animals & Co. 26-MP92".
Value: $650-800

Duck
unmarked.
Value: $40-50

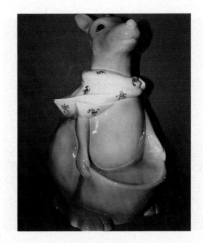

Kangaroo
marked "Arnel's Mold".
Value: $150-175

Alien Pig
14 1/2" high, marked "Copyright 1968 Pacific
Stoneware Inc. USA 3611 Flower, Scarpino".
Value: $175-250

Cat with Bird
marked "Copyright Pacific Stoneware",
(the jar at the right is a larger variation).
Value: $175-250   **Larger Jar Value: $225-275**

Owl
marked "Pacific Stoneware Copyright 1958".
Value: $150-175

Clown with Bow Tie
Los Angeles Potteries.
Value: $60-75

Christmas Tree
Los Angeles Potteries.
Value: $125-150

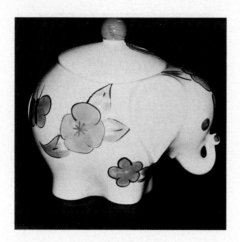

Elephant
Los Angeles Potteries.
Value: $125-150

Gingerbread Jar
Los Angeles Potteries.
Value: $150-175

Flirty Flossie

as shown in next three pictures

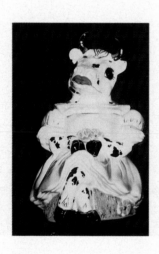

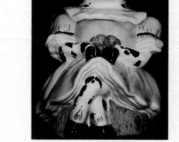

Flirty Flossie
"Clayworks Made in USA, Limited Edition, by L. Amiot".
Value: $200-250

Clown
marked "USA", unknown.
Value: $50-60

Happy Easter
unmarked.
Value: $125-150

Raggedy Ann
unknown, this is a Twin Winton copy.
Value: $95-110

Humpty Dumpty
unmarked.
Value: $250-300

Windmill
14 1/2" high, unmarked,
also available in brown.
Value: $125-155

Witch
marked "USA", made by Holiday Designs.
Value: $75-85

Tuggle Bank
marked "USA".
Value: $55-65

Pigs Going to Market
also a bank with slot for coins in mouth, glass jar,
(two different views shown).
Value: $50-55

King
unknown, marked "USA HM 53".
Value: $150-175

Taxi Cab
City Cab Company,
sold on Home Shopping Channel.
Value: $350-450

Clown
unmarked.
Value: $65-75

1930 Model T
the top part is a bank, signed "F.O. More
CHRISSBAUN Arts, Adrian Art, Roseville, Ohio".
(A very unusual jar, two views shown here).
Value: $450-525

Penguin Waiter
marked "Made in California".
Value: $65-70

Little Lady
unmarked.
Value: $60-65

Humpty Dumpty
unmarked.
Value: $200-250

Space Clown
12 1/2" high, marked "USA".
Value: $195-225

McCoy Indian Head Reproduction
limited edition of 300 pieces, issued by
George Williams III.
Value: $300-350

Clown
hand crafted in Ceramics Class by
David Klein, Boca Raton, FL Age 11.
Marked "David Klein 1994".
Value: Priceless

Ye Olde Cottage
made in England.
Value: $150-250

Humpty Dumpty
unmarked.
Value: $500-600

Carousel
marked "MET" in raised lettering.
Value: $150-200

Lamb on Cylinder
unmarked, possibly ABC or Ungemach.
Value: $150-175

Chick with Bonnet
unmarked.
Value: $175-200

Nummy Cookie
incised "Haeger Copyright".
Value: $225-250

Teddy Bear
unknown.
Value: $65-75

Cookie Chef
unmarked.
Value: $110-145

Duck
unmarked.
Value: $65-95

Train
reads "Kookie Express" on lid.
Value: $60-70

Oriental Man
made in California.
Value: $150-200

Colonial Woman
unmarked.
Value: $150-175

Colonial Man
unmarked.
Value: $150-175

Dutch Woman
11 ¹/²" high, unmarked, (two different color variations shown here).
Value: $150-175

Gleep
marked "Copyright Haeger"
incised in pottery.
Value: $500-650

Flower Cylinder
made by Ransburg Pottery, Indianapolis, Indiana,
(three differnt colors shown here).
Value: $60

 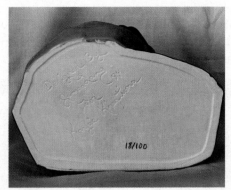

Cowboy Lude
15" high, limited Edition of 100, (two views shown here).
Made by Bob & Pam Timm of Ovid, Colorado, of Kaye's Kreations, owned and operated since 1982.
Value: $125

Roseabell Mammy
13" high, gold trim, marked "R Molds", (also available in various color dresses),
Kaye's Kreations, limited edition of 100, (two views shown here).
Value: $75

Chef Arden
14" high, marked "R Molds",
Kaye's Kreations, Limited Edition of 50.
Value: $75

Mrs. Rabbit
15" high, Kaye's Kreations, Mayco Mold.
Value: $55

National Potteries Corporation

National Potteries Corporation, NAPCO, of Cleveland, Ohio was founded in 1939. For many years, they operated out of Bedford, Ohio before moving to Jacksonville, Florida in 1984. NAPCO jars are very nice quality and are highly collectible.

Cookies Jar
marked "Napco".
Value: $40-50

Cookie Wagon
unmarked.
Value: $85-150

Carousel
marked "Napco".
Value: $150-225

Spaceship
10" high, Cookies out of this World,
marked "Napco".
Value: $900-1,100

Cookie Chef Ketchup, marked "Napco". – **Value: $55**

Cookie Chef Jam, marked "Copyright 1960 Napco". – **Value: $55**

Cookie Chef Mustard, marked "Copyright 1960 Napco". – **Value: $55**

Cookies Chef, marked "Napco". – **Value: $250-300**

Cookie Chef Salt & Pepper Shakers, marked "Napco". – **Value: $45 a set**

Cookie Chef Creamer, marked "Napco". – **Value: $30**

Cookie Chef Spice Set, marked "5F4677". – **Value: $110-120 a set**

Cinderella
9 3/4" high, marked "JC Napco 1957 K2292".
Value: $350-425

Little Red Riding Hood
9 1/2" high, marked "Napco".
Value: $350-425

Little Bo Peep
stamped "Napco".
Value: $350-425

Miss Cutie Pie
8 1/2" high, marked "Napco",
(two different color variations shown here, left is pink, right is blue).
Value: $300-375

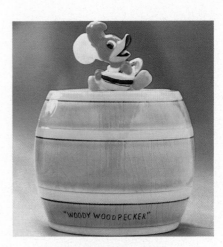

Miss Cutie Pie Salt & Peppers
(blue).
Value: $85-95 a set

Bulldog Police
marked "Napco, Japan".
Value: $200-250

Winking Santa
marked "Napco, Japan KX2352".
Value: $150-165

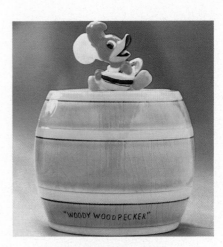

Woody Woodpecker
marked "A3391-WW Napco".
Value: $625-700

Hummel-Like Children
marked "Napco, Japan A 4101".
Value: $125-140

Cookie Castle
marked "Copyright 1961 Napco
Bedford OH A 5286-L".
Value: $125-150

Cookie Corporal
8" high, marked "Napco".
Value: $250-375

Snail
sticker marked "Napco".
Value: $75-110

Omnibus

Omnibus is a division of Fitz & Floyd.

Humpty Dumpty
marked "OCI", 1993,
produced for only one year.
Value: $150

African American Grandma
marked "OCI 1993", giving out cookies
in front of a Christmas tree.
Value: $75

African American Grandma
reading a book in front of a Christmas tree.
Value: $65

Santa
1989, sticker.
Value: $75-95

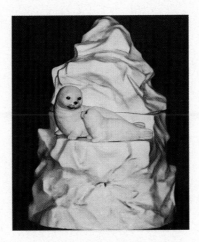

Two Seals on an Iceberg
1988, marked "OCI".
Value: $65-75

Rabbit on Cabbage
candy bar.
Value: $40-50

Pirate Captain
marked "OCI 1993".
Value: $75

Hippo On A Scale
marked "OCI".
Value: $65

Moo Juice
1993.
Value: $50-65

Dalmatian in Fire Truck
1993, marked "OCI".
Value: $65-75

Safari Wagon
1993.
Value: $60-75

Keystone Cop
Value: $40-60

U.S. Cookie Mailbox
marked "OCI 1993".
Value: $40-60

The Referee
1993 marked "OCI".
Value: $40-60

Scandinavian Santa
1991 marked "OCI".
Value: $75-95

Edible Express
1993, marked "OCI".
Value: $40-60

The Eats Diner
marked "OCI 1993".
Value: $45-55

Cowboy Cat
1989, sticker marked "OCI".
Value: $95-125

The Chili Cow
1993, marked "OCI".
Value: $55-75

Arlo and Friends
1992 marked "OCI".
Value: $45-55

Santa Around the World
1993 marked "OCI".
Value: $65-85

ABC Cookie Jar
marked "Copyright OCI 1991".
Value: $65-85

Daisy Cow
marked "OCI 1990".
Value: $55-75

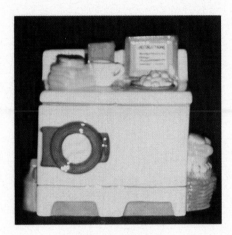

Washing Machine
marked "1994 OCI".
Value: $65-75

Russian Santa
marked "OCI ".
Value: $85-125

Snow Gentlemen
sticker, marked "OCI".
Value: $85-95

Yule Hog
original paper label, marked "Omnibus".
Value: $75-95

Other Characters

Clarabelle Clown
marked "American Greeting Cards".
Value: $250

Tom on Hamburger Bank
marked "Metro Goldwyn
Mayer (MGM) 1981, Enesco".
Value: $125

Tom & Jerry
7" tall, England, marked "Copyright 90
Turner Entertainment Company Exclusive
Harry James Design, Enesco".
Value: $300-375

Tom & Jerry
marked "Copyright MGM Film
Company 1981, Enesco", made in Japan.
Value: $300-350

Tom & Jerry
marked "Metro Goldwyn Mayer, from Gift
World of Gorum, Made in Japan".
Value: $900-1,100

Woody Woodpecker Bank
Walter Lance marked "Enesco".
Value: $75-125

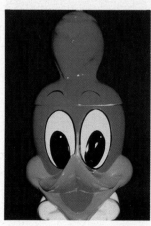

Woody Woodpecker Head
(sold on the Home Shopping Channel),
marked "Walter Lance 1967 All Rights Reserved,
Enesco, Made in Japan".
Value: $1,000-1,500

Garfield Bank
marked "United Features Syndicate, Enecso".
Value: $50-65

Garfield in a Club Chair
marked "Retired",
"United Features Syndicate Enesco".
Value: $200-250

Garfield Playing Golf Bank
marked "United Features Syndicate, Enecso".
Value: $150-175

Garfield Tea Pot
marked "United Features Syndicate, Enecso".
Value: $225-250

Garfield Cookie Jar
marked "Copyright 1978, United Features
Syndicate,Inc. All Rights Reserved Worldwide,
Licensee Enecso Corp. Made in Indonesia".
Value: $100

Garfield Bank
marked "United Features Syndicate, Enecso".
Value: $50-75

Garfield in an Airplane Bank
very hard to find, made in England,
marked "Enecso".
Value: $200-250

Garfield on Stack of Cookies
marked "Copyright 1978, 1981 United Features
Syndicate,Inc. Licensee Enecso".
Value: $400-475

Garfield
marked "Enecso".
Value: $175-225

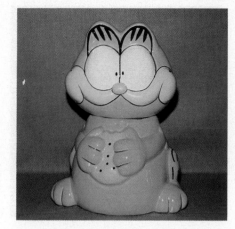

Garfield with Hands in Cookie Bag
(two different color variations).
Value: $425-475

Garfield Loose in the Kitchen
very rare jar, marked "Garfield Copyright 1978,
United Syndicate Features, Inc. Made in Taiwan
for Molly Housewares LTD".
Value: $295-350

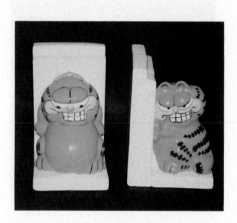

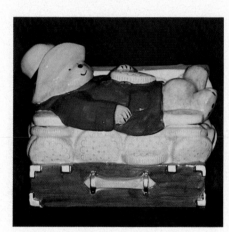

Garfield Book Ends
marked "Garfield Copyright 1978,
1981 United Features Inc.
Licensee Enesco, Enesco Designed Giftware Korea".
Value: $400-475

Paddington Bear
marked "Eden's Toys, Inc. 1978".
Value: $1,100

Paddington Bear
created by Children's Author, Michael Bond,
8" high, marked "Toscany Eden 1987, Japan".
Value: $900-1,100

Paddington Bear
marked "By Toscany, Copyright Eden 1987".
Value: $800-950

Paddington Bear Lamp
paper label, 9" tall, marked "Paddington Bear By
Nojo, Copyright Eden 1991 E 111715".
Value: $250-275

Howdy Doody Cookie Go Round
marked "Luce Manuf. Groton VT, US Pat,
#2548168, Copr. Kagran Corp.".
Value: $125-175

Motorcycle Dog – Sargeant Murphy
marked "Richard Scarry,
Made by O.G.G.I., Taiwan".
Value: $35-50

Mr. Frumble
marked "Richard Scarry,
Made by O.G.G.I., Taiwan".
Value: $35-50

Hippo Hilda
marked "Richard Scarry,
Made by O.G.G.I., Taiwan".
Value: $35-50

Bananas Gorilla
marked "Richard Scarry,
Made by O.G.G.I., Taiwan".
Value: $35-40

Lowly Worm
marked "Richard Scarry,
Made by O.G.G.I., Taiwan".
Value: $35-40

C3PO
from the Star Wars Movies,
Made by Roman Ceramics.
Value: $500-550

R2D2
from Star Wars Movies, Roman Ceramics.
Value: $175-250

Darth Vader Musical Lamp
unmarked, (plays the Star Wars theme)
Value: $85-95

Darth Vader
marked "Copyright 1977 20th Century Fox Film
Corp. USA Star Wars TM".
Value: $125-150

Topo Gigo
marked "Maria Parego, Distributed
by Ross Products, NY".
Value: $250-325

Sherlock Holmes
paper label marked "Made in Italy by Comoys".
Value: $800-900

The Cathy Jar
marked McMe Productions,
CA, Made by Treasure Craft".
Value: $150

The Cathy Jar
marked "Copyright 1982, Universal Press
Syndicate, The Good Company,
Made in Taiwan".
Value: $700-850

Hopalong Cassidy
Peter Pan Products, unmarked.
Value: $600-750

Hopalong Cassidy
unmarked.
Value: $900-1,100

Peanuts Banks
hard to find, marked
"United Features Syndicate".
Value: $150-175 each

Little Orphan Annie Bank
unmarked.
Value: $50-65

Top Cat on Garbage Can
marked "Copyright 1990
Hanna Barbera Productions, Inc."
Value: $175-225

Ziggy Book Ends
marked "Designer Collection, by Tom Wilson,
Press Syndicate, Made in Korea".
Value: $500-550

Ziggy on Stack of Cookies
Value: $450-575

Ziggy Cylinder
marked "Made by Marsh".
Value: $150-175

Thomas the Tank Engine & Friends
produced by Schmid, 1994.
Value: $85-100

Emmett Kelly on Circus Tent
marked "Emmett Kelly World's Greatest Clown,
Copyright Emmett Kelly Estate, Royal Garden".
Value: $700-900

Tom & Jerry
unknown, marked "Japan".
Value: $225-295

The Cookie Barrel
part of the Daisy Mae and The Bum Collection.
Value: $450-500

The Bum
inside lid, marked "USA".
Value: $450-500

Daisy Mae
marked "made in USA"
inside the lid, "Daisy Mae"
Value: $800-900

McGruff on Cookie Jar
marked "Sigma – The Taste Setter".
Value: $350-400

Beany

Cecil

(This is the front and back view of the same jar),
marked "Kellens-Pasadena, Copyright 53, Bob Clampett".
Value: $1,800

Sherman on the Mount
marked "American Greetings".
Value: $600-750

Mrs. Berenstein Bear
marked "Ebeling & Company".
Value: $475-525

Benny
England, 7" high, marked "Copyright 1990, Hanna
Barbera Productions Harry James Design".
Value: $325-375

Homer Simpson
Harry James Design, marked "Copyright
1990 20th Century Fox Film Corp., Taiwan".
Value: $1,500-1,800

Bart Simpson with Cookie
made by Treasure Craft.
Value: $75

Big Bird on Nest
marked "Newcor Copyright Muppets, Inc."
Value: $65-75

Big Bird on Nest
marked "Demand Marketing, Henderson, KY,
Made in USA, Copyright Muppets".
Value: $75-85

Cookie Monster
marked "Demand Marketing, Henderson, KY,
Made in USA, Copyright Muppets".
Value: $75-85

Oscar the Grouch
marked "Demand Marketing, Henderson, KY,
Made in USA, Copyright Muppets".
Value: $75-85

Cookie Monster
marked "Made by Enesco 1993-1994".
Value: $60-75

Cookie Monster Box
notice the unusual foreign markings
on inside of box.
No Value

Cookie Monster
unmarked.
Value: $95-125

Yogi Bear
England, 10" high, marked "Copyright 1990
Hanna Barbera Productions
An Exclusive Harry James Design".
Value: $600-750

Boo Boo
England, 7" high, marked "Copyright 1990,
Hanna Barbera Productions
An Exclusive Harry James Design".
Value: $750-900

Yogi Bear
unknown, marked "Hanna Barbera
Productions 1979".
Value: $850-1,100

Snoopy Chef
Value: $300-350

Snoopy
marked "Holiday Design 4890".
Value: $125-140

Snoopy with Straw Hat
marked "Copyright 1958-1966
United Features Syndiate".
Value: $250-300

Snoopy on Brown Bag
marked "1958-1966, United Features
Syndicate, for Conagg".
Value: $150-195

Snoopy & Woodstock
marked "Willettes, Snoopy 1958-1966,
United Features Syndicate".
Value: $325-395

Snoopy Chef
marked "G-1958-1966, United Features
Syndicate, Made in Japan".
Value: $225-250

Snoopy Chef
large jar, marked "G-1958-1966,
United Features Syndicate, Made in Japan".
Value: $350-395

Porky Pig
Duncan Mold.
Value: $150-175

Porky Pig
Duncan Mold.
Value: $125-150

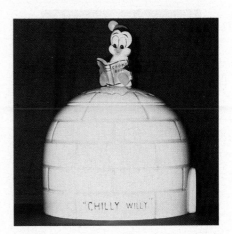

Alf
unmarked, (two different designs).
Value: $200-250

Alf
unmarked.
Value: $300-425

Cool Cat
nice, heavy jar, unmarked.
Value: $500-550

Little Bo Peep
made in Japan, unmarked.
Value: $300-395

Chilly Willy
marked "1958 Walter Lance
Productions, A-3391-CW".
Value: $2,000-2,500

Nintendo – Mario
marked "1994 Musical, Welcome Industrial
Corp., Made in Taiwan".
Value: $50

Yoshi
marked "1994 Musical, Welcome Industrial
Corp., Made in Taiwan".
Value: $50

The Princess
marked "1994 Musical, Welcome Industrial
Corp., Made in Taiwan".
Value: $50

Toad
marked "1994 Musical, Welcome Industrial
Corp., Made in Taiwan".
Value: $50

Ms. Piggy
unknown, unmarked.
Value: $175-250

Raphael
Teenage Mutant Ninga Turtles, marked
"Copyright 1991 Mirage Studios USA
Exclusively Licensed by Surge Licensing Inc.
International Silver Co., Made in Taiwan".
Value: $150-175

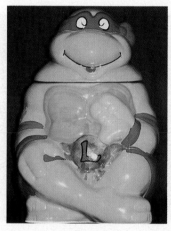

Leonardo
Teenage Mutant Ninga Turtles, marked
"Copyright 1991 Mirage Studios USA
Exclusively Licensed by Surge Licensing Inc.
International Silver Co., Made in Taiwan".
Value: $150-175

Michaelangelo
Teenage Mutant Ninga Turtles, marked
"Copyright 1991 Mirage Studios USA
Exclusively Licensed by Surge Licensing Inc.
International Silver Co., Made in Taiwan".
Value: $150-175

Donatello
Teenage Mutant Ninga Turtles, marked
"Copyright 1991 Mirage Studios USA
Exclusively Licensed by Surge Licensing Inc.
International Silver Co., Made in Taiwan".
Value: $150-175

Fred Flintstone House
marked "Certified International".
Value: $75-95

Standing Fred Flintstone
marked "Certified International".
Value: $75-95

Standing Barney Rubble
marked "Certified International".
Value: $75-95

Dino & Pebbles
marked "Certified International".
Value: $75-95

Fred Flintstone
made in England, marked "Copyright 1990
Hanna Barbera Prod. Inc. An
Exclusive Harry James Design".
Value: $250-300

Barney Rubble
marked "An Exclusive Harry James Design".
Value: $150-175

Strawberry Shortcake
marked "Made by American Greetings Corp. Cleveland, OH MCMLXXXIII",
(two views of this jar).
Value: $1,200-1,500

Bully
marked "Lori's Originals Copyright",
signed "Dick".
Value: $150

Smokey the Bear
made by Norcrest
Value: $900-1,000

Smokey the Bear
very rare jar, possibly American Bisque.
Value: $2,500-3,000

Smokey the Bear Bank
unmarked.
Value: $125-175

Smokey The Bear
reads "Prevent Forest Fires".
Value: $900-1,000

Smokey The Bear Candy Jar, unmarked, made by Norcrest. – **Value: $125-175**
Smokey The Bear Bank – **Value: $125-175**
Smokey The Bear Bank – **Value: $125-175**
Smokey The Bear Standing Shakers, unmarked. – **Value: $150-175 a set**
Smokey The Bear Head Shakers, unmarked. – **Value: $150-175 a set**

Care Bear
marked "Funshine Bear American Greeting
Corp., Made in Korea"
Value: $350-450

Care Bear
marked "Tenderheart Beat American
Greetings Corp. Made in Korea".
Value: $350-450

Nose Marie Pound Puppy
marked "Pound Puppies Taiwan".
Value: $140-175

Howler Pound Puppy
marked "Pound Puppies Taiwan".
Value: $125-150

Pound Puppy with Cane & Derby
marked "Pound Puppies Tonka Corp. Taiwan".
Value: $125-150

Nose Marie Pound Puppy
marked "Pound Puppies Tonka Corp. Taiwan".
Value: $125-150

Chef Puppy
marked "Pound Puppies Tonka Corp. Taiwan".
Value: $150-195

Pound Puppy with Present
marked "Pound Puppies Tonka Corp. Taiwan".
Value: $150-195

Happy Memories Collectibles

Loretta and William Hamburg, Woodland Hills California, founded their business, Happy Memories Collectibles in 1986, originally dealing in collectible toys. Loretta was a cookie jar collector for many years, then tried dealing in pottery and cookie jars with much success. These are the first of their own original designs made by Treasure Craft Inc. Future jars will include Elvis, Marilyn Monroe, Scarlett O'Hara, and Rhett Butler.

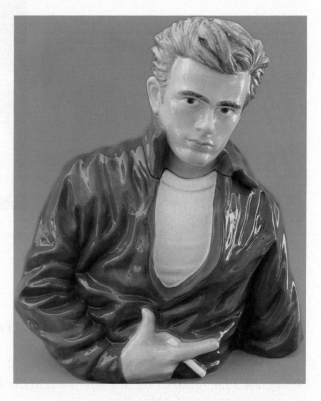

Hopalong Cassidy & Topper
15 1/2" high, x 14 1/2" wide, Limited Edition of 500 Jars.
Marked "Happy Memories Collectibles – Hollywood Legends Series",
"Authorized & Licensed by the U.S. Television Office, Inc.".
Value: $400

James Dean
16" high, x 15" wide, Limited Edition of 500 Jars.
Marked "Happy Memories Collectibles – Hollywood Legends Series", "Trademark Copyright 1994 James Dean Foundation".
Value: $300

Negatha Peterson

Negatha Peterson operates as Erwin Pottery, and is located in Erwin, Tennessee, where she continues to produce cookie jars and other pottery items in her home. Negatha was a 16 year veteran of Southern Potteries, until the company closed their doors in 1957. She bought the Gold Tooth Mammy mold from Acme Craft Ware of Wellsville, Ohio, at their closing.

Gold Tooth Mammy
with a scarf, marked "Erwin Potteries, Erwin, TN",
(four different color scarves).
Value: $150

Gold Tooth Mammy

(description and priced as shown above)

The Pfaltzgraff Company of York

The Pfaltzgraff Company of York, Pennsylvania was founded in 1811 by German immigrant George Pfaltzgraff. Pfaltzgraff Company later bought the Treasure Craft Company of California and are now the producers of Treasure Craft Cookie jars.

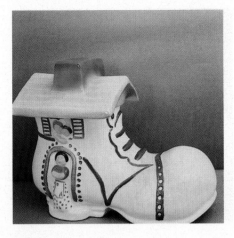

The Old Woman and The Shoe
unmarked, (shown here with two different color roofs).
Value: $300+

Handy Harry
utility jar, stamped "Handy Harry Muggsy –
The Pfaltzgraff Pottery Co., York, PA,
Designed by Jessop".
Value: $350-450

Derby Dan Mugsie
8 1/2" high, marked "Derby Dan Mugsie –
The Pfaltzgraff Pottery Co., York, PA
Designed by Jessop".
Value: $350-495

Little Bo Peep
possibly Pfaltzgraff, a few companies
made these same jars.
Value: $300-350

Little Miss Muffet
unmarked.
Value: $350-450

Mother Goose
unmarked, same type of bottom
as Little Bo Peep.
Value: $500-550

Cooky Girl
experts say, Pfaltzgraff, unmarked.
Value: $195-250

Clown with Drum
unmarked.
Value: $550-600

Chef
unmarked.
Value: $475-525

Sack of Cookies
unmarked.
Value: $225-275

Train
9" high, marked "USA".
Value: $225-300

Cookie Time Clock
10" high, marked "USA".
Value: $200-250

Cookie Cop
produced in 1950, made in
two different color variations.
Value: $700+

Stagecoach
raised lettering, marked
"CJ-4 Pfaltzgraff USA Copyright".
Value: $525-600

Blue Crock
Value: $75-100

Renita Pines of Oakland, California

Renita Pines of Oakland, California, is an art teacher and a collector of Black Memorabilia. She has been designing the Cookie Doll for several years, striving for perfection.

Cookie Doll
brown skin, hand designed and sculpted
by Renita Pines. Limited Edition of 100,
(a very heavy jar).
Value: $350

Cookie Doll
this is a similar jar, with black skin.
Value: $350

Pottery Guild of America

Pottery Guild of America was manufactured by the Cronin China Company, Minerva, Ohio.

Little Red Riding Hood
12 3/4" high, unmarked.
Value: $150-195

Dutch Boy
blue, unmarked.
Value: $150-195

Dutch Girl
12 1/4" high, blue, unmarked.
Value: $150-195

Dutch Girl
12 1/4" high, pink, unmarked.
Value: $150-195

Dutch Boy
pink, unmarked.
Value: $150-195

Old King Cole
12 3/4" high, hard to find,
marked "Pottery Guild".
Value: $700-800

Old King Cole
12 3/4" high, unmarked.
Value: $700-800

Little Girl
11 1/4" high, hand painted,
marked "Pottery Guild of America".
Value: $350-400

Boy with Fruit
unmarked.
Value: $175-200

Balloon Lady
Value: $175-200

Red Wing Stoneware Company

When Red Wing Stoneware Company began producing on a large scale in 1878, the pottery began to become known beyond the local area. By 1936, the company changed its name to Red Wing Potteries, Inc. Red Wing produced pottery for George Rum Rill of Arkansas during the 1930's. These pieces can be identified with a paper label of a Rum Rill mark. Red Wing kept the contract with the Mr. Rum Rill until it was later given to the Shawnee Pottery Company of Zanesville, Ohio. Red Wing also produced stoneware for the Sleepy Eye Milling Company of Sleepy Eye, Minnesota. By the middle of the 1940's all stoneware had been completely discontinued. The cookie jars were produced in the later years of the company. Red Wing Potteries closed their doors permanently in 1967. The Red Wing factory was used for many years as a storage and warehouse facility before it was demolished in 1994.

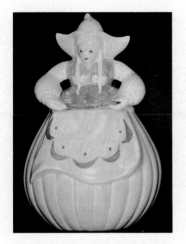

Katrina Dutch Girl
10 1/2" high, yellow, stamped "Red Wing",
impressed in bottom "Red Wing USA".
Value: $140-150

Katrina Dutch Girl
10 1/2" high, blue, stamped "Red Wing",
impressed in bottom "Red Wing USA".
Value: $125-140

Katrina Dutch Girl
10 1/2" high, green, stamped "Red Wing",
impressed in bottom "Red Wing USA".
Value: $250-300

Katrina Dutch Girl
white, incised "Red Wing USA".
Value: $300+

Katrina Dutch Girl
blue, hand painted, stamped "Standing Wing",
embossed "Red Wing USA".
Value: $150

Katrina Dutch Girl
yellow, stamped "Standing Wing",
incised "Red Wing USA".
Value: $150

Katrina Dutch Girl
green, stamped "Standing Wing",
incised "Red Wing USA".
Value: $400

Katrina Dutch Girl
beige, stamped "Standing Wing",
incised "Red Wing USA".
Value: $200

Katrina Dutch Girl
white, 3/8" shorter and 3/4" less in diameter
than regular Katrinas, however quite rare.
Value: $250

Grapes
10" high, turquoise, marked "Red Wing USA".
Value: $175-225

Grapes
10" high, turquoise, marked "Red Wing USA".
Value: $225-300

Orange

*(description and price the same as in the
next three pictures).*

Grapes
bottom stamped "Red Wing USA", (shown here in four different colors).
Value: $300-350

Yellow   **Green**   **Pink**

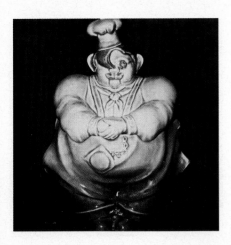

Pierre Chef
11 1/2" high, unmarked.
Value: $250-300

Green

Mustard Yellow

Pierre Chef
yellow, marked "Red Wing Pottery
Hand Painted Patent".
Value: $95-125

Pierre Chef
unmarked, (shown here in two different colors).
Value: $125-150

Pierre Chef
blue speckled, hard to find,
marked "Red Wing USA".
Value: $300-400

Pierre Chef
white, incised "Red Wing USA",
red is cold painted.
Value: $400+

Pierre Chef
beige, marked "Standing Wing".
Value: $200

Pierre Chef
speckled pink, incised "Red Wing USA".
Value: $400+

Pierre Chef
speckled mustard color,
incised "Red Wing USA".
Value: $550

Pierre Chef
black, incised "Red Wing USA",
hand painted by a collector in Texas.
Value: $350

Pierre Chef
stamped "Standing Wing Red Wing Pottery
Hand Painted D130328". Pierre, Katrina, and
Friar Tuck were designed by Charles Murphy,
noted red wing designer and wildlife artist.
Value: $300+

Rooster Casserole
marked "Red Wing".
Value: $100-125

Bananas
9" high, pink,
bottom stamped "Red Wing USA".
Value: $250-300

Bananas
yellow, bottom stamped "Red Wing USA".
Value: $250-300

Bananas
bottom stamped "Red Wing USA".
Value: $300-350

Orange

Green

Turquoise

Bananas
cobalt blue, bottom stamped "Red Wing USA".
Value: $400

Cattails Stoneware Jar
blue, stamped "Red Wing Art Pottery".
Value: $400

Cattails Stoneware Jar
green, unmarked.
Value: $500

Cattails Stoneware Jar
brown, stamped "Red Wing Art Pottery".
Value: $400

Cattails Stoneware Jar
turquoise, stamped "Red Wing Pottery".
Value: $450

Cattails Stoneware Jar
multicolored, stamped "Red Wing Pottery".
Value: $450

Fish Casserole
6" high, marked "Red Wing USA".
Value: $75-85

Saffron Jar
marked "Made in Red Wing".
Value: $400+

Saffron Jar without Band
advertising shown,
bottom stamped "Red Wing Saffronware"
Value: $400+

Saffron Jar with Band
advertising shown,
bottom stamped "Red Wing Saffronware".
Value: $400+

Saffron Jar
from the 1930's, stamped "Red Wing Saffronware",
bottom stamped "Red Wing Saffronware".
Value: $150

Saffron Barrel
plain, bottom stamped "Red Wing Saffronware".
Value: $100

Saffron Barrel
squat shaped, bottom stamped
"Red Wing Saffronware".
Value: $75-100

Saffron Jar
hand painted decorations, bottom stamped
"Red Wing Saffronware".
Value: $150

Saffron Jar
unusual shape, bottom stamped
"Red Wing Saffronware".
Value: $150

Saffron Jar
barrel shape, bottom stamped
"Red Wing Saffronware".
Value: $150

Saffron Jar
barrel shape, plain, bottom stamped
"Red Wing Saffronware".
Value: $150

Saffron Barrel with Blue Bands
bottom stamped "Red Wing Saffronware".
Value: $200

Saffron Jar
hand painted floral design, bottom stamped
"Red Wing Saffronware".
Value: $200

Gray Line
on the bottom "Made in Red Wing".
Value: $1,250+

Saffron Jar
(made from the same mold as the Gray Line Jar,
but slightly larger due to the differences in
clay). Bottom stamped "Red Wing Saffronware".
Value: $250+

Saffron Barrel
hand painted, bottom stamped
"Red Wing Saffronware".
Value: $125

Saffron Barrel
decorated with flowers,
bottom stamped "Red Wing Saffronware".
Value: $100

Saffron Barrel
squat shape,
bottom stamped "Red Wing Saffronware".
Value: $250+

Friar Tuck
10 3/4" high, beige, marked "Red Wing USA".
Value: $95-125

Friar Tuck
blue, stamped "Standing Wing Red Wing
Pottery Hand Painted".
Value: $200-250

Friar Tuck
green, stamped "Standing Wing ",
incised "Red Wing USA".
Value: $300

Friar Tuck
brownish color, incised "Red Wing USA".
Value: $225+

Friar Tuck
yellow, stamped "Standing Wing",
with three patent numbers.
Value: $150

Friar Tuck
white, incised "Red Wing USA".
Value: $300+

Carousel
white, marked "Slanted Wing Red
Wing Hand Painted".
Value: $1,000+

Carousel
speckled blue, marked "Slanted Wing
Red Wing Hand Painted".
Value: $1,000

Carousel
speckled mint green, unmarked.
Value: $1,000

Sponge Crock
possibly Red Wing, unmarked.
Value: $100-125

Green Ball Cookie Jar
8" high, plain pattern of Gypsey Trail
Dinnerware, made in 1935, unmarked.
Value: $75-100

Ivory Ball Cookie Jar
unmarked.
Value: $75-100

Orange Ball Cookie Jar
unmarked.
Value: $75-100

Cobalt Blue Ball Cookie Jar
Value: $75-100

Fondosso
from Dinnerware Line, First Produced in 1938,
fairly rare, bottom incised, marked "Red Wing
Potteries Inc., Design Pending Copyright".
Value: $175+

Spruce
platter of contemporary dinnerware,
2 1/2 quart cookie jar.
Value: $75

Canister Jar
Value: $50-75

Cylinder with Flowers
very old, circa 1900's,
marked "Red Wing Stoneware Company".
Value: $100-150

King of Tarts
10" high, pink speckled,
stamped "Red Wing USA".
Value: $1,500+

King of Tarts
blue, incised "Red Wing USA".
Value: $1,200

King of Tarts
unusual cinnamon color,
incised "Red Wing USA".
Value: $3,000

King of Tarts
cream speckled, incised "Red Wing USA".
Value: $1,200

King of Tarts
blue speckled, incised "Red Wing USA".
Value: $1,500+

King of Tarts
pale lime green, incised "Red Wing USA".
Value: $1,200

King of Tarts
multicolored, incised "Red Wing USA".
Value: $1,00-1,200

King of Tarts
yellow, incised "Red Wing USA".
Value: $1,100-1,200

Short Jack Frost
unmarked.
Value: $750+

Tall Jack Frost
marked "Red Wing USA".
Value: $825-900

Flared Barrel Stoneware
with rose decorations, incised "Red Wing", (three different color variations shown here).
Value: $100

Stoneware Jar
no cattails, cream with rose decoration,
circle stamp "Red Wing Saffronware".
Value: $250

Stoneware Jar
unmarked, not Saffron
Value: $150

Stoneware Barrel
Value: $125

Fruit Jar
straight sided, unmarked.
Value: $100

Fruit Munch Jar
unmarked.
Value: $50

Cream Sponged Barrel
unmarked.
Value: $225

Green Sponged Barrel
unmarked, (two different jars shown here).
Value: $125

Flared Barrel Stoneware
better paint, rose decorations,
incised "Red Wing".
Value: $100

Fruit Munch Jar
Value: $50

Fruit Bowl
shown upside down.
Value: $50

Peasant Fruit Bowl
marked "Red Wing USA".
Value: $40-50

Peasant Munch Jar
Value: $50

Brown Peasant Jar
10" high, incised "Red Wing USA",
made in the 1940's
Value: $75-95

Aqua Peasant Jar
incised "Red Wing USA".
Value: $75-95

Peasant Jar
incised "Red Wing USA", (shown here in three different colors).
Value: $100-125

Beige   **Green**   **Cream**

304

Pineapple
9" high, orange color,
bottom stamped "Red Wing USA".
Value: $250+

Pineapple
turquoise, bottom stamped "Red Wing USA".
Value: $200+

Pineapple
pink, bottom stamped "Red Wing USA".
Value: $250+

Pineapple Jam Jar
bottom stamped "Red Wing USA".
Value: $60

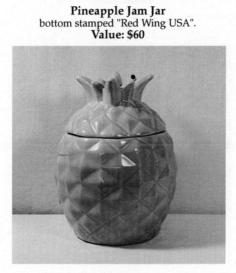

Pineapple
cobalt blue, bottom stamped "Red Wing USA".
Value: $400+

Pineapple
green, bottom stamped "Red Wing USA".
Value: $250

Pineapple
yellow, bottom stamped "Red Wing USA".
Value: $250

Round-Up
from the dinnerware line,
introduced in 1958.
Value: $325+

Bob White Bird Cylinder
from the dinnerware line,
introduced in 1956, unmarked.
Value: $125

Crock/Cylinder
"Lunch Hour Jar", introduced in 1955, bottom
marked "Red Wing USA J.O.", one of a kind.
Value: $250+

White Casual Line
bottom marked "Red Wing USA".
Value: $100

Reproduction for the St. James Hotel
made from an original Red Wing mold by
Artists in the Park, Deer Park, Wisconsin.
Value: $150

Apple
8 1/2" high, green, bottom stamped "Red Wing USA".
Value: $225

Covered Sugar Apple
yellow, bottom stamped "Red Wing USA".
Value: $80-100

Apple
bottom stamped "Red Wing USA", (two different colors shown here).
Value: $250

Apple
cobalt blue, bottom stamped "Red Wing USA".
Value: $300

Orange

Pink

Apple
bottom stamped "Red Wing USA", (two different colors shown here).
Value: $200

Yellow

Turquoise

Happy The Children Jar
white speckled, unmarked. Poem on the jar
reads "Happy the Children Wherever They Are
Who Live in a House With a Cookie Jar".
Value: $200-250

Happy the Children Jar
(three different color variations shown here).
Value: $300+

Speckled Blue

Decorated

Speckled Mustard Color

Cabbage
orange color, very rare.
Value: $2,500

Cabbage
cobalt blue, stamped on bottom
"Red Wing USA", (very rare).
Value: $3,000

Drummer Boy
Value: $1,000-1,250

Pear
bottom stamped "Red Wing USA", (three different color variations shown here).
Value: $200-250

Pink

Turquoise

Green

Pear
yellow, bottom stamped "Red Wing USA".
Value: $250-300

Pear
cobalt blue, bottom stamped "Red Wing USA".
Value: $300-350

Sierra Design
green.
Value: $100

Sierra Design
cream color, large jar,
marked "Red Wing USA 725 L".
Value: $75-100

Sierra Design
cream color, medium jar,
marked "Red Wing USA 724 M".
Value: $75-100

Sierra Design
cream color, small jar,
marked "Red Wing USA 723 S".
Value: $75-100

Sierra Design
large jar, marked "Red Wing USA 725 L".
Value: $75

Sierra Design
medium jar, marked "Red Wing USA 725 M".
Value: $75

Sierra Design
small jar, marked "Red Wing USA 725 S".
Value: $75

Sweet Shop Design
large jar, marked "Red Wing USA 715 L".
Value: $75-100

Sweet Shop Design
medium jar, marked "Red Wing USA 714 M".
Value: $75-100

Sweet Shop Design
small jar, marked "Red Wing USA 713 S".
Value: $75-100

Mosaic Design
large jar, marked "Red Wing USA 715 L".
Value: $75-100

Mosaic Design
medium jar, marked "Red Wing USA 714 M".
Value: $75-100

Mosaic Design
small jar, marked "Red Wing USA 713 S".
Value: $75-100

Regal China Company

Regal China Company began producing cookie jars in the early 1940's. Their pottery is extremely valuable and is desired by many collectors. Most of their jars are porcelain. Originally located in Chicago, Regal China moved to Anitoch, Illinois, in 1940. Regal China closed its doors in June 1992.

Little Red Riding Hood
Advertising Plaque
extremely rare, only a few known to exist.
Value: $10,000+

Little Red Riding Hood Cookie Canister
marked "Patent Design #135889", very rare.
Value: $4,000-4,500

Little Red Riding Hood Peanut Canister
marked "Patent Design #135889", very rare,
only one known to exist.
Value: $4,000-4,500

Little Red Riding Hood Cookie Canister
marked "Patent Design #135889", very rare,
(shown alone in this picture), many other
canister jars are available.
Value: $4,000-4,500

Little Red Riding Hood
fired on poppy decals, marked "#135889 Pat.
Applied For".
Value: $500-600

Little Red Riding Hood
fired on poppy, red shoes.
Value: $400-450

Little Red Riding Hood
three bushels of poppies on skirt,
marked "Pat. Des. #135889".
Value: $400-450

Little Red Riding Hood
marked "967 Hull Ware Little Red Riding Hood
Pat. App. for USA".
Value: $450-500

Little Red Riding Hood
marked "967 Hull Ware Little Red Riding
Hood Pat. App. for USA".
Value: $550-600

Little Red Riding Hood
marked "967 Hull Ware Little Red Riding
Hood Pat. App. for USA".
Value: $500-550

Little Red Riding Hood
marked "967 Hull Ware Little Red Riding
Hood Pat. App. for USA".
Value: $600-650

Little Red Riding Hood
marked "967 Hull Ware Little Red Riding
Hood Pat. App. for USA".
Value: $400-450

Little Red Riding Hood
marked "967 Hull Ware Little Red Riding
Hood Pat. App. for USA".
Value: $450-500

Little Red Riding Hood
marked "Little Red Riding Hood Pat.
Design 135889 USA".
Value: $350-400

Little Red Riding Hood
hand painted marked "967 Hull Ware Little
Red Riding Hood Pat. App. for USA".
Value: $300-325

Little Red Riding Hood
marked "967 Hull Ware Little Red Riding
Hood Pat. App. for USA".
Value: $350-425

Little Red Riding Hood
marked "Little Red Riding Hood Pat.
Design 135889 USA".
Value: $350-400

Little Red Riding Hood
marked "Little Red Riding Hood Pat.
Design 135889 USA".
Value: $350-400

Little Red Riding Hood
marked "Little Red Riding Hood Pat.
Design 135889 USA".
Value: $450-500

Little Red Riding Hood
marked "Little Red Riding Hood Pat.
Design 135889 USA".
Value: $650-700

Large Poinsettia Little Red Riding Hood
marked "Little Red Riding Hood
Pat. Design 135889 USA".
Value: $1,000-1,100

Medium Poinsettia Little Red Riding Hood
marked "Little Red Riding Hood
Pat. Design 135889 USA".
Value: $1,000-1,100

Small Poinsettia Little Red Riding Hood
marked "Little Red Riding Hood
Pat. Design 135889 USA".
Value: $1,000-1,100

Medium Salt & Pepper Shakers
shown with large Poinsettia Jar,
marked "Pat. Des. 135889".
Value: $900-1,000 a set

Little Red Riding Hood
marked "967 Hull Ware Little Red Riding
Hood Pat. App. for USA".
Value: $800-900

Little Red Riding Hood
marked "967 Hull Ware Little Red Riding
Hood Pat. App. for USA".
Value: $800-900

Little Red Riding Hood
marked "967 Hull Ware Little Red Riding Hood
Pat. App. for USA".
Value: $800-900

Little Red Riding Hood
marked "Little Red Riding Hood Pat.
Design 135889 USA".
Value: $450-500

Little Red Riding Hood
marked "967 Hull Ware Little Red Riding
Hood Pat. App. for USA".
Value: $550-600

Little Red Riding Hood
marked "967 Hull Ware Little Red Riding
Hood Pat. App. for USA".
Value: $350-400

Little Red Riding Hood
decal, marked "967 Hull Ware Little Red Riding
Hood Pat. App. for USA".
Value: $500-550

Little Red Riding Hood
marked "Little Red Riding Hood Pat.
Design 135889 USA".
Value: $350-400

Little Red Riding Hood
marked "Little Red Riding Hood Pat.
Design 135889 USA".
Value: $450-500

Wolf Jar
marked "USA".
Value: $900-1,000

Hanging Wall Bank
marked "Pat. Design 135889 USA".
Value: $2,000-2,500

Little Red Riding Hood
marked "Little Red Riding Hood
Pat. Design 135889 USA".
Value: $350-400

Gem Refractories Little Red Riding Hood
unmarked.
Value: $300-400

Little Red Riding Hood
decal, marked "967 Hull Ware Little Red
Riding Hood Pat. App. for USA".
Value: $200-225

Little Red Riding Hood Dresser Jar
marked "Hull Ware".
Value: $600-650

Little Red Riding Hood
bronze cape, marked "Little Red Riding
Hood Pat. Design 135889 USA".
Value: $550-600

Little Red Riding Hood Cracker Jar
marked "Pat. Des. 135889".
Value: $700-750

Little Red Riding Hood Single Shaker
blue and white single shaker.
Value: $125

Little Red Riding Hood Single Shaker
all gold.
Value: $300

Little Red Riding Hood Single Shaker
clear glaze.
Value: $50

Little Red Riding Hood Single Shaker
white with platinum trim.
Value: $300

Little Red Riding Hood Single Shaker
common shaker.
Value: $50

Uncle Mistletoe
the jar on the left is made by Peter Pan Products,
unmarked.
Value: $800-1,000

Uncle Mistletoe
marked "Pat. Copyright 50028 Produced by
Regal China for Marshall Field".
Value: $2,500-3,000

Uncle Mistletoe
(a view of the previous jar shown here alone).
marked "Pat. Copyright 50028 Produced by
Regal China for Marshall Field".
Value: $2,500-3,000

Alice in Wonderland Cookie Jar
marked "Copyright Walt Disney Productions
Alice in Wonderland".
Value: $2,500-3,200

Mad Hatter Teapot
marked "Mad Hatter Copyright
Walt Disney Productions".
Value: $3,000

Tweedle Dee & Tweedle Dum Salt & Peppers
marked "Walt Disney Productions".
Value: $1,000-1,100 a set

Alice in Wonderland Salt & Peppers
Value: $750

King of Hearts Milk Pitcher
marked "King of Hearts Walt Disney Productions"
Value: $1,200-1,400

White Rabbit Covered Sugar
marked "Walt Disney Productions".
Value: $700-750

White Rabbit Creamer
marked "Walt Disney Productions".
Value: $700-750

Mad Hatter Teapot
marked "Mad Hatter Copyright
Walt Disney Productions".
Value: $3,000

White Rabbit Covered Sugar
marked "Walt Disney Productions".
Value: $700-750

Alice in Wonderland Salt & Peppers
Value: $750

King of Hearts Milk Pitcher
marked "King of Hearts Walt Disney Productions".
Value: $1,200-1,400

White Rabbit Creamer
marked "Walt Disney Productions".
Value: $700-750

King of Hearts Milk Pitcher
marked "King of Hearts
Walt Disney Productions".
Value: $1,200-1,400

Tweedle Dee & Tweedle Dum Salt & Peppers
marked "Walt Disney Productions".
Value: $1,000-1,100 a set

White Rabbit Covered Sugar
marked "Walt Disney Productions".
Value: $700-750

White Rabbit Creamer
marked "Walt Disney Productions".
Value: $700-750

Clown
marked "Translucent Vitrified China
Copyright C. Miller 54-439A".
Value: $800-850

Clown
marked "Translucent Vitrified China
Copyright C. Miller 54-439A".
Value: $800-850

Harpo Marx
looks like Regal, feels like Regal,
but probably is not.
Value: $1,500

Harpo Marx
white hair.
Value: $1,500

Monkey Bank
marked "Copyright C. Miller".
Value: $150-175

Monkey Bank
single color, marked "Copyright C. Miller".
Value: $95-110

Humpty Dumpty
11 1/2" high, marked "Humpty Dumpty 707",
(Abingdon also made a very similar jar).
Value: $350-375

Peek-A-Boo Salt & Peppers
large, white with gold trim, marked "Van
Telligen Copyright Pat. Pend. Peek-A-Boo".
Value: $600-650 a set

Peek-A-Boo Salt & Peppers
white with gold trim, marked "Van Telligen".
Value: $250-300 a set

Peek-A-Boo
11 3/4" high, marked "Peek-A-Boo
Copyright Van Telligen."
Value: $1,400-1,500

Dutch Girl
12" high, marked "54-200" hard color to find.
Value: $800-900

Dutch Girl
12" high, marked "54-200".
Value: $750-800

Dutch Girl Salt & Peppers
matches previous jar.
Value: $350-400 a set

A Nod to Abe Salt & Peppers with Nodders
marked "6th S & P Conv. 1991 Chicago, IL
Designed by Regal China Copyright USA".
Value: $350-400 a set

Hubert the Lion
produced for the Harris Bank in Chicago, IL
in 1982, marked "Hubert Made in the USA".
1,500 were produced, notice with wire glass frames.
Value: $1,200-1,250

316

Majorette
11 1/2" high, unmarked, a very popular jar.
Value: $495-550

Diaper Pin Pig
12" high, marked "404".
Value: $675-750

Davy Crockett
11 3/4" high, marked "Translucent Vitrified
China Copyright C. Miller 55-140 B".
Value: $700-750

Fi Fi the French Poodle
marked "Copyright C. Miller 1163".
Value: $900-950

Toby Cookies
unmarked.
Value: $1,200-1,400

Little Miss Muffett
marked "Little Miss Muffett #705"
Value: $350-400

Goldilocks
12 1/2" high, marked "405 Goldilocks Pat. Pend.".
Value: $425-475

Goldilocks Shaker
clear glaze and trimmed in gold.
Value: $150 each

Goldilocks Salt & Peppers
full color to match cookie jar.
Value: $300 a set

Goldilocks Salt & Peppers
very rare green & yellow color.
Value: $300-325 a set

French Chef
12" high, marked "54-192", (two different color variations shown here).
Value: $400-450

Three Bears
marked "Three Bears 704".
Value: $400-450

Regal China Advertising Sign
Value: $500-600

French Chef Shakers
(shown with chef)
Value: $250-300

French Chef
12" high, solid white trimmed in gold.
Value: $500-525

Barn Cookie Jar
marked "Pat. Pend. 381".
Value: $400-450

Uncle Sam
unmarked, (could this be Regal China?), (two different color variations shown here).
Value: $3,500-4,000

Churn Boy
12" high, unmarked,
similar to American Bisque's Jar.
Value: $350-400

Oriental Lady
unmarked, (two different color variations shown here).
Value: $700-750

Regal Cat
12 1/4" high, unmarked,
very similar to Shawnee Pottery's Jar.
Value: $400-450

Goldilocks
very rare and unusual color design, (two views shown here).
Value: $1,200-1,400

Fi Fi Salt & Peppers
4 3/4" high, rare.
Value: $450

Robinson Ransbottom Pottery Company

Robinson Ransbottom Pottery Company started in 1920 and is still in business today in Roseville Ohio, however, they stopped producing cookie jars quite a few years ago. They do still produce stoneware crocks, garden ware, and flower pots.

Ole' King Cole
10 1/4" high, (hard to find color),
marked "RRP Co. Roseville, OH".
Value: $600-675

Ole' King Cole
10 1/4" high, marked "Roseville O USA RRP Co."
Value: $450-475

Bud
11 1/4" high, unmarked.
Value: $350-395

Bud
11 1/4" high, the head is a bank, notice the slot, unmarked.
(Front and Back views shown here).
Value: $475-550

Jack
11" high, unmarked.
Value: $350-395

Hey Diddle Diddle
9 3/4" high, marked "RRP Co., Roseville, OH #411",
(two different color variations).
Value: $275-350

Hey Diddle Diddle
9 3/4" high, gold trim, marked "RRP Co.,
Roseville, OH #317",
Value: $400-425

Wise Bird
12" high, gold trim,
marked "RRP Co., Roseville, OH 359".
Value: $195-250

Wise Bird
12" high, marked "RRP Co., Roseville, OH 359".
Value: $175-195

Chef
11" high, marked "RRP Co., Roseville, OH #411",
(also available with gold trim).
Value: $150-175

Dutch Girl
12" high, marked "RRP Company, Roseville, OH".
Value: $275-350

Dutch Girl
12" high, gold trim,
marked "RRP Co., Roseville, OH".
Value: $375-475

Dutch Boy
12 1/2" high, unmarked.
Value: $275-350

Dutch Boy
12 1/2" high, gold trim,
marked "RRP Co., Roseville, OH #423".
Value: $375-475

Dutch Boy
12 1/2" high, gold trim, (different color variation).
marked "RRP Co., Roseville, OH".
Value: $375-475

Frosty the Snowman
14" high, marked "RRP Company,
Roseville, OH USA".
Value: $700-875

Sheriff Pig
12 1/2" high, marked "RRP Co., Roseville, OH #363".
(Two different color hats).
Value: $125-150

Whale
7 3/4" high, marked "RRP Company,
Roseville, OH", hard to find jar.
Value: $750-850

Oscar
10" high, (two different color hats),
shown in a 1943 catalog.
Value: $150-195

Cylinder
8 1/2" high, marked "RRP Company,
Roseville, OH #350".
Value: $60-70

Bowl with Peaches
8 1/2" high, gold trim,
marked "RRP Company, Roseville, OH #312".
Value: $95-125

Bowl with Peaches
8 1/2" high, marked "RRP Company, Roseville, OH".
Value: $60-75

Jocko
11 1/2" high, marked "RRP Company,
Roseville, OH USA".
Value: $450-475

Peter, Peter Pumpkin Eater
8 3/4" high, marked "RRP Company,
Roseville, OH #1502".
Value: $350-400

Peter, Peter Pumpkin Eater
8 3/4" high, gold trim, marked "RRP Company,
Roseville, OH #1502".
Value: $425-525

The New Rose Collection

The New Rose Collection – Rose and Gary Saxby of Warren, Illinois. Rose is a long time ceramicist that designs and produces Limited Edition cookie jars with her husband Gary's help.

Little Black Sambo
marked "The New Collection of Rose, Warren, IL". Limited Edition of 100,
(two different views shown here).
Value: $150-195

Mallard Duck
Limited Edition.
Value: $40-50

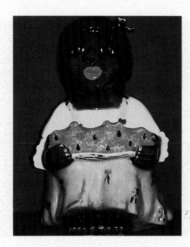

Watermelon Girl
Limited Edition of 100.
Value: $195

Watermelon Boy
Limited Edition of 100, sculpted from lawn
ornament marked "The New Collection of Rose".
Value: $195

Whistler
white face, one of thier first jars,
limited edition of 100,
marked "The Collection of Rose".
Value: $150-300

Whistler
black face, (two differnt color variations shown here),
limited edition of 100,
marked "The Collection of Rose #66".
Value: $350-400

The Count of Sesame Street
limited reproduction, limited edition.
Value: $125-150

Bert of Sesame Street
also known as "Ernies Friend"
limited edition, marked "Ernies Friend".
Value: $125-150

Martin Luther King
limited edition of 500, (only 100 were sold to
collectors, the other 400 were sold to NAACP".
Value: $150-195

I Have A Dream/Martin Luther King
limited edition.
Value: $150-175

Little Angel
limited edition,
marked "New Rose Collection #12".
Value: $125-150

Cow Head
limited edition.
Value: $65-95

Steer Head
limited edition.
Value: $100-125

Purple Cow
limited edition.
Value: $50-85

Cookie Bus
marked "Parlor Car Bus Tours", (front and back views shown here).
Value: $95-125

Paul Bunyan
marked "Designed by Rose Saxby,
RNC Exclusive", limited edition of 150.
Value: $150

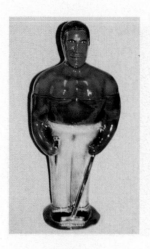

John Henry
marked "Designed by Rose Saxby,
RNC Exclusive", limited edition of 150.
Value: $125

Little Black Santa
Sandstone Finish, limited edition.
Value: $30-40

Shawnee Pottery Company

Shawnee Pottery Company was incorporated in December 1936. Over the years, many different pieces of pottery were produced, including kitchen and pantry ware, decorative art pottery, and dinnerware. The Shawnee Pottery Company was located on Linden Avenue in Zanesville, Ohio. Shawnee closed its doors in 1962. Shawnee Pottery has been probably the most sought after collectible over the past 25 years.

Smiley Pig
11 1/4" high, gold trim, decals, under lid marked
"gylcerine AEIG 123", marked "U.S.A."
Value: $550-650

Smiley Pig
11 1/4" high, red bandana, apples, gold trim,
marked "U.S.A."
Value: $950-1,100

Smiley Pig
11 1/4" high, blue bandana, black hair, gold trim,
with flower decals, marked "U.S.A."
Value: $1,250-1,400

Smiley Pig
11 1/4" high, yellow bandana, gold trim, hand painted flowers.
Bugs painted on head under glaze, (front and back views shown here), marked "U.S.A."
Value: $750-800

Smiley Pig
11 1/4" high, green bandana, red hair,
with chrysanthemums, marked "U.S.A."
Value: $1,500-1,800

Smiley Pig
11 1/4" high, red bandana, roses, decals,
gold trim, marked "U.S.A."
Value: $650-700

Smiley Pig
11 1/4" high, red bandana, gold trim,
with bouquet of flowers, marked "U.S.A."
Value: $650-700

Smiley Pig
11 1/4" high, yellow bandana, gold trim,
hand painted flowers all over jar with decals,
marked "U.S.A."
Value: $1,100

Smiley Pig
11 1/4" high, blue bandana, gold and decals,
hand painted flower on collar, marked "U.S.A."
Value: $1,100

Smiley Pig
11 1/4" high, yellow bandana, black hair,
original sticker, gold and decals, marked "U.S.A."
Value: $1,250-1,400

Smiley Pig
11 1/4" high, yellow bandana, barbor shop hair,
gold and decals, big fly on face, marked "U.S.A."
Value: $1,250-1,500

Smiley Pig
11 1/4" high, red bandana, gold trim,
tulips, marked "U.S.A."
Value: $750-800

Smiley Pig
11 1/4" high, yellow bandana,
marked "Smiley" in gold block letters,
decals with bangs on head, marked "U.S.A."
Value: $1,150

Smiley Pig
11 1/4" high, blue bandana, brown hooves and
brown feet, no gold, marked "U.S.A."
Value: $450-525

Smiley Pig
11 1/4" high, red bandana, chrysanthemum
flowers, no gold, marked "U.S.A."
Value: $400-450

Smiley Pig
11 1/4" high, blue bandana, black buttons, black
hooves, gold and decals, marked "U.S.A."
Value: $650-700

Smiley Pig
11 1/4" high, red bandana, no gold,
tulips, marked "U.S.A."
Value: $525-600

Smiley Pig
11 1/4" high, red bandana, red collar,
gold trim, chrysanthemums,
original sticker on collar, marked "U.S.A."
Value: $700-800

Smiley Pig
11 1/4" high, green bandana, gold trim,
with shamrock flowers, marked "U.S.A."
Value: $600-675

Smiley Pig
11 1/4" high, green bandana, no gold,
with shamrock flowers, marked "U.S.A."
Value: $400-450

Smiley Pig
11 ¹/⁴" high, red bandana, no gold,
with clover bud, marked "U.S.A."
Value: $600-650

Smiley Pig
11 ¹/⁴" high, yellow bandana, red feet, gold trim
and decals, marked "U.S.A."
Value: $650-725

Smiley Pig
11 ¹/⁴" high, yellow bandana, gold and decals,
marked "U.S.A."
Value: $650-725

Smiley Pig
11 ¹/⁴" high, green bandana, gold trim
with roses, marked "U.S.A."
Value: $650-700

Smiley Pig
11 ¹/⁴" high, red collar, cold painted,
(this is the original), marked "U.S.A."
Value: $125

Smiley Pig
11 ¹/⁴" high, chrysanthemum flowers, red collar,
hand painted bug, gold trim, marked "U.S.A."
Value: $750-900

Smiley Pig
11 ¹/⁴" high, very rare, poppy decals,
gold trim, marked "U.S.A."
Value: $975-1,100

Smiley Pig Cookie Jar Bank Head
11 ¹/⁴" high, butterscotch pants,
trimed in gold, marked "#60 U.S.A."
Value: $850-950

Smiley Pig Cookie Jar Bank Head
11 ¹/⁴" high, no gold, brown pants,
marked "Smiley #60, U.S.A."
Value: $550-625

Smiley Pig Cookie Jar Bank Head
11 1/4" high, gold trim, brown pants,
marked "U.S.A. #60".
Value: $850-950

Winnie Pig Cookie Jar Bank Head
11 1/2" high, gold trim, brown coat,
marked "Shawnee Winnie 61 U.S.A."
Value: $850-950

Winnie Pig
11 1/2" high, brown coat, no bank in head,
marked "Shawnee Winnie U.S.A."
Value: $1,100

Winnie Pig
11 1/2" high, brown coat, view of top of hat,
(should have been a bank, but for some reason was decided against).
Marked "USA", (two views shown).
Value: $1,100

Winnie Pig Cookie Jar Bank Head
11 1/2" high, butterscotch coat,
marked "Shawnee Winnie 61, U.S.A."
Value: $550-625

Winnie Pig
11 1/2" high, green coat, gold trim, very rare,
marked "U.S.A."
Value: $1,500-1,900

Winnie Pig
11 1/2" high, gold trim, clover bud in hat,
green collar, hard to find, marked "U.S.A."
Value: $1,400-1,600

Winnie Pig
11 1/2" high, gold trim, original sticker,
blueberries in hat, harder to find, marked "U.S.A."
Value: $950-1,100

Winnie Pig
11 1/2" high, bright green collar, very rare jar, peach flower in hat, gold trim, marked "U.S.A."
Value: $1,400-1,600

Winnie Pig
11 1/2" high, peach collar, gold trim, marked "U.S.A."
Value: $900-1,000

Winnie Pig
11 1/2" high, maroon collar, clover blooms in hat, very unusual, marked "U.S.A."
Value: $1,200

Winnie Pig
11 1/2" high, clover blossoms, harder to find, no gold, marked "U.S.A."
Value: $700-800

Winnie Pig
11 1/2" high, gold trim, red collar, marked "U.S.A."
Value: $750-850

Winnie Pig
11 1/2" high, unusual design in lid, China paint red collar, gold trim, red feet, marked "U.S.A."
Value: $1,100-1,250

Winnie Pig
11 1/2" high, peach collar, no gold, marked "U.S.A."
Value: $375-425

Winnie Pig
11 1/2" high, blue collar, no gold, marked "U.S.A."
Value: $375-425

Winnie Pig
11 1/2" high, green collar, no gold, marked "U.S.A."
Value: $375-425

Winnie Pig
11 1/2" high, blue collar, gold trim,
marked "U.S.A."
Value: $750-850

Owl Cookie Jar
11 1/2" high, no gold, marked "U.S.A."
Value: $150-175

Owl Cookie Jar
11 1/2" high, gold trim, all brushed
in brown, marked "U.S.A."
Value: $350-425

Chef Baker
8 1/2" high, marked "U.S.A."
Value: $150-195

Chef Baker
8 1/2" high, all green, marked "U.S.A."
Value: $195-250

Chef Baker
8 1/2" high, butterscotch, marked "U.S.A."
Value: $195-250

Muggsy
11 3/4" high, blue scarf, gold trim,
marked "U.S.A."
Value: $550-600

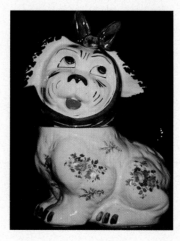

Muggsy
11 3/4" high, gold trim, flowered decals,
marked "Patented Muggsy U.S.A.", (two different variations shown here).
Value: $895-1100

Muggsy
11 3/4" high, gold trim,
unusual rose decals, marked "U.S.A."
Value: $950-1,200

Muggsy
11 3/4" high, green scarf, gold trim,
flowered decals, very rare, marked "U.S.A."
Value: $2,200-2,400

Muggsy
11 3/4" high, gold trim,
unusual design, marked "U.S.A."
Value: $1,600-1,800

Happy
gold trim, flowered decals, marked "U.S.A."
Value: $375-425

Happy
gold trim, red tie, blue pants
with patches, marked "U.S.A."
Value: $450-525

Happy
gold trim, striped pants, flowered decals,
marked "U.S.A.".
Value: $400-450

Happy
gold trim, striped pants, petit point flower
decals, marked "U.S.A."
Value: $400-450

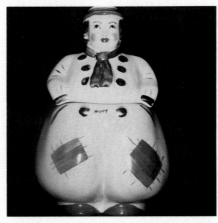

Happy
gold trim, blue pants with patches,
marked "U.S.A."
Value: $450-525

Happy
gold trim, flowered decals on
pants with patch, unusual, marked "U.S.A."
Value: $495-525

Happy
gold trim, yellow pants,
flowered decals, marked "U.S.A."
Value: $395-450

Happy
gold trim, blue pants with patches,
blond hair, marked "U.S.A."
Value: $495-525

Dutch Boy
striped pants, no gold, marked "U.S.A.".
Value: $195-295

Dutch Boy
double striped pants, no gold,
marked "U.S.A.".
Value: $500-650

Dutch Boy
cold painted, yellow pants, marked "U.S.A.".
Value: $95-125

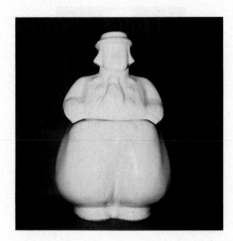

Dutch Boy
cold painted, blue pants, marked "U.S.A.".
Value: $95-125

Dutch Boy
cold painted, blue tie,
brown buttons, marked "U.S.A.".
Value: $95-125

Dutch Boy
striped pants, blue tie,
original sticker, marked "U.S.A.".
Value: $195-295

Great Northern Dutch Boy
butterscotch pants, yellow jacket, blue buttons,
marked "Great Northern 1025".
Value: $450-550

Great Northern Dutch Girl
green dress, blond hair,
marked "Great Northern 1026".
Value: $450-550

Great Northern Dutch Girl
blue and white dress, brown hair,
marked "Great Northern 1026".
Value: $400-475

Cooky
12 ¹⁄₄" high, gold trim, blue hat,
blond hair, tulip, flower decals, marked "U.S.A.".
Value: $450-495

Cooky
gold trim, blue hat, brown hair, tulip, flower
decals, marked "U.S.A.".
Value: $450-495

Cooky
very, very rare, all hand painted,
unusual flower designs all over skirt,
soft muted colors, marked "U.S.A.".
Value: $600+

Cooky
beautiful maroon hat, gold trim, beautiful spray
of flower design decals, marked "U.S.A.".
Value: $550-650

Cooky
green hat, yellow dress, gold trim,
bouquets of flowers, marked "U.S.A."
Value: $350-425

Cooky
green hat, yellow dress, gold trim, flower decals,
hand painted border, marked "U.S.A."
Value: $495-525

Cooky
blue hat, yellow dress, gold trim,
flowered decals, marked "U.S.A."
Value: $495-525

Cooky
gold trim, flowered decals,
marked "U.S.A."
Value: $300-350

Cooky
blue dress, gold trim, decals, marked "U.S.A."
Value: $395-425

Dutch Girl
12" high, no gold, tulip on skirt,
marked "U.S.A."
Value: $295-325

Dutch Girl
cold paint, blue hat, yellow skirt,
marked "U.S.A."
Value: $95-125

Dutch Girl
cold painted, yellow hat, yellow skirt,
marked "U.S.A."
Value: $95-125

Carousel Cookie Jar
designed by Robert Heckman,
red and yellow, marked "U.S.A. S4".
Value: $300-375

Pennsylvania Dutch Jug
8 1/4" high, tulips and heart design,
marked "U.S.A. 75".
Value: $195-225

Cottage House Cookie Jar , marked "U.S.A. #6". – **Value: $1,100-1,300**

Cottage House Teapot, marked "U.S.A. #7". – **Value: $650-800**

Cottage House Sugar Bowl, 6 3/4" high, marked "U.S.A. #8". – **Value: $450-500**

Cottage House Salt & Pepper Shakers, marked "U.S.A. #9". – **Value: $300-400**

Carousel Cookie Jar
designed by Robert Heckman,
pink and blue, marked "U.S.A. S4".
Value: $300-375

Lucky the Elephant
12" high, (rear view and front view shown here),
hand painted flowers all over back of jar.
Value: $1,200

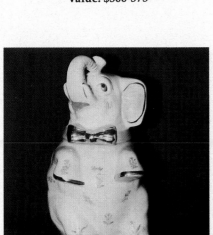

Lucky the Elephant
12" high, gold and decals, marked "U.S.A.".
Value: $950-1,100

Fernware Cookie Jar
8 3/4" high, marked "U.S.A."
Value: $45-85

King Corn Cookie Jar
10 1/2" high, marked "#66, U.S.A.".
Value: $195-250

Corn Queen Cookie Jar
10 1/2" high, original sticker,
marked "#66 U.S.A.".
Value: $250-295

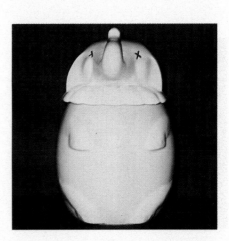

Octagon Cookie Jar
decals, gold trim, marked "U.S.A."
Value: $125-195

Pink Elephant Cookie Jar/Ice Bucket
10 1/2" high, white collar, no gold,
marked "Shawnee #60".
Value: $200-250

Jug
8 1/4" high, marked "U.S.A.",
(two different color variations shown here).
Value: $195-225

Jo Jo The Clown
9 1/2" high, gold trim, hard to find,
Shawnee #12.
Value: $950-1,100

Jo Jo The Clown
9 1/2" high, no gold, Shawnee #12.
Value: $450-550

Drum Major
10" high, no gold, marked "U.S.A. #10".
Value: $550-600

Drum Major
10" high, gold trim, hard to find,
marked "U.S.A. #10".
Value: $950-1,100

Sailor Boy
blond hair, gold trim, flowered decals, marked "U.S.A."
Value: $1,200-1,400

Sailor Boy
blond hair, gold trim, no decals, larger in size,
very unusual, marked "U.S.A."
Value: $1,200-1,400

Sailor Boy
black hair, gold trim, hard to find,
marked "U.S.A."
Value: $1,200

Sailor Boy
black hair, gold trim, original
painter's palette label, marked "U.S.A."
Value: $1,200

338

Sailor Boy
cold painted, blue scarf, marked "U.S.A."
Value: $150-195

Sailor Boy
blond hair, gold trim,
flower decals, marked "U.S.A."
Value: $1,200-1,400

Sailor Boy
blond hair, gold trim, blue collar,
flower decals, original label marked "U.S.A."
Value: $1,200-1,400

Puss-n-Boots
10 ½" high, thick gold trim, flowered decals, tail
over foot, marked "U.S.A."
Value: $575-650

Puss-n-Boots
10 ¼" high, short tail, maroon bow,
marked "Puss-In-Boots U.S.A."
Value: $195-225

Puss-n-Boots
gold trim, maroon bow, flowered decals,
marked "U.S.A."
Value: $550-650

Puss-n-Boots
10 ¼" high, gold trim, white bow,
flowered decals, marked "U.S.A."
Value: $700-800

Puss-n-Boots
plain, tail over the foot, marked "U.S.A."
Value: $195-225

Puss-n-Boots
gold trim, flowered decals,
slight variation in design, marked "U.S.A."
Value: $550-650

Shawnee Commemorative Cookie Jars

Shawnee Commemorative Cookie Jars were first produced in 1992, from the idea that it was Smiley's 50th birthday and that we should help celebrate his birthday by doing a Commemorative Happy 50th Birthday Smiley Cookie Jar. The response from the collectors was incredible. Everyone kept asking for more. Most of the jars were in Limited Editions of 150 pieces, except for the Sailor Boy which was done at 100 pieces with blond hair and 100 pieces with black hair. At the present time, we are now designing the 1995 Edition of the Strawberry Winnie and Smiley Cookie Jars. All editions sold out immediately and have sold very well on the secondary market. The jars are made by Shirley Corl of the Corl Pottery Company of Caro, Michigan. Each jar is hand decorated, and at the bottom of each, impressed into the pottery reads, "Mark Supnick's Commemorative Edition", the year, the name of the jar, USA, Mark Supnick's signature, the jar number, and Shirley Corl's signature. There is no way that these jars can be tampered with.

 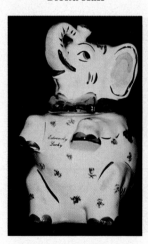 

Sailor Boy
Celebrating 50 Years of Service, 1942-1992, Ltd. Ed. of 100 Jars,
marked "Designed by S. A. Corl, Produced by Mark Supnick Sailor Boy 1992".
(different hair color variation).
Value: $400+

Sailor Boy
blond hair, Celebrating 50 Years of Service,
1942-1992, Ltd. Ed. of 100 Jars, marked
"Designed by S. A. Corl, Produced by Mark
Supnick Sailor Boy 1992", made especially for
Mark Supnick, (different hair color variation).
Value: $400+

Black Hair   **Blond Hair**

 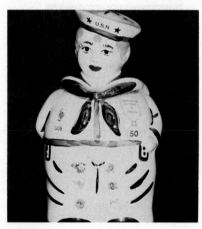 

Wonderful Winnie
solid gold collar, clover bud design, limited
edition of 150, marked "Wonderful Winnie 1993"
Value: $400+

Extremely Lucky
limited edition of 150, marked
"Extremely Lucky 1993".
Value: $400+

Purr-fect Puss-n-boots
limited edition of 150, marked
"Purr-fect Puss-in-boots 1993".
Value: $400+

Smiley's Stash Cookie Jar/Bank Head
marked "Purr-fect Puss-in-Boots 1993",
test pattern color, .
Value: $400+

Mugnificent Muggsy
red scarf, test glaze,
marked "Mugnificent Muggsy 1992".
Value: $400+

Mugnificent Muggsy
green scarf, limited edition of 150,
marked "Mugnificent Muggsy 1992".
Value: $400+

**Bank on Muggsy
Cookie Jar Bank Head**
limited edition of 150, larger size than 1992 edition, marked "Mugnificent Muggsy 1994",
(two views shown here).
Value: $400+

**Windfall Winnie
Cookie Jar Bank Head**
marked "Windfall Winnie 1994".
Value: $400+

Windfall Winnie
**test colors, not produced, blue coat, peach
collar, marked "Windfall Winnie 1994".
No Value**

Smiley's Stash Cookie Jar/Bank Head
150 in Edition, marked "Smiley's Stash 1994".
Value: $400+

Happy 50th Birthday Smiley
blue collar, test glaze, only 1 produced.
First jar in Commemorative Series,
marked "Smiley 1992".
Value: $400+

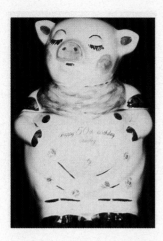

Happy 50th Birthday Smiley
blue collar, limited edition of 150,
marked "Smiley 1992".
Value: $400

Happy 50th Birthday Smiley
yellow collar, black hair, only 15 jars were
produced, marked "Smiley 1992".
Value: $550+

Happy 50th Birthday Smiley
green collar, black hair, made for Mark & Ellen
Supnick 1992, marked "Smiley 1992".
Value: $550+

Happy 50th Birthday Smiley
blue collar, black hair, "Sunshine Collectibles"
in gold, made for Mark & Ellen Supnick 1992,
marked "Smiley 1992".
Value: $550+

Happy 50th Birthday Smiley
pink collar, test glaze, only 1 produced.
First jar in Commemorative Series,
marked "Smiley 1992".
Value: $400+

Berry Winnie
limited edition of 100, hand painted
Strawberries, blond hair, gold collar,
marked "Berry Winnie 1995".
Value: $185 Issue Price

Wonderful Winnie
with hand painted Strawberries, gold collar, Christmas gift to Supnicks from Bill & Shirley Corl,
marked "Wonderful Winnie 1993", (two different views of same jar).
Value: $185

Berry Smiley
limited edition of 100, hand painted Strawberries, blond hair,
marked "Berry Smiley 1995", (two different views shown here).
Value: $185 Issue Price

Sierra Vista

Sierra Vista, was a family business and co-owned by Reinhold Lenaburg and his son William. They operated out of Pasadena, California from 1944 until 1951, when Mr. Lenaburg retired and sold his part of the business to William. William moved the business to Phoenix, Arizona. After he moved, they stopped producing cookie jars. Starnes is located in Los Angeles, California. Not much knowledge is known about this company, but you often see the Starnes Paper Label on Sierra Vista cookie jars and also on American Bisque Company items. Starnes was believed to be a jobber.

Squirrel
10 1/2" high, Starnes paper label,
marked "Sierra Vista Ceramics Pasadena CA".
Value: $225-250

Rooster
12" high, Starnes paper label, marked "Sierra
Vista CA", also available in earth tones.
Value: $75-95

Doghouse with Howling Cat Finial
Starnes paper label,
marked "Genuine Hand Made Starnes CA".
Value: $350-450

Rag Doll
original Starnes paper label,
marked "Starnes".
Value: $350-400

Train
9 3/4" high, Starnes paper label,
marked "Sierra Vista CA",
(also available with gold trim).
Value: $175-250

Rooster Cylinder
marked "Sierra Vista CA".
Value: $95-100

Queen Bee
original Starnes paper label,
marked "Starnes, Made in CA".
Value: $475-575

Boy with Crown
unmarked.
Value: $750-900

Girl with Crown
original Starnes paper label,
marked "Starnes, Made in CA".
Value: $750-900

Family Circus Billy
unmarked, believed to be Starnes, (two different color variations).
Value: $750-850

Family Circus Dolly
unmarked, believed to be Starnes.
Value: $750-850

Tuggles
9 1/4" high, marked "Sierra Vista".
Value: $175-250

Tuggles
9 1/4" high, marked "Sierra Vista CA USA".
Value: $175-250

Owl
10 1/2" high, marked "Sierra Vista CA Copyright".
Value: $95-125

French Poodle
marked "Sierra Vista Ceramics,
Pasadena, CA Copyright 1956".
Value: $275-325

Clown
11" high, marked "Sierra Vista CA",
(also available in brown tones).
Value: $75-95

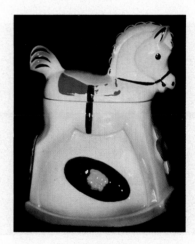

Hobby Horse
paper label, marked "Starnes".
Value: $375-475

Clock
unmarked.
Value: $350-450

Noah's Ark
original Starnes paper label,
marked "Starnes, Made in USA",
"Pat. Pend. Starnes CA Copyright".
Value: $325-375

Noah's Ark
unusual colors, original Starnes paper label,
marked "Starnes, Made in USA",
"Pat. Pend. Starnes CA Copyright".
Value: $450-475

Pinnochio on Whale
unmarked, believed to be Starnes.
Value: $750-825

Froggy Goes a Courtin'
unmarked, believed to be Starnes.
Value: $575-650

Old Jalopy
paper label, marked "Starnes".
Value: $350-375

Humpty Dumpty
11 3/4" high, marked "Sierra Vista Ceramics Copyright 57 Pasadena CAL",
(two different variations shown here).
Value: $525-575

Dog on a Drum
marked "Sierra Vista CA".
Value: $350-375

Cottage
marked "Sierra Vista CA
Copyright 53 CA 1953 USA".
Value: $175-225

Cottage
marked "Sierra Vista CA
Copyright 53 CA 1953 USA".
Value: $225-250

Castle
marked "Sierra Vista Pasadena CA".
Value: $550-650

Stagecoach
marked "Sierra Vista Pasadena
CA USA Copyright 1956".
Value: $425-495

Spaceship
marked "Sierra Vista Ceramics
Pasadena CA Copyright 57 USA".
Value: $700-800

Davy Crockett
marked "Sierra Vista of Calif. Copyright".
Value: $1,100-1,400

ABC Bear
original Starnes paper label,
marked "Sierra Vista Ceramics CA USA".
Value: $300-350

Dutch Girl
marked "Sierra Vista Ceramics
Pasadena Copyright 1957".
Value: $225-250

Monkey on Pot
marked "Sierra Vista CA", hard jar to find.
Value: $325-350

Sigma

Sigma was an import business company that did many different types of pottery, but were very well known for their beautiful cookie jars that include Jim Henson Muppet Jars, Storybook characters, as well as other unusual jars.

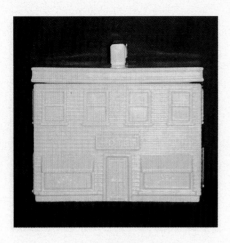

Hotel
marked "American Roadside John Beeder
for Sigma, the Tastesetter".
Value: $225-250

Pix Theater
marked "American Roadside John Beeder
for Sigma, the Tastesetter".
Value: $250-275

Peter Max
stamped "Peter Max", paper label
"Copyright Peter Max 1989 Made in Japan".
Value: $525-575

Fat Cat
marked "Sigma the Tastesetter".
Value: $365-425

Hortense
marked "Sigma the Tastesetter".
Value: $225-275

Rabbit
marked "Sigma the Tastesetter".
Value: $250-295

Mrs. Tiggy-Winkle
marked "From the Tale of Mrs Tiggy-Winkle by
Beatrix Potter, Illus. by Allen Atkinson,
Sigma, the Tastesetter".
Value: $450-525

Kabuki Dancer
marked "Kabuki Copyright
Sigma the Tastesetter".
Value: $275-325

Hearts and Flowers
marked "Tastesetter by Sigma",
designed by Nanci Goldstein.
Value: $250-325

Vend-A-Cart Lady
paper label reads "Tastesetter by Sigma".
Value: $600-725

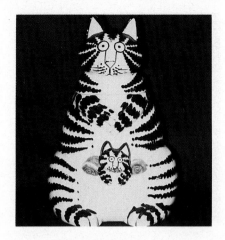

Fireman Dog
marked "Sigma the Tastesetter MCMLXXXIV".
Value: $325-350

Kilban Cat
10 3/4" high, marked "Copyright Sigma the Tastesetter Designed by Copyright B. Kilban".
Value: $425-450

Kilban Cat Playing Guitar
marked "B. Kilban Tastesetter Sigma".
Value: $250-295

Kilban Cat in Tall Pants
marked "B. Kilban Tastesetter Sigma".
Value: $275-300

Kilban Cat in Top Hat
marked "B. Kilban Tastesetter Sigma".
Value: $275-325

Miss Piggy on Cushion
paper label, marked "Jim Henson Muppets, Sigma the Tastesetter".
Value: $125-150

Kermit on TV
marked "Sigma the Tastesetter, Copyright Henson & Assoc. Made in Japan".
Value: $700-850

Miss Piggy Bank
incised "Sigma", marked "Tastesetter Copyright Sigma Made in Japan".
Value: $65-95

Kermit on Stack of Mattresses
paper label marked "Jim Henson Muppets
Copyright Sigma".
Value: $175-250

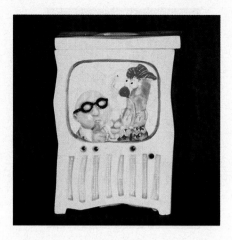

**Dr. Benson Honeydew &
Assistant Beaker"**
paper label reads "Sigma the Tastesetter
Copyright Jim Henson & Assoc."
Value: $175-250

Muppets' Old Men in Balcony
marked "Jim Henson – The Muppets, Copyright,
Sigma the Tastesetter".
Value: $200-250

**Miss Piggy & Friend in TV
From The Show Pigs in Space**
marked "Jim Henson – The Muppets,
Sigma the Tastesetter".
Value: $200-250

Kermit Creamer & Muppet Sugar Bowl
marked "Jim Henson Muppets, Sigma".
Value: $225-250 a set

Miss Piggy on Top of Piano with Rowlf
marked "Jim Henson, Muppets,
Sigma the Tastesetter".
Value: $350-395

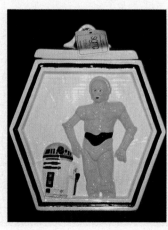

Star Wars Turnabout
10 1/2" high, C3PO & R2D2 on one side, the other side is Darth Vader, (both sides shown here).
Marked "Copyright Lucas Film Ltd. Trademarks Owned by Lucafilm Ld. and
Used by Sigma the Tastesetter Under Authorization TM".
Value: $150-195

Circus Man
marked "Sigma the Tastesetter".
Value: $175-225

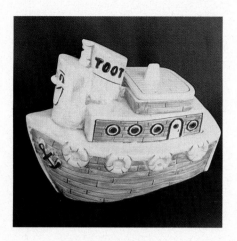

Tootie the Tugboat
marked "Sigma the Tastesetter".
Value: $325-350

Agatha
marked "Agatha, Tastesetter by Sigma,
Designed by David Strauss".
Value: $275-350

Panda Chef
marked "Sigma the Tastesetter".
Value: $275-325

Last Elegant Bear
marked "The Last Elegant Bear,
Dennis Kyte, for Sigma the Tastesetter,
Copyright MCMLXXXIV".
Value: $350-375

Goose Cylinder
marked "Sigma the Tastesetter".
Value: $150-175

Circus Lady
marked "Circus, David Strauss, Tastesetter,
Copyright Sigma, Made in Japan", hand decorated.
Value: $350-395

Theodore Dog
marked "Sigma the Tastesetter".
Value: $375-425

Planetary Pal
marked "Planetary Pals by David Hyman for
Sigma the Tastesetter Copyright MCMLXXXIV".
Value: $300-375

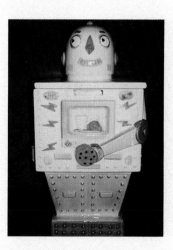

Planetary Pal
marked "Planetary Pals by David Hyman for
Sigma the Tastesetter Copyright MCMLXXXIV".
Value: $300-375

Baby Pig Clown
marked "Cara Marks for Sigma the Tastesetter".
Value: $350-395

Mixing Bowl Duck
marked "Cara Marks for Sigma the Tastesetter".
Value: $225-275

Fireman Beaver
marked "Cara Marks for
Sigma the Tastesetter 'R'".
Value: $275-350

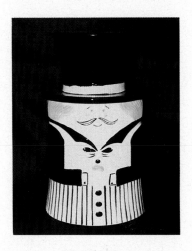

Tuxedo Man
marked "Sigma the Tastesetter Copyright".
Value: $325-350

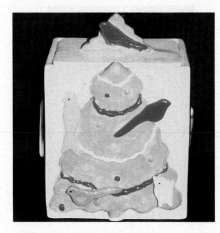

Christmas Tree
marked "Sigma the Tastesetter".
Value: $225-250

Hortense
marked "Sigma the Tastesetter ".
Value: $225-275

Victoria
marked "Sigma the Tastesetter ".
Value: $325-375

Millicent
marked "Sigma the Tastesetter ".
Value: $350-400

Agatha
marked "Sigma the Tastesetter ".
Value: $275-350

Peter Rabbit
marked "Sigma the Tastesetter, Peter Rabbit ".
Value: $275-350

Pig Cylinder
marked "Sigma the Tastesetter ",
designed by KATJA.
Value: $250-325

Snitching Cylinder
marked "Sigma the Tastesetter ".
Value: $150

Kilban Cat with a Kiss on its Face
marked "B. Kilban Sigma the Tastesetter".
Value: $475-500

Storyteller Ceramics

Storyteller Ceramics, El Paso, Texas was created by Rachel Elizondo in 1985. Rachel is a resident of Santa Fe, New Mexico. She produces a complete line of decorative and functional earthenware, along with partner, Lori Johnson. The company continues to develop new ideas to satisfy the demand of an ever-expanding market place for their products. Rachel and Lori look forward to working with their customers in the future and bring them the quality designs that have enjoyed and expect from Storyteller Ceramics.

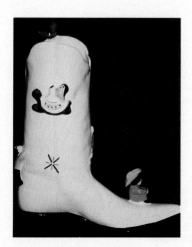

Cowboy Boot
paper label, marked "Storyteller, El Paso TX".
Value: $95-110

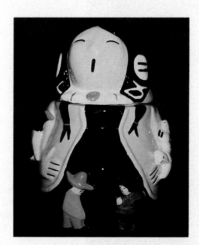

Navajo Woman
paper label, marked "Storyteller, El Paso TX".
Value: $95-110

Storyteller Jar
paper label, marked "Storyteller, El Paso TX".
Value: $125-150

Storyteller Jar
different color pants, paper label, marked
"Storyteller, El Paso TX".
Value: $125-150

Cactus
paper label, marked "Storyteller, El Paso TX".
Value: $40-50

Teepee
paper label, marked "Storyteller, El Paso TX".
Value: $80-110

Denise Teeter

Fred Flintstone, Denise Teeters' first creation, was a great success! Denise and her husband raise horses in Canton, Ohio. Denise has been a cookie jar collector for many years. We hope that Fred Flintstone is not the last, but the first of many wonderful cookie jars to come!

Fred Flintstone Head Jar
created and designed by Denise Teeters, of
Canton, OH, a fabulous jar,
limited edition of 200.
Value: $250-300

Terrace Ceramics

Terrace Ceramics was founded by John Bonistal of Zanesville, Ohio. Mr. Bonistal was the former President of the Shawnee Pottery Company until they closed their doors. Terrace Ceramics used many of the same molds from Shawnee. Terrace was located in Marietta, Ohio before closing in 1974.

Smiley the Pig
11 3/4" high, marked "Terrace Ceramics USA".
Value: $125-150

Winnie the Pig
12 1/4" high, marked "Terrace Ceramics USA".
Value: $125-150

Muggsy
12" high, marked "Muggsy
Terrace Ceramics USA 6256".
Value: $150-195

Teddy Bear
12" high, marked "USA 42514X52".
Value: $110-140

Treasure Craft Company

Treasure Craft Company of Compton, California was founded by Alfred A. Levin in 1945. The family owned and operated the business until November 1988, when it was purchased by the Pfaltzgraff Company of York, Pennsylvania. The older Treasure Craft jars are very sought after by many cookie jar collectors across the country.

The Coach
marked "Treasure Craft Copyright USA",
base is marked "David Kirschner Prod.
All Right Reserved".
Value: $1,100-1,400

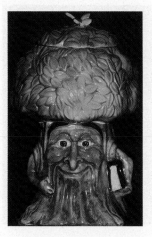

Tree of Knowledge
marked "Treasure Craft Copyright USA",
base is marked "David Kirschner Prod.
All Right Reserved".
Value: $1,200-1,400

Football Coach
8" high, marked "Treasure Craft Copyright USA",
base is marked "Copyright 1983 David Kirschner
Prod. 1983 All Right Reserved".
Value: $425-475

Rose Petal Teapot
marked "Treasure Craft USA",
base is marked "David Kirschner Prod. 1983",
from Rose Petal Place Movie,
Picture on the front is a decal.
Value: $650-775

Seymour the Snail
marked "Treasure Craft Copyright Made in the
USA", "1983 David Kirschner
Prod. All Right Reserved".
Value: $750-900

Hedgehog
marked "Treasure Craft Copyright Made in the
USA", "David Kirschner Prod. 1983
All Right Reserved". Jar comes in two different
ways, marked or unmarked on bottom.
(This jar has markings).
Value: $750-900

Treasure Craft Sign
marked "Made in USA".
Value: $20-25

Old Red Truck Collector Series
1 of 100, Limited Edition, (two views shown here).
This jar was made for Mark & Ellen Supnick as a reissue of Limited Edition of 100 pieces
and 25 Artist Proofs, all were signed by Treasure Craft owner, Bruce Levin.
Value: $450-500

Antique Truck
marked "Treasure Craft Made in USA".
Value: $85-95

Katrina
Only 75 jars were made originally before being
discontinued. Bruce Levin, Past President of Treasure Craft found approx. 40 more pieces of Bisque
and sold 17 to Ellen Supnick and 17 to Carol Piatt,
6 did not make it through the production. Jars are
marked "Treasure Craft USA".
Value: $900-1,100

Baseball Boy
marked "Treasure Craft USA".
Value: $65-75

Nanna Collector Series
test glaze, not produced, one of a kind.
Value: $900-1,100

Nanna Collector Series
high gloss finish, test glaze, one of a kind.
Value: $900-1,100

Nanna Collector Series
high gloss finish, test glaze, one of a kind.
Value: $900-1,100

Nanna
blue dress, matte finish, mass produced.
Value: $75-90

Nanna Collector Series
with a green dress, limited edition of 100,
marked "Treasure Craft USA", made for
Mark & Ellen Supnick.
Value: $325-450

Fox
marked "Treasure Craft USA".
Value: $60-75

Conductor Bear
marked "Treasure Craft USA".
Value: $60-75

Dog on Sled
marked "Treasure Craft USA".
Value: $125-150

Basketball
marked "Treasure Craft USA".
Value: $85-90

Baseball
marked "Treasure Craft USA".
Value: $85-90

Football
marked "Treasure Craft USA".
Value: $85-90

Eight Ball
marked "Treasure Craft USA".
Value: $150-175

Soccer Ball
marked "Treasure Craft USA".
Value: $85-90

Golf Ball
marked "Treasure Craft USA".
Value: $85-90

Log Cabin
marked "Treasure Craft USA".
Value: $60-70

Cowboy with Lasso
marked "Treasure Craft USA".
Value: $60-70

Cowboy Boot
marked "Treasure Craft USA".
Value: $75-85

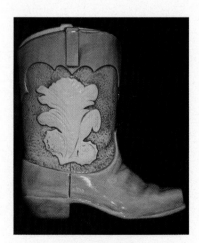

Cowboy Boot
marked "Treasure Craft USA".
Value: $95-110

Indian Tee Pee
marked "Treasure Craft USA".
Value: $60-70

Covered Wagon
marked "Treasure Craft USA".
Value: $60-70

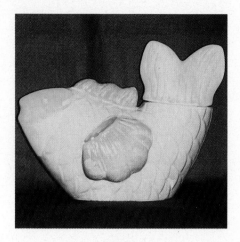

Fish
marked "Treasure Craft USA".
Value: $75-85

Sugar
15 1/2" high, marked "Treasure Craft USA".
Value: $55-65

Spice
15 1/2" high, marked "Treasure Craft USA".
Value: $55-65

Leopard
older jar, marked "Treasure Craft Made in USA".
Value: $95-125

Toucan
marked "Treasure Craft USA".
Value: $75-80

Gingerbread House
10 1/2" high, marked "Treasure Craft USA".
Value: $85-95

Miss Piggy
marked "Treasure Craft Made in Mexico".
Value: $60-75

Wurlitzer Jukebox
11 1/2" high, marked "Treasure Craft USA",
original release.
Value: $125-175

Wurlitzer Jukebox
11 1/2" high, marked "Treasure Craft USA",
newer release, however it was
discontinued shortly after issue.
Value: $125-175

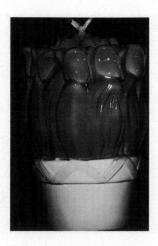

Tulip Time
marked "Treasure Craft Made in USA".
Value: $55-60

Lila the Lamb
marked "Treasure Craft Made in Mexico".
Value: $55-60

Kermit the Frog
marked "Treasure Craft Made in Mexico".
Value: $60-75

Hank Holstein
marked "Treasure Craft Made in Mexico".
Value: $45-55

Oliver Oink
marked "Treasure Craft Made in Mexico".
Value: $55-65

Slot Machine
marked "Treasure Craft Made in USA".
Value: $125-150

Dalmatian with Glass Bowl
marked "Treasure Craft Made in USA".
Value: $60-75

Pig with Overalls
marked "Treasure Craft Made in USA".
Value: $70-75

Victorian House
11 3/4" high, also available in
various color and slight design changes.
Marked "Treasure Craft Made in USA".
Value: $60-75

Cactus
12" high, marked "Treasure Craft Made in USA".
Value: $65-70

Potbellied Stove
marked "Treasure Craft Made in USA".
Value: $75-95

Potbellied Stove
marked "Treasure Craft Made in USA".
Value: $60-65

Monkey
12 1/2" high, marked "Treasure Craft 1968
Copyright Compton CA".
Value: $55-65

Puppy Face Cylinder
marked "Treasure Craft
Copyright Made in USA".
Value: $45-50

Standing Puppy
10" high, marked "Treasure Craft Made in USA",
there is a canister set available in this style.
Value: $65-75

Sienna Stove
marked "Treasure Craft Made in USA".
Value: $185-195

Old Fashioned Radio
marked "Treasure Craft Copyright Made in USA",
(two different variations shown here).
Value: $125-150

Cookie Van
marked "Treasure Craft Made in USA", (two different color variations).
Value: $110-150

Grandma
yellow dress, older version,
marked "Treasure Craft Made in USA".
Value: $125-175

Grandma
blue dress, marked "Treasure Craft Made in USA".
Value: $65-75

Grandma
Afro American, (this jar is a test pattern,
and the only one known to exist).
Value: $1,200-1,400

Honey Bear
marked "Treasure Craft Made in USA".
Value: $95-125

Boot with Gun
incised in pottery "Treasure Craft Copyright
Made in USA".
Value: $75-125

Jack in the Beanstalk
marked "Treasure Craft Made in USA Jack-in-the-Beanstalk".
(on the left is the jar and on the right is the lid by itself).
Value: $200-225

Cookie Cop
marked "Treasure Craft
Copyright Made in USA".
Value: $150-225

Toot Toot Tugboat
marked "Treasure Craft
Copyright Made in USA".
Value: $195-225

Trolley
9 1/2" high, marked "Treasure Craft
Copyright Made in USA".
Value: $150-175

Home Ice Company Truck
marked "Treasure Craft Made in USA".
Value: $110-150

Cat
marked "Treasure Craft Compton CA USA".
Value: $55-65

Lamb
11 1/2" high, marked "Treasure Craft 1968
Copyright Compton CA".
Value: $55-65

Rabbit with Baseball Bat
marked "Treasure Craft
Copyright Compton CA".
Value: $55-65

Cookie Balloon
marked "Treasure Craft Made in USA".
Value: $350-425

Owl
11 ¼" high, marked "Treasure Craft
Made in Compton CA USA".
Value: $40-45

Recipe Books
marked "Treasure Craft Made in USA".
Value: $150-195

Cat
marked "Treasure Craft Made in USA".
Value: $45-50

Teddy Bear
marked "Treasure Craft Made in USA".
Value: $55-60

Monkey
marked "Pet Shop Collection Treasure
Craft Made in USA".
Value: $150-175

Cat
marked "Pet Shop Collection
Treasure Craft Made in USA".
Value: $150-175

Dog
marked "Pet Shop Collection
Treasure Craft Made in USA".
Value: $150-175

Cat
marked "Pet Shop Collection
Treasure Craft Made in USA".
Value: $150-175

Dog
marked "Pet Shop Collection
Treasure Craft Made in USA".
Value: $150-175

Cat
marked "Pet Shop Collection
Treasure Craft Made in USA".
Value: $175-200

Dog
marked "Pet Shop Collection
Treasure Craft Made in USA".
Value: $175-200

Pig
marked "Pet Shop Collection
Treasure Craft Made in USA".
Value: $175-200

Rabbit
marked "Pet Shop Collection
Treasure Craft Made in USA".
Value: $175-200

Cookie Club Mushroom House
marked "Treasure Craft
Copyright Made in USA".
Value: $95-110

Police Chief Bear
marked "Treasure Craft
Copyright Made in USA".
Value: $95-110

Cat with Cookies
marked "Treasure Craft
Copyright Made in USA".
Value: $75-85

Liberty Barn
marked "Treasure Craft Made in USA".
Value: $140-175

Cookie Cylinder
marked "Treasure Craft
Copyright Compton CA".
Value: $35-40

Teddy Bear with Bow Tie
marked "Treasure Craft
Copyright Compton CA".
Value: $55-60

Elf
marked "Treasure Craft
Copyright Compton CA".
Value: $75-80

Dinosaur
marked "Treasure Craft Made in USA".
Value: $75-85

Cowboy with Gun
marked "Treasure Craft
Copyright Made in USA".
Value: $125-150

Owl
marked "Treasure Craft Copyright Compton CA".
Value: $55-60

Owl Shakers
Value: $18-25 a set

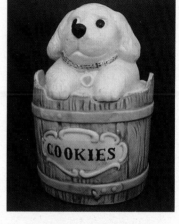

Puppy in Basket
marked "Treasure Craft
Copyright Made in USA".
Value: $75-85

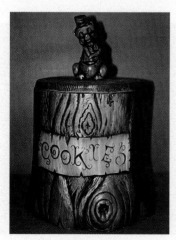

Pig on Stump
marked "#425 Treasure Craft
1964 Copyright CA".
Value: $40-45

Clown
marked "Treasure Craft
Copyright Made in USA".
Value: $125-150

Clown
marked "Treasure Craft
Copyright Made in USA".
Value: $85-95

USN Elephant
marked "Treasure Craft
Copyright Made in USA".
Value: $95-110

Bear with Red Bow
marked "Treasure Craft
Copyright Made in USA".
Value: $55-60

Mrs. Owl
marked "Treasure Craft
Copyright Made in USA".
Value: $45-55

Hobo
paper label reads "Treasure Craft
Copyright Compton CA Made in USA".
Value: $95-110

Cookie Chef
12 1/2" high, marked "Treasure Craft
Copyright Made in USA".
Value: $65-75

Cookie Chef
12 1/2" high, marked "Treasure Craft
Copyright Made in USA".
Value: $75-95

Bear with Drum
marked "Great American Pottery Company
Copyright USA", part of Treasure Craft.
Value: $75-80

Duck
wood tone, marked "Treasure Craft
Copyright Made in USA".
Value: $45-55

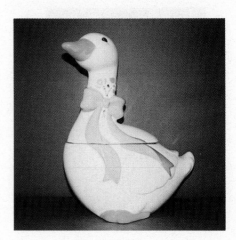

Mother Goose
marked "Treasure Craft
Copyright Made in USA".
Value: $50-55

Covered Wagon
marked "Treasure Craft
Copyright Made in USA".
Value: $55-65

Treasure Chest
marked "Treasure Craft
Copyright 1961 Compton CA".
Value: $125

Noah's Ark
marked "Treasure Craft
Copyright Made in USA".
Value: $125-140

Mother Goose
marked "Treasure Craft
Copyright Made in USA".
Value: $110-125

Blue Ribbon Goose
marked "Treasure Craft Copyright
Compton CA Made in USA".
Value: $95-110

B & R Railroad Train
8" high, marked "Treasure Craft
Copyright Made in USA".
Value: $125

B & R Railroad Train
8" high, marked "Treasure Craft
Copyright Made in USA".
Value: $65-75

Rooster
marked "Treasure Craft Copyright Made in USA",
(two different color variations shown here).
Value: $65-75

Black & White   **Blue & White**

Multicolor Rooster
marked "Treasure Craft
Copyright Compton CA".
Value: $65-75

Cow
marked "Treasure Craft
Copyright Made in USA".
Value: $50-55

Cow
marked "Treasure Craft
Copyright Made in USA".
Value: $55-65

Cat with Mouse Finial
marked "Treasure Craft
Copyright Made in USA".
Value: $85-95

Sheep Dog
7 1/2" high, with butterfly finial,
marked "Treasure Craft
Copyright Made in USA".
Value: $75-95

The Twin Winton Company

The Twin Winton Company was started in 1935 by twins, Don and Ross Winton. In 1946, a third brother, Bruce, joined the company. The Twin Winton Company then moved from Pasadena to San Juan Capistrano and El Monte, California. Cookie jars were produced in a Limited scale in 1951 and were all done in a wood tone finish. In 1974, a Collector Series was introduced. Twin Winton came to an end in 1977 and the molds were purchased by the Treasure Craft Company. Today, Craig Winton, with the guidance of his father, Don Winton, have again entered the field of producing cookie jars.

Dutch Girl Napkin Holder
marked "A.D. Snyder".
Value: $75-125

Dutch Girl
13" high, incised into pottery
"Twin Winton Copyright CA USA".
Value: $225-250

Dutch Girl
13" high, high gloss, highly decorated,
incised "Twin Winton".
Value: $125-150

Dutch Girl
marked "Twin Winton Copyright CA USA".
Value: $160-195

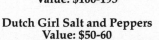

Dutch Girl Salt and Peppers
Value: $50-60

Dutch Girl
under glaze, marked "Twin Winton
Copyright CA USA".
Value: $300-375

Noah's Ark
11" high, orange color,
marked "Twin Winton California Copyright USA".
Value: $195-225

Noah's Ark
11" high, mustard color.
Value: $195-225

Noah's Ark
11" high, high gloss,
marked "Twin Winton California USA".
Value: $300-395

Noah's Ark
blue, marked "Twin Winton Copyright
San Juan Capistrano CA USA".
Value: $195-225

Noah's Ark
brown, marked "Twin Winton
Copyright CA USA".
Value: $195-225

Noah's Ark
brown, paint under glaze,
marked "Twin Winton Copyright CA USA".
Value: $225-350

Cookie Safe
marked "Twin Winton".
Value: $85-95

Pirate Fox Jar
Value: $125-150

Pirate Fox Salt & Peppers
Value: $55-65

Ranger Bear Salt & Pepper Shakers
marked "Japan".
Value: $65

Ranger Bear Wall Pocket
unmarked.
Value: $90-100

Ranger Bear
12 1/4" high, Collector Series, stamped "Twin
Winton Copyright Juan
Capistrano California USA".
Artist's initials, "JL", 1974.
Value: $300-325

Ranger Bear
12 1/4" high, 1975, wood tone.
Value: $60-65

Ranger Bear
marked "Twin Winton California USA".
Value: $150-160

Ranger Bear
gold seal, marked "Beautiful Handcrafted
Ceramics", paper label "Twin Winton CA
San Juan Capistrano".
Value: $85-95

Ranger Bear
green.
Value: $125

Ranger Bear Lamp
marked "Twin Winton",
(these items are very difficult to find).
Value: $450-550

Wheelbarrow
marked "Twin Winton Copyright
San Juan CA USA".
Value: $225-300

Lion Salt & Pepper Shakers
unmarked.
Value: $95 a set

Lion
13 1/2" high, marked "Twin Winton
Copyright California USA".
Value: $195-210

Cookie Time Clock
14 1/4" high, marked "Twin Winton California",
shown in 1965 catalog.
Value: $65-70

Cookie Time Clock
incised "Twin Winton Copyright
60 Made in USA".
Value: $65-70

Train
marked "TW89 Twin Winton
Copyright California USA".
Value: $95

Duck with Mixing Bowl
marked "Twin Winton Copyright
California USA".
Value: $150-165

Teepee
marked "Twin Winton
Copyright California USA".
Value: $300-350

Indian Salt & Peppers
Value: $50-60

Tugboat
unmarked.
Value: $375-400

Dobbin Donkey
14 1/4" high, marked "Twin Winton Made
in San Juan Capistrano". Jar on left is grey in
color and is harder to find.
Value: $200-225 grey only

Dobbin Donkey
14 1/4" high, marked "Twin Winton
Made in USA". (Three Jars on Right).
Value: $150-175 ea.

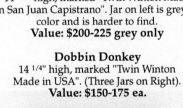

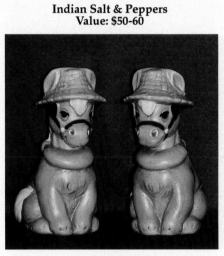

Dobbin Salt & Pepper Shakers
marked "Twin Winton".
Value: $95-110 a set

Castle
under glaze paint, incised "The Twin Wintons",
very unusual and rare jar.
Value: $900-1,100

Bakery
12 1/4" high, inkstamp, gold seal "Beautiful
Hand Crafted Ceramics Made in USA Twin
Winton CA Capistrano 92675", 1965.
Value: $125-150

Owl
11 3/4" high, Collector Series, marked "Twin Winton
Collector Series Copyright California USA".
Value: $95-110 a set

Owl
11 3/4" high, 1965, incised and stamped "Twin
Winton San Juan Capistrano, California".
Value: $65-85

Owl Salt & Peppers
Value: $50-60

Owl
gray, incised "Twin Winton Copyright CA USA".
Value: $65-85

Owl
white, inkstamp "Twin Winton Copyright
CA San Juan Capistrano CA USA".
Value: $65-85

Cookie Cable Car
available in various colors, unmarked.
Value: $85-95

Cookie Cable Car
mustard color.
Value: $85-95

Cookie Cable Car
avacado finish, unmarked.
Value: $85-95

Gunfighter Rabbit Salt & Pepper Shakers
marked "Twin Winton California".
Value: $65-75

Gunfighter Rabbit Cookie Jar
13 1/2" high, Collector Series, incised and
stamped "Twin Winton San Juan Capistrano"
Value: $295-325

Teddy Bear
gray, marked "Twin Winton Copyright
San Juan Capistrano".
Value: $125

Teddy Bear
marked "Twin Winton Copyright
California USA".
Value: $95

Ye Olde Sugar Bucket
part of canister set,
marked "Twin Winton California".
Value: $85-95

Ye Olde Cookie Bucket
7 1/2" high, green color,
marked "Twin Winton Copyright 59".
Value: $75-85

Ye Olde Cookie Bucket
wood tone, marked "Twin Winton Copyright 59".
Value: $75-85

Baby Elephant
marked "Twin Winton Pasadena California".
Value: $175

Train Candy Jar
marked "Twin Winton California".
Value: $90

Dinosaur
marked "1994 Designed by Don Winton,
Produced by Craig Winton".
Value: $150-195

Rooster
Collector Series, marked "Twin Winton
Collector Series Copyright CA USA".
Value: $150-175

Rooster
wood tone, marked "Twin Winton CA".
Value: $100-125

Rooster Salt & Peppers
Value: $50-60

Rooster
paint under glaze, incised "Twin Winton
Copyright", marked "59" in base.
Value: $125

Crooked Shack
12" high, gray, marked "Made in USA
Twin Winton Copyright CA".
Value: $150-160

Crooked Shack
12" high, stamped "Twin Winton Copyright CA".
Value: $95-125

Happy Bull
marked "Twin Winton California Copyright USA".
Value: $85-125

Crooked Shack
incised "Twin Winton Copyright CA USA", (two different color variations shown here).
Value: $125-150

Green   **Orange**

Happy Bull Salt & Pepper Shakers
marked "Twin Winton California Copyright USA".
Value: $65-70

Chipmunk
marked "Twin Winton California Copyright USA".
Value: $125

Friar Tuck Bank
marked "Twin Winton California Copyright USA".
Value: $150

Friar Tuck
12" high, stamped "Twin Winton
Capistrano California USA".
Value: $75-85

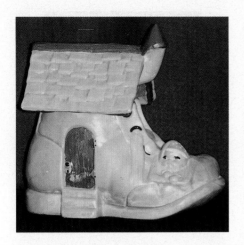

Child in Shoe
10 1/2" high, marked "Twin Winton Copyright
California USA", notice the paint detail,
(shown in 1965 catalog).
Value: $60-65

Child in Shoe
"Twin Winton California USA".
Value: $60-65

Child in Shoe
green, marked "Twin Winton California USA".
Value: $110-115

Mother Goose
13 3/4" high, marked "Twin Winton 1964
Calif. USA Copyright".
Value: $175

Mother Goose Shakers
Value: $85-95 a set

Mother Goose
incised "Twin Winton Collector
Series USA 1962".
Value: $350-375

Mother Goose
gray, marked "Twin Winton Copyright
Made in USA 1962".
Value: $165-195

Cookie Barn
marked "Twin Winton California USA".
Value: $150

Cookie Barn
marked "Beautiful Hand Crafted Ceramics
Made in USA San Juan Capistrano Twin Winton
CA 92675", gold paper label,
cold paint trim under glaze.
Value: $150-175

Cookie Barn
Collector Series, stamped "Twin Winton
Copyright San Juan Capistrano USA",
"Collector Series".
Value: $250-300

Flour Stable
marked "Twin Winton California USA".
Value: $60-65

Sugar Dairy Canister
marked "Twin Winton California USA".
Value: $60-65

Coffee Coop Canister
marked "Twin Winton California USA".
Value: $60-65

Barn Tea Sty
marked "Twin Winton".
Value: $40-45

Barn Salt & Pepper Shakers
marked "Twin Winton".
Value: $55 a set

Flour, Sugar, Coffee, Tea Set
special bright orange color.
Value: $195-225 a set

Sailor Elephant
11 1/2" high, all white stamped "Twin Winton San
Juan Capistrano CA USA".
Value: $125-140

Sailor Elephant Salt & Pepper Shakers
unmarked.
Value: $50-60

Sailor Elephant
Collector Series, stamped "Twin Winton
Copyright San Juan Capistrano USA".
Value: $200-225

Sailor Elephant
incised "Twin Winton Copyright #60
Made in USA".
Value: $150-165

Pot Bellied Stove
marked "Twin Winton California USA".
Value: $130-140

Pot Bellied Stove
bright orange, marked "Twin Winton
San Juan Capistrano CA USA".
Value: $195

Pot Bellied Stove
slightly different design.
Value: $125-140

Cookie Elf
13" high, marked "Twin Winton
California", 1965.
Value: $95-100

Elf Salt & Pepper Shakers
marked "Twin Winton".
Value: $85-95

Cookie Elf
avacado color, unmarked.
Value: $150-175

Cookie Elf
ink stamped "Twin Winton CA USA".
Value: $100-110

Cookie Elf
white, marked "Twin
Winton CA USA Copyright".
Value: $95-100

Cookie Elf
stamped "Twin Winton San Juan Capistano",
incised "Twin Winton CA USA".
Value: $300-325

Cookie Elf
orange.
Value: $100-110

Kittens with a Churn
marked "Twin Winton California USA".
Value: $150-175

Walrus
marked "Twin Winton California USA".
Value: $300-325

Grandma's Cookies
marked "Twin Winton California".
Value: $125-150

Grandma's Cookies Salt & Peppers
Value: $65-75

Grandma's Cookies
marked "Copyright Twin Winton".
Value: $125-150

Persian Cat
marked "Twin Winton California Copyright 63".
Value: $200-225

Persian Cat Salt & Pepper Shakers
marked "Twin Winton".
Value: $65-70 a set

Squirrel on Nut
marked "Twin Winton Copyright CA USA".
Value: $75-95

Cookie Coach
unmarked.
Value: $175-200

Cookie Coach
marked "Twin Winton California USA".
Value: $125-150

Raggedy Ann
Collector Series,. ink stamped
"San Juan Capistrano CA USA".
Value: $275-325

Raggedy Andy
marked "Twin Winton Collector
Series CA Copyright USA", 1975.
Value: $275-325

Cookie Stove
brown, marked "Twin Winton California
USA", available in various colors.
Value: $85-110

Cookie Stove
red, unmarked.
Value: $150

Hotei
stamped "Twin Winton Copyright
California USA", 1965, artist signed.
Value: $100-125

Hotei Salt & Peppers
Value: $50-60

Hotei
inkstamped "Twin Winton Copyright
San Juan Capistrano CA USA".
Value: $175-225

Coffee Grinder
unmarked.
Value: $195-200

Candy House
unmarked.
Value: $50-55

Suspenders Hillbilly Ice Bucket
marked "Twin Winton California USA".
Value: $300-375

Wood Finish Hillbilly Ice Bucket with Jug
marked "Twin Winton Made
in California USA 1962".
Value: $300-350

Hillbilly Taking A Bath
marked "Twin Winton Copyright
1962 Made in California USA".
Value: $400-450

Hillbilly "Bottoms Up"
marked "Twin Winton Copyright CA USA".
Value: $400-450

Hillbilly Outhouse
unmarked.
Value: $375-425

Grandma
a hard to find jar, marked "Twin Winton
California USA", 1962.
Value: $125-165

Santa with Bag of Toys
marked "Don Winton" in script on side of jar,
under glaze paint, (wonderful jar).
Value: $700-900

Santa with Bag of Toys
designed by Don Winton, first jar for new
company, painted & produced by Craig Winton.
Value: $175+

Deer on Stump
marked "Twin Winton California USA".
Value: $150-195

Cookie Catcher
marked "Twin Winton Pasadena California".
Value: $150-175

Cookie Catcher
gray, unmarked.
Value: $125

Dog on a Drum
marked "Twin Winton Copyright California USA".
Value: $300-350

Dog in Basket
circular stamp "Twin Winton Copyright
El Monte California".
Value: $80-85

Cat in Basket
circular stamp "Twin Winton Copyright
El Monte California".
Value: $80-85

Tortoise & The Hare
marked "Twin Winton California
USA Copyright 63".
Value: $150-175

Howard Johnson's Restaurant
the rarest of the rare of Twin Winton, marked "Twin Winton USA", most sought after jar.
(two views shown here).
Value: $2,500+

Little Lamb
Collector Series, stamped "Twin Winton
Copyright San Juan Capistrano USA",
incised "Twin Winton USA".
Value: $250-300

Cable Car Candy Jar
high gloss, extremely rare piece, documented by Don Winton,
Found by Donna Gainey in Oklahoma City.
(two views shown here one of the jar and one of the bottom showing the markings).
Value: $400+

Hobby Horse
stamped "Twin Winton Collector Series
Copyright CA USA".
Value: $300-325

Sailor Mouse
under glaze, marked "Twin Winton CA San Juan
Capistrano CA 92675" golf gold paper label.
Value: $175-250

Sailor Mouse
marked "Twin Winton USA".
Value: $75-95

Sailor Mouse
11 1/4" high, 1975, marked "Twin Winton
Collector Series USA".
Value: $300-325

Frog
marked "Twin Winton California USA".
Value: $250-295

Keystone Cop
13" high, 1965, marked "Twin Winton USA".
Value: $95-110

Keystone Cop Salt & Peppers
Value: $50-60

Keystone Cop
marked "Twin Winton San Juan Capistrano".
Value: $275-325

Pirate Fox
Collector Series, marked "Twin Winton Made in California USA", stamped "Twin Winton Capistrano".
Value: $350-375

Butler Napkin Holder
hard to find piece, marked "Twin Winton Copyright California", 1965.
Value: $150-195

Butler
incised "Twin Winton Copyright CA USA".
Value: $275-300

Cookie House Jar
unmarked.
Value: $225-250

Cookie House Salt & Peppers
Value: $95-125

Mallard Duck
stamped "Twin Winton Copyright San Juan Capistrano CA USA".
Value: $200-225

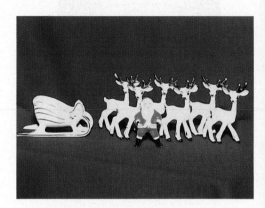

Santa and Reindeer Figurines
only two known to exist, marked "Twin Winton Ceramics Pasadena CA".
Value: $500+

Wagon Salt & Pepper Shakers
Value: $65-75 a set

Cookie Wagon
incised and stamped "Twin Winton Pasadena California".
Value: $225-250

Cow
marked "Twin Winton California USA".
Value: $75-95

Tommy Turtle
8 1/2" high, marked "Twin Winton San Juan
Capistrano California USA", Made in 1965.
Value: $150-175

Tommy Turtle Salt & Peppers
Value: $50-60

Squirrel Salt & Pepper Shakers
marked "Twin Winton".
Value: $50-60 a set

Squirrel with Cookie
white, ink stamped "Twin Winton Copyright
San Juan Capistrano USA".
Value: $65-75

Squirrel with Cookie
10 3/4" high, marked "Twin Winton Copyright
El Monte California USA"
Value: $60-65

Squirrel Napkin Holder
Value: $60-75

Poodle at Cookie Counter Jar
marked "Twin Winton Copyright USA".
Value: $150-165

Poodle at Cookie Counter Salt & Peppers
Value: $65-75

Twinton Figurines Dealer Plaque
hard to find piece,
marked "Twinton Copyright 1972 T-21".
Value: $350-475

Twin Winton Creations Dealer Plaque
Value: $350-475

Standing Pig
marked "Twin Winton Copyright CA USA".
Value: $175-225

Guard House
unmarked.
Value: $400-525

Old King Cole
marked "Twin Winton Copyright CA USA".
Value: $500+

Hen
Value: $125-175

Hen Salt & Peppers
Value: $50-65

Sheriff Bear
11" high, marked "Copyright California USA".
Value: $65-85

Sheriff Bear
11" high, marked "Twin Winton
Collector Series USA".
Value: $275-325

Kangaroo Jar
marked "Twin Winton CA USA".
Value: $325-375

Kangaroo Salt & Peppers
Value: $150

Apple
unmarked.
Value: $175-200

Apple
orange, ink stamped "Twin Winton
Copyright San Juan Capistrano".
Value: $175-200

Donkey Cookie Cart
unmarked.
Value: $110-125

Donkey Jar
marked "Twin Winton Copyright CA USA".
Value: $150-165

Donkey Salt & Peppers
Value: $75-85

Donkey Jar
marked "Twin Winton Collector Series".
Value: $275-325

Pot O'Cookies
marked "Twin Winton Copyright CA USA".
Value: $60-65

Pot O'Cookies
under glaze "Beautiful Handcrafted Ceramics",
"Twin Winton Collector Series Copyright CA
San Juan Capistrano USA 92675", gold paper label.
Value: $200-225

Pot O'Cookies
pineapple finish, marked "Twin Winton
Collector Series Copyright CA USA".
Value: $125-150

Fire Engine
brown, marked "Twin Winton
Copyright CA USA".
Value: $75-95

Fire Engine
red, marked "Twin Winton California USA".
Value: $95-125

Vandor

Vandor is an importer/distributor, based in Salt Lake City, Utah, and has been in business for 37 years.

Howdy Doody Head Bank
marked "Vandor, Made in Japan".
Value: $75

Howdy Doody Bumper Car
8 1/2" high, marked "1988 Vandor, Copyright".
Value: $425-475

Howdy Doody Head Jar
10" high, paper label
"Vandor, Made in Japan".
Value: $350-450

Fred & Pebbles in Chair
10" high, paper label
"Vandor, 1988, Made in Japan".
Value: $450-550

Standing Fred Flintstone
paper label reads"Vandor 1989",
paper label reads "Made in Korea".
Value: $175-275

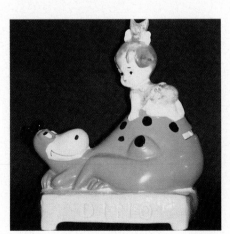

Dino & Pebbles Bank
unmarked.
Value: $150

Betty Boop
paper label reads "Copyright 1983,
KFC Corp., Vandor".
Value: $150

Betty Boop
marked "Copyright 1985, King
Features Syndicate Inc."
Value: $1,100-1,200

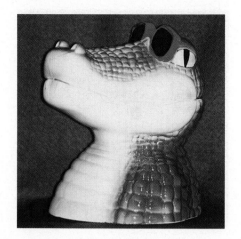

Crocagator
marked "Vandor".
Value: $95-125

Jukebox
marked "Vandor".
Value: $175-200

The Radio
marked "Vandor".
Value: $75-95

Beethoven's Piano
marked "Vandor".
Value: $60-75

Cowmen Moo-Randa
9 3/4" high, marked "Copyright Vandor 1988".
Value: $250-325

Cowmen Moo-Randa Matching Shaker
Value: $125s

Baseball Cookie Jar
marked "The Great American Game, Copyright
1991 Pelzman Designs Taiwan, Vandor".
(Many other accessories available).
Value: $60

Swee' Pea Bank
marked "Vandor".
Value: $225-300

Popeye
8 1/2" high, **paper label "Copyright 1980 King Features Syndicate".**
Value: $500-550

Cowboy Cookie Jar
stamped "American Frontier Copyright, 1991 Pelzman Designs Taiwan, Vandor".
Value: $65-75

Mona Lisa
Vandor, 1992, Pelzman Designs, Made in Sri Lanka.
Value: $65-75

Socks the First Cat
marked "1994, Vandor".
Value: $50-65

The Court Jester
marked "Vandor".
Value: $900-1,100

Walt Disney Productions

Walter Disney, born in Chicago, Illinois on December 5, 1901, worked as a commercial artist and cartoonist. His first movie, Steamboat Willie, was made in 1928. This was the start of an incredible career. Many different companies over the years have been given licenses for producing various types of Disney products. At the present time, Disney products are marked simply "Disney" and are extremely sought after in the collectible world of pottery.

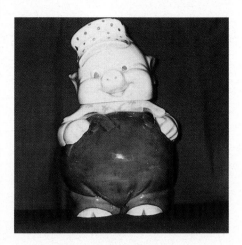

Practical Pig
made for Disney by Hagen Renaker,
marked "Walt Disney Productions".
Value: $1,500-1,800

Snow White Cylinder
very rare jar, marked "Made in Japan",
beautiful quality, 1940's origin.
Value: $1,100-1,500

Pinnochio
marked "Walt Disney, Productions, Copyright,
Cuernavaca, Mexico".
Value: $1,200-1,400

Joe Carioca
single, not a turnabout, from the Three
Caballeros, marked "Walt Disney U.S.A. Made
by Leeds China Co., Chicago, IL".
Value: $750

Joe Carioca
turnabout, Made by Leeds China Co., Chicago,
marked "Walt Disney U.S.A."
Value: $200-225

Joe Carioca
turnabout, Made by Leeds China Co., Chicago,
marked "Walt Disney U.S.A.",
(a different color combination).
Value: $200-225

Winnie the Pooh Hunny Pot
Made by California Originals,
marked inside lid "#907".
Value: $200-250

Donald Duck/Joe Carioca Turnabout
original paint, very unusual, Made by Leeds China Company, marked "Walt Disney U.S.A."
(two views shown here).
Value: $250-350

Big Al
light brown finish, made by Treasure Craft,
marked "Walt Disney Productions".
Value: $150-200

Big Al
common finish.
Value: $150-200

Big Al
underglaze finish.
Value: $150-200

Winnie the Pooh
marked "Copyright Sears Roebuck & Co.
1982, Made in Japan".
Value: $450-575

Winnie the Pooh
Made in Mexico, 1992.
Value: $150-200

Winnie the Pooh's Treats
marked "Made by Enesco Japan".
Value: $400-450

Mickey Driving the Car
marked "Copyright Walt Disney Productions,
Made for Sears Roebuck & Company 1978 Japan".
Value: $400-450

Winnie the Pooh
cold paint, marked "#900 Walt Disney Productions U.S.A., Made by California Originals".
Value: $150-250

Winnie the Pooh
paint under glaze, marked "#900 Walt
Disney Productions U.S.A.,
Made by California Originals".
Value: $225-275

Chef Mickey
marked "Made by Treasure Craft,
Made in the U.S.A., 1991".
Value: $175

Standing Donald Duck
12 ³/₄" high, Made by Leed's Pottery, unmarked.
Value: $450-525

Standing Donald Duck
marked "Copyright Walt Disney U.S.A."
Value: $600-750

Snow White and the Seven Dwarfs
original gold foil tag, marked
"Walt Disney Productions Enesco".
Value: $1,100

Snow White Napkin Holder
(shown with previous jar),
marked "Walt Disney Productions Enesco"
Value: $600-700

Snow White Salt & Peppers
marked "Walt Disney Production, Enesco".
Value: $450-600

Bulldog Cafe
made by Treasure Craft, 1992, from the movie,
"The Rocketeer", marked "Walt Disney,
Treasure Craft, Made in the U.S.A."
Value: $150-200

Alice Through the Looking Glass
made in Japan, unmarked.
Value: $900-1,100

Jack Skellington R.I.P.
also known as Jack's Tombstone, made for the
movie, The Night Before Christmas, marked
"Treasure Craft, Made in USA Walt Disney".
Value: $85

Mickey and Bag of Toys
sold through catalog, marked "Disney 1993".
Value: $250-300

Mickey Mouse with Flour Sack
marked "Copyright The Walt Disney
Company, Hoan Ltd."
Value: $90-110

Donald Duck
marked "Copyright The Walt Disney
Company, Hoan Ltd."
Value: $90-110

Eeyore
Made by California Originals #901,
marked "Copyright Walt Disney Productions".
Value: $1,500

Mrs. Potts
Made by Treasure Craft for the Movie "The
Beauty and the Beast", marked "Treasure Craft,
Disney, Made in the U.S.A."
Value: $75

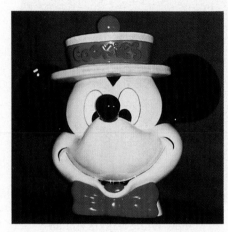

Mickey Mouse with Straw Hat
Made in 1994, limited production, made by
Enesco, marked "Disney".
Value: $70-125

Mickey with Santa Hat
1994, made by Enesco, marked "Disney".
Value: $70-110

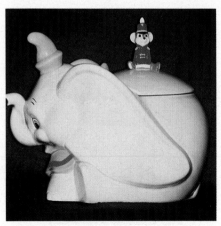

Dumbo
1992, marked "Disney".
Value: $150-200

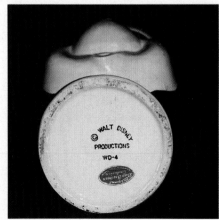

Mickey Mouse Candy Jar with Derby
unusual, marked "Walt Disney Production Copyright WD-4 Original Dan Brechner".
(A view of the jar and a view of the markings shown here).
Value: $900-1,100

Pinnochio
marked "Copyright Walt Disney Productions,
Made by Enesco".
Value: $375-450

Pinnochio with Fish Bowl
marked "Treasure Craft, Disney, U.S.A."
Value: $85-125

Snow White
1994, marked "Treasure Craft,
Disney, Made in Mexico".
Value: $60-75

Ludwig Von Drake
marked "Copyright 1961, Walt Disney
Productions WD-6".
Value: $900-1,100

Mickey & Pluto Cylinder
marked "Treasure Craft USA".
Value: $150-225

Mickey with Leather Ears
marked "Copyright Walt Disney Productions",
paper label reads "Enesco".
Value: $475-550

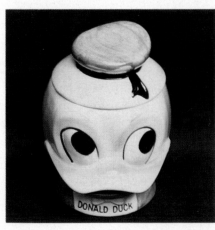

Donald Duck
marked "Walt Disney Productions WD-5", original Dan Brechner label.
(Both of these jars are the same except for
the different type of eyes, both jars are 7 1/4" high).
Value: $650-750

Mickey on Birthday Cake
produced for Mickey's 50th Birthday,
marked "Walt Disney Productions".
Value: $850-1.000

Mickey Mouse Clubhouse
marked "Copyright Walt Disney Productions", (two different color variations shown here).
Value: $400-450

Genie
Disney, Made in Mexico, sold in Disney stores.
Value: $175-250

Genie
made by Treasure Craft 1993, marked
"Treasure Craft, Disney, U.S.A."
Value: $85-125

Genie
marked "Disney, Taiwan".
Value: $250-300

Goofy
made by Treasure Craft 1995, marked
"Treasure Craft, Disney, U.S.A."
Value: $75

 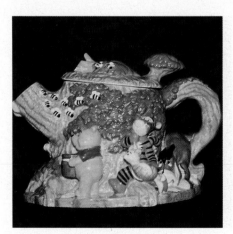 

Mr. Sander's Tree House
Holiday 1994, marked "Disney Made in China".
Issue Price: $55   Market Value: $200-295

Mr. Sander's Tea Pot
Holiday 1994, marked "Disney China".
Value: $125

Mickey Clock
made by Enesco, marked "W.D.E.-219, Walt
Disney Productions" on face of clock.
Value: $375-450

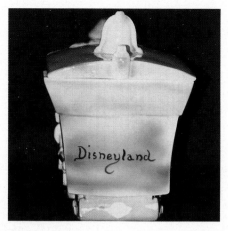

Disneyland Train
(front & back views shown of this jar)
The front says "Casey Jr.", the back of the jar reads "Disneyland".
Value: $400-500

Pinnochio with Fish Bowl
antique finish, marked "Copyright
Walt Disney Productions, #867, U.S.A.
Made by California Originals".
Value: $1,300-1,500

Pinnochio with Fish Bowl
full color finish, marked "Copyright
Walt Disney Productions, #867, U.S.A.
Made by California Originals".
Value: $1,800-2,200

Dumbo Turnabout
cold painted, marked "Patented Turnabout #4-1
Dumbo Copyright Walt Disney, Made by Leeds China",
(two different views shown here).
Value: $200-250

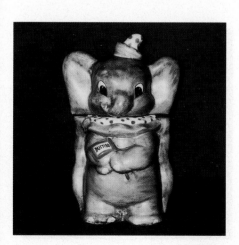

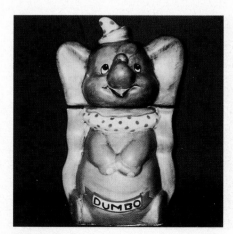

Dumbo Turnabout
original fired-on paint under glaze very rare,
marked "Copyright Walt Disney".
Value: $450-650

Christmas Tree Mickey & Friends
Annual Holiday Jar,
marked "Disney, Made in 1993".
Value: $400-450

Donald on a Pumpkin
marked "Walt Disney Productions #805, Made by California Originals".
(two different variations of the jar shown here).
Value: $375-425

Mickey on a Drum
marked "Walt Disney Productions #864,
Made by California Originals".
Value: $450-575

Antique Finish

Mickey Mouse Cookie Tin
9" high, marked "C. Chein & Company,
Burlington New Jersey".
Value: $125

Donald Duck Cylinder
possibly American Bisque.
Value: $135-150

Donald Duck Cylinder
9 3/4" high, unmarked.
Value: $125-150

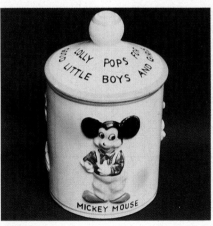

Lollypop Jar
7 1/2" high, (shows two different views),
marked "Copyright 1961, Walt Disney Productions".
Value: $375-450

Lollypop Jar
trimmed in pink, marked "Copyright 1961,
Walt Disney Productions".
Value: $375-450

Uncle Scrooge Bank
marked "Copyright Walt Disney Productions,
Ceramica de Cvernavaca".
Value: $600-800

Mary Poppins
very hard to find, marked "Copyright
MCMLXIV Walt Disney Productions".
Value: $1,500-1,800

Mary Poppins Teapot
original paper label, marked "Copyright
MCMLXIV Walt Disney Productions".
This teapot pictured at the right is musical.
Value: $450-550

Dopey
marked "Treasure Craft, Disney, Made in U.S.A.".
Value: $95-125

Sneezy & Bashful Salt & Pepper Shakers
Made by Treasure Craft, marked
"Walt Disney Productions".
Value: $35-45

Bambi
magnificent jar, made in japan,
marked "Walt Disney Productions".
Value: $900-1,300

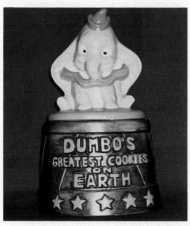

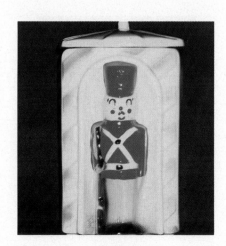

Dumbo's Greatest Cookies on Earth
made by California Originals, (two different color variations shown here).
Marked "Copyright Walt Disney Production,m U.S.A. #969".
Value: $1,500-1,800

Babes in Toyland
Value: $1,000-1,300

Professor Ludwig Von Drake
Made by American Bisque, marked
"Walt Disney Productions".
Value: $1,400-1,500

Donald Duck Basket Handled Cookie Jar
very rare, made in Japan, unmarked.
(two views shown here), the back view shows Chip & Dale.
Value: $1,500-1,800

Pinnochio
made by California Originals, (two different color variations shown here).
Marked "G-131 USA".
Value: $1,200-1,400

101 Dalmatians Cylinder
marked "Treasure Craft,
Made in the USA Disney".
Value: $125

Disney Parade Tin
marked "Walt Disney Productions
Cheinco Housewares
J. Chein & Co. Burlington, NJ".
Value: $125-150

Bambi on Tree Stump
Antique finish, made by California Originals,
marked "Copyright Walt
Disney Productions, U.S.A. 868".
Value: $750-900

Bambi on Tree Stump
full color, marked "Copyright Walt
Disney Productions, U.S.A. 868".
Value: $1,800

Minnie Mouse/Mickey Mouse Turnabout
14 1/2" high, Leed's China, Four-in-One
marked "Walt Disney". (Both views shown here).
Value: $125-175

Roly Dalmatian
marked "Treasure Craft, U.S.A. Disney".
Value: $85-110

Tigger
made by California Originals,
marked "Walt Disney Productions #902".
Value: $200-250

Snow White
very hard to find jar, Made by California Originals,
marked "Walt Disney Productions #902", Shown with the Seven Dwarfs,
display by Nyla & Phil Thurston.
Value: $3,000-3,500

Snow White
marked "Walt Disney Productions #866 USA".
Value: $2,500-2,800

Antique Finish   **All White**

Figaro
made by Hagen Renaker,
marked "Walt Disney Productions".
Value: $2,500-3,200

Alice in Wonderland
9 3/4" high, possibly made by American Bisque,
marked "Walt Disney Productions #866, U.S.A."
Value: $125-150

Ringmaster
Gepetto Pottery, from Walt Disney's "Pinnochio",
made by Brayton Laguna, California, marked
"Trademark Reg. U.S. Pat. Office".
Value: $3,000-3,500

Mickey Mouse Candy Jar
Dan Brechner Original Label, no music,
marked "Walt Disney Productions".
Value: $650-750

Simba
from the Lion King Movie,
marked "Made by Treasure Craft", 1994,
marked "Treasure Craft Disney Mexico".
Value: $65

Mother Goose Cookie Bus
hard jar to find,
marked "Walt Disney Productions".
Value: $900-1,100

Mickey Mouse Cookie Bus
marked "Walt Disney Productions".
Value: $650-1,000

Mickey Mouse
marked "Treasure Craft, Mexico".
Value: $75

Minnie Mouse
marked "Treasure Craft, Mexico".
Value: $75

Classic Pooh
marked "Treasure Craft, Mexico".
Value: $75

Donald Duck Turnabout
made by Leed's China, another side of this
jar is Joe Carioca. Marked "Walt Disney U.S.A."
Value: $200-225

Sitting Donald Duck
made by American Bisque, marked
"R.E.G. US Patent Office Celebrate Made in
U.S.A., Walt Disney Productions".
Value: $450

Snow White & Dwarfs Cylinder
marked "860-C Walt Disney Prod.", by
California Originals.
Value: $175-200

Pinocchio Cylinder
marked "860-C Walt Disney Prod.",
by California Originals.
Value: $175-200

Disney Channel
marked "Copyright made in USA by
Treasure Craft Walt Disney Productions".
Value: $250-325

Disney Channel
matching mug shown with previous jar.
Value: $25-30

Warner Brothers

Warner Brothers never produced any of the cookie jars themselves, but they issued a license to certain companies all over the United States to produce their characters as cookie jars or parts of canister sets etc.

Pepe Cylinder
marked "1994".
Value: $150

Bugs Cylinder
marked "1994".
Value: $150

Taz Cylinder
marked "1994".
Value: $150

Roadrunner Cylinder
discontinued, marked "1994".
Value: $150

Tazmanian Devil
Looney Tunes Certified International
New York 1994, some of these Looney Tune Jars
have been reintroduced by the Enesco Corp.
Value: $50

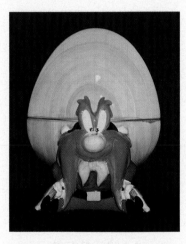

Yosemite Sam
Looney Tunes Certified International New York
1993, some of these Looney Tune Jars
have been reintroduced by the Enesco Corp.
Value: $50

Foghorn Leghorn
Looney Tunes Certified International New York
1993, some of these Looney Tune Jars have been
reintroduced by the Enesco Corp.
Value: $50

Bugs Bunny
Looney Tunes Certified International New York
1993, some of these Looney Tune Jars
have been reintroduced by the Enesco Corp.
Value: $50

Wile E. Coyote & Roadrunner
Looney Tunes Certified International New York
1993, some of these Looney Tune Jars
have been reintroduced by the Enesco Corp.
Value: $50

Sylvester & Tweety Bird
marked "Looney Tunes Certified
International New York 1993".
Value: $50

Bugs Moo-Randa
marked "Warner Brothers 1994".
Value: $150

Marvin the Martian
marked "Looney Tunes Certified International
New York 1993".
Value: $95-125

Tazmanian Devil
made by the Applause Company 1994,
marked "Applause Warner Brothers".
Value: $65-75

Sylvester & Tweety
made by the Applause Company 1994,
marked "Applause Warner Brothers".
Value: $65-75

Bugs Bunny on Burlap Bag
unmarked.
Value: $450-600

Bugs Bunny
marked "Copyright Warner Brothers Inc. 1981".
Value: $950-1,200

Champ
made by DeForest, this is a character from the
Sylvester Cartoon, very rare, unmarked.
Value: $3,000

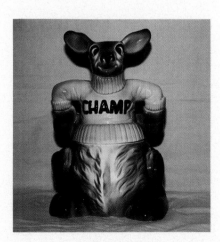

Champ
made by DeForest, this is a character from the
Sylvester Cartoon, very rare, unmarked.
Value: $3,000

Christmas Tweety
marked "Looney Tunes Certified International,
Holiday 1994". Limited production,
"Warner Brothers 1994".
Value: $50-65

Bugs Bunny with Candy Cane
marked "Looney Tunes Certified International,
Holiday 1994". Limited production,
"Warner Brothers 1994".
Value: $50-65

Sylvester & Tweety in Bird Cage
marked "Warner Brothers 1989, The Good
Company, City of Industry, CA".
Value: $1,100

Acme TNT
the elusive 12th jar of the series, marked
"Looney Tunes Certified International, 1993,
Copyright, made in Taiwan".
Value: $600-800

K-9 Dog
Marvin the Martian's Dog, marked
"Warner Brothers 1994".
Value: $125-195

Sylvester on Garbage Can
Looney Tunes, paper label.
Value: $125-200

Porky Pig Bank
marked "Warner Brothers".
Value: $125-200

Football Player Taz
marked "Warner Brothers",
with Dallas Cowboys Helmet.
Value: $95-125

Tazmanian Devil
marked "Warner Brothers 1989, The Good
Company, All Rights Reserved, Woodland
Hills, CA, Made in Korea".
Value: $325-375

Rick Wisecarver

Rick Wisecarver of Roseville, Ohio, specializes in Black Americana and Indian Art pottery.

Mammy Bust
9 3/4" high, limited edition, marked "Copyright
Rick Wisecarver Originals, R. Sims".
Value: $150

Pappy Bust
11 1/4" high, limited edition, marked "Copyright
Rick Wisecarver Originals, R. Sims".
Value: $150

Morning Aggravation
11" high, limited edition,
marked "#79 1991 RS".
Value: $225-250

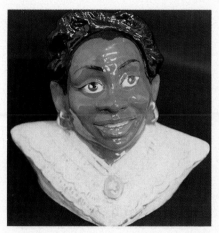

Mammy with Churn
13 1/2" high, limited edition.
Value: $150-195

Colonial Mammy
14" high, marked "Wihoa's Cookie Classic
by Rick Wisecarver, NO-44-91 RS".
Value: $150

Mrs. Claus
limited editon, African American.
Value: $195-250

Little Red Riding Hood & Big Bad Wolf
several different versions of this jar have
been made by Rick Wisecarver, limited edition.
Value: $295-350

Santa Claus
12" high, marked "Wihoa's Original Cookie
Classic by Rick Wisecarver R. Sims".
Value: $195-250

Santa Claus
12" high, marked "Wihoa's Original Cookie
Classic by Rick Wisecarver R. Sims".
Value: $195-250

Cook Stove Mammy
12" high, limited edition.
Value: $195-250

Witchy Flo
11 1/2" high, marked "Wihoa's Cookie Classic
by Rick Wisecarver No-34-91 RS", limited edition.
Value: $75-95

Indian Tee Pee
limited edtion, marked "Wihoa's Cookie
Classic by Rick Wisecarver of Rosev ille, OH".
Value: $225-250

Indian Maiden
9 1/2" high, limited edition, marked "Wihoa's
Cookie Classic by Rick Wisecarver".
Value: $150-175

Indian Chief
10 1/2" high, limited edition, 1989.
Value: $150

Saturday Bath
limited edition, marked "Wihoa's Cookie Classic
by Rick Wisecarver 1990, R. Sims".
Value: $150

Saturday Bath
limited edition, different color,
marked "Wihoa's Cookie Classic by Rick
Wisecarver 1990, R. Sims".
Value: $150

Geronimo
10 1/2" high, limited edition, marked "Chiricahua Warrior, Old Age 105, Wihoa's Original Cookie
Classic, Roseville, OH, NO-1-89, Rick Wisecarver, 1989 R. Sims".
(Shown here in different color variations).
Value: $150-175

Indian Head
only 12 jars were produced,
marked "Rick Wisecarver".
Value: $150

Wolfe Studio

Wolfe Studio is located in West Bloomfield, Michigan. Wolfe Studios is owned and operated by Kathy and Doug Wolfe. They sculpt and manufacture cookie jars and salt and pepper shakers. Both Kathy and Doug enjoy the creative end of the business and doing specialty jars. The bottoms of their cookie jars are stamped with "Wolfe Studios, Made in Michigan". The shakers are stamped with Wolf Paw Print. Licensed or trademarked items include "The Big Boy" cookie jar and shakers, "Jazze Junque", Purdue "PETE" University Mascot, and "San Jose Shark Goalie", an NHL team. All of Kathy and Doug's creations are Limited Editions.

Witch Head
limited edition of 100,
sculpted by Kathy Wolfe.
Value: $125

Snow Bear
commerical mold.
Value: $85-100

Popeye & Spinach Can
Value: $200

Hattie
limited edition.
Value: $150

The Cookie Girl
limited edtion, (two different designs shown here).
Value: $125-150

Hattie
limited edition, (three different designs shown here).
Value: $150 ea.

Witch with Arms Around Pumpkin
commercial mold.
Value: $200

Witch
custom, made from Brayton mold.
Value: $250+

Human Skull
limited edition of 100, unmarked.
Value: $100

Grandma Dubois
commerical mold, (front and back view of same jar shown here).
Value: $135

Big Boy
prototype, on the jars that went to
Elias Brothers in 1992.
Value: $1,500+

Big Boy
marked "Made for Elias Brothers 1992", limited
edition, marked "Sculpted by Kathy Wolfe".
Value: $500+

Purdue Boilermaker
prototype, sculpted by Doug,
this one was rejected.
Value: $195

Purdue Boilermaker
marked "Sculpted by Doug, Licensed Product
of Purdue University, IN", Limited Edition.
Value: $195

USA Hockey Goalie
limited edition of 150, sculpted by Doug.
Value: $150

San Jose Shark
limited edition of 100, Licensed Product.
Value: $175

Coffee Cup with Donut
sculpted by Kathy, can be personalized.
Value: $130

Santa Head
limited edition of 100.
Value: $95

Santa in Chair with Coke Bottle
Limited edition of 100,
marked "AP 1992 Kathy Wolfe".
Value: $195

Black Santa Head
limited edition of 100.
Value: $95

Snowman
commercial mold.
Value: $65

Statue of Liberty
gold trim, marked "Wolfe Studio Original,
Sculpted by Kathy", limited edition of 150.
Value: $175

Wolf Head
marked "Wolfe Studio Original,
Limited Edtion", Paw Print.
Value: $150

Kilban Cat
commercial mold.
Value: $100

Electric Car
licensed by General Motors,
very few produced, marked "KW".
Value: $200-250

4th of July
Brayton Reproduction.
Value: $150

Brayton Mammy
reproduction.
Value: $150

Brayton Mammy
reproduction.
Value: $150

Luzianne Mammy
reproduction, commercial mold.
Value: $125

Mammy
reproduction.
Value: $125

Ruby's Roadhouse
custom jar, gold trim, sculpted by Kathy.
Value: $250+

Index

417

426

428

Tale of A Cat

Puss N Boots was a famous cat,
The greatest of all by far.
But he wasn't aware of how great he was,
'Til they put him on a cookie jar.
Oh, it really didn't happen quite that fast,
It took 50 years or more.
In '41 on my Honeymoon, I won him at the Jersey shore.
I didn't know how famous he'd be,
I loved him for himself,
I was married a week and I thought "How Chic"
He would look there on my shelf.
Half a century now has gone,
And what do you think of that!
The only four things I never replaced,
Was my husband, my kids, and the cat!
But time and tide have their own rewards,
So proud and so very respectable,
My beloved jar has now become
A bonafide collectible.
He lives with my son and his Hall of Fame
For all to come and see.
Surrounded by thousands of cookie jars,
The head of a dynasty!

Epilogue

My Puss N Boots is not just a jar
My Puss N Boots is what we are
A home filled with love and sweet reflections
What better reason for starting collections.

Written by Pearl Supnick 1919-1995